PEARL HARBOR'S
FINAL WARNING

Pearl Harbor's Final Warning: A Man, A Message, and Paradise Lost

Non-fiction

History/WWII HIS 027100

Library of Congress Control Number: 2021903167

ISBN: 978-1-7367066-3-3 (paperback)

"We might have possessed the genius to break the Purple code, but in 1941, we didn't have the brains to know what to do with it." – Henry C. Clausen and Bruce Lee

Quote from *Pearl Harbor: Final Judgement* by Henry C. Clausen and Bruce Lee, Copyright 1992, is reprinted with permission from Da Capo Press. Eprinted version is fair use and available at Open Road Distributors (openroad.com).

Cover design: Germancreative at Fiverr.com

Voleander Press

Sisters, Oregon

voleanderpress@gmail.com

Also by the author

Non-Fiction

Money Eater: Bernard Otto Kuehn

Blog

The Footfalls of History at www.valarieanderson.com

For

George Street, Jr., Barbara (Street) Olsen, and all those who lived and died on Pearl Harbor Day

Principal Characters

Civilians

President Franklin D. Roosevelt

Secretary of State Cordell Hull

Secretary of the Navy Frank Knox

Secretary of War Henry L. Stimson

David Sarnoff, president of RCA

George Street, RCA district manager Hawaii

George Street, Jr., son of George Street (age 19)

Barbara Jean Street, daughter of George Street (age 17)

Special Envoy Saburo Kurusu, Asst. Japanese Ambassador

Tadao Fuchikami, RCA messenger #9

Joe Unger, RCA engineer

William (Bill) Steed, RCA night manager

Robert Shivers, FBI special agent in charge

Bernard Kuehn, German sleeper agent for Japanese Intelligence

Dr. and Mrs. Motokazu Mori

U. S. Military

1941 Rank and Duty

General George C. Marshall, U.S. Army — Chief of Staff of the U.S. Army, Washington, D.C.

Admiral Harold R. Stark, U.S. Navy — Chief of Naval Operations, Washington, D.C.

Admiral Husband E. Kimmel, U.S. Navy — Commander in Chief, Pacific Fleet, Hawaii

Lt. General Walter C. Short, U.S Army — Commanding General, Hawaiian Dept. H

Colonel Rufus S. Bratton, U.S. Army — Chief, Far Eastern Section, Military Intelligence, Washington, D.C.

Lt. Colonel Carrol A. Powell, U.S. Army — Head of Army Signal Corps, Ft. Shafter, Oahu

Lt. Cdr. Alvin D. Kramer, U.S. Navy — Head of Naval Translation Group, Washington, D.C.

Captain Irving H. Mayfield, U.S. Navy — Hawaiian District Intelligence Officer (counter-espionage)

Lt. Colonel G. Bicknell, U.S. Army — U.S. Army Intelligence Officer, Hawaii

Captain L.F. Stafford, U.S. Navy — Head of Cryptographic Division, Washington, D.C.

Commander J. J. Rochefort, U.S. Navy — Officer in charge of HYPO at Pearl Harbor

Commander Edwin T. Layton, U.S. Navy — Chief Intelligence Officer for Admiral Kimmel, Hawaii

Japanese Military

General Hideki Tojo

Prime Minister of Japan, October 1941, Tokyo

Admiral Kichisaburo Nomura

U.S. Ambassador, Washington, D.C.

Admiral Isoroku Yamamoto

Commander in Chief of the Combined Fleet, Tokyo

Consul General Nagao Kita

Japanese consulate, Honolulu

Ensign Takeo Yoshikawa

Japanese Intelligence, Japanese consulate, Honolulu; Code Name: Tadashi Morimura

Captain Kanji Ogawa

Chief of American Section Japanese Naval Intelligence, Tokyo

Table of Contents

Preface

The Red Suitcase

I really did not want to be doing what I was doing — preparing my parents' house for an estate sale. My mother had died unexpectedly, having kept her heart condition a secret until decisions had to be made. Then Dad died three and a half months later. Mom was always secretive about the things she thought would upset her children, no matter their ages. I never understood her reasons, and I learned to despise secrets. They rob people of the truth, of understanding, and, as in this case, of being prepared.

As I continued the task of sorting through their things, Mom's life surrounded and smothered me. She was such a contradiction, while Dad was an open book. Mom lived in the present, but she saved everything from her past. She stuffed every card, every bird list, or bit of poetry she'd written into drawers, boxes, and pockets. It was as if she wanted to define herself or preserve a past she longed to relive. More than once, she'd told me she felt like she'd never accomplished anything. Were these bits and pieces her trophies? Why did she bury herself in a puzzle of memories? What was she trying to find? And what was I looking for — the parents I had lost so abruptly?

Then I found the red suitcase under the guest room bed.

It was a 1970s Samsonite hard case — a suitcase my Mom had said she wanted to save when I was there on a previous visit. When

I snapped open the torpedo-shaped clasps, the smell of ages long gone made me sneeze. As I probed, I found yellowing letters, old newspaper clippings, Radio Corporation of America (RCA) telegrams, and carbon copies of memos. When I saw the copy of a telegram with random four-letter groupings and the word "Marshall" typed at the bottom of the text, I realized what I had found. It was my family's Pearl Harbor story.

I was vaguely aware that my grandfather, George Street, was manager of Honolulu's RCA Communication office in 1941 and that his office had received and delivered Washington's last warning message to the military command of Hawaii. I also knew my mother and her brother lived with him at the time, but I did not know much more.

Mom refused to talk about what she did on the day of the attack, even when I conducted a formal interview in 2010 for a sociology class. She only said her father had told her never to write about what happened. So she didn't — and now she couldn't. Curiosity piqued, I began to read the contents of the suitcase.

Frustration, and even anger, oozed from the typed, tissue-thin pages. Scattered throughout were handwritten comments attesting to my grandfather's desire to "keep the record straight ... in the interest of historical accuracy and ... keep it honest." Historians, politicians, authors, and movie producers were not portraying the complete story as he knew it. Why not? Why did my grandfather's notes differ from the historical record? How did Pearl Harbor's final warning message end up with him, a civilian? What had he, my mom, and uncle done that day? Why had the story been buried in a red suitcase under a guest-room bed? Realizing the suitcase might hold answers, I stuffed the paperwork into a cardboard box and shipped it home.

Later, after all the horrible business of death was done, I called my mother's brother, George Street Jr. Eighteen months older than Mom, now in his late 90s, he was still fit, and sharp as a tack. I was surprised to learn that he had never seen some of the items squirreled away in the red suitcase. With his support and enthusiasm, his step-daughter, Pat March, and I organized his father's and my mother's papers. Six four-inch binders and two containers later, we had a history. Together, we produced *A Compendium of the Life and Times of George Street, Sr.* for the family. However, some of my questions surrounding Pearl Harbor's final warning message remained unanswered, including the compelling one of how it ended up with my grandfather.

So I dug through the contents of the red suitcase again. I compared them with Pearl Harbor's investigative hearings in the *Congressional Record*, and with as many early accounts as I could find. I drilled down into citations, crosschecked contradictory statements, talked to people who were there, and solicited the help of my siblings, former Air Force Captain James R. Olsen, Kathryn M. (Olsen) Klattenhoff, and Commander Bill Olsen, USN (Retired). They provided research assistance and clarification, confirmed memories, and more. It was George Street, Jr.'s memories that filled the gaps and brought the story to life. The more I unearthed, the more I realized that I needed to supplement the historical record with the details my mother had secreted.

The result is this work of nonfiction. The quotes in this book are unaltered, except as noted. The pictures and documents chronicling events are scans from my grandfather's archives. The people mentioned are real, some still living. This account is as close to the truth as I could get.

I am honored to share the story of my mother, grandfather, and uncle, now that the benefit of time forgives indiscretions and mistakes. In the end, the red suitcase answered some questions. A lot of research answered others — but not all.

Valarie J. (Olsen) Anderson

Sisters, Oregon

Prologue

Japanese Imperial Year 2591

Captain Ito Risaburo sighed, bent over, and plucked an escaped screw off the concrete floor. Typewriter guts, wires, and rotors cluttered his workbench. Japan's naval ministry wanted an encoding machine, and it was his responsibility to make it happen because the ministry did not like being embarrassed — ever.

Herbert Yardley, an American cryptologist, had slapped Japan's national pride in the face when he revealed to the world that his decryption unit had cracked their code, which allowed U.S. delegates at the 1921 Washington Armament Conference to undermine Japan's negotiations. Then in 1929, newly appointed secretary of state, Henry L. Stimson, cut off Yardley's funding because "Gentlemen do not read other people's mail." Angry at having sixteen years of his work shuttered, Yardley spelled out his unit's code-cracking details in *The American Black Chamber*.[1] His exposé took the world by storm — and Japan never forgave nor forgot.

So, Ito worked out calculations, sketched and plotted, and his cipher machine took form. He fashioned a half-rotor with Latin alphabetic letters — twenty-six contacts on one side, twenty-six contact strips on the other. He separated the vowels. Each cluster needed one, because telegraph companies charged less for letter groupings that were pronounceable.

Slip rings connected the rotor to the wheel face. There were sixty of them. Wires spaghettied one to the other. Ito developed a brake wheel to control the rotation of the rotor. Forty-seven pins in the gear did the trick. He could scramble the pattern by removing pins.[2]

Ito's J-91 code from the new encryption machine hit the airwaves within months of Yardley's book release. The U.S. Army dubbed the mysterious code "Red" to match the color of the file folders used to sort their intercepts. The U.S. Navy referred to the code as "M3" or "A." The Red code proved too complex to break manually, so military intelligence went to work.

Intrigue, clandestine meetings, and a sexual tryst unearthed the plans of the J-91 "Red" cipher machine. With the blueprints in hand, the Office of Naval Intelligence (ONI) replicated five machines. Pearl Harbor and the Philippines each received one. The U.S. sent one to London in a top-secret trade for the German Enigma cipher machine key.[3] Army and Navy intelligence retained the remaining two.

By 1937, Captain Ito suspected that the Red machine had been compromised, so he went to work on the next generation — Type No. J-97, again, named after the Japanese Imperial year of its invention — 2597. This time he was determined to make it impregnable, and he succeeded — for a while.

When Ito's new mechanical code hit the airwaves, America called it "Purple." U.S. decoders determined that Japan now used the Red machine for low-level diplomatic messages — supply lists, personnel issues, and the like. Top-secret traffic between Japan's embassies in Washington, D.C., London, Moscow, and Tokyo was in the new Purple code.

For over two years, Japan cranked out the uncrackable Purple code. Then in 1940, a young civilian cryptologist, Harry L. Clark, had a eureka moment. He deduced that Ito employed telephone stepping switches instead of rotors to set the code. Letters changed positions in a cascade of rotating switches with remarkable complexity. The letter A became the letter G in the next line of text and so forth.[4] America quickly manufactured replicas. Now the team had to figure out how to set the switches. They needed a key.

Soon, Genevieve Marie Grotjan, a brilliant mathematician who preferred numbers to people, placed a worksheet in front of her boss and circled two letters, one on an intercept and one on a crib sheet. Then she proceeded to circle another combination, then another, and another until a pattern emerged.[5] They had the key, and the game was on again.

To process and man the Purple replicates, the Army and Navy formed a joint unit in the Munitions Building in Washington, D.C. They called the new unit "Magic" because the Purple cipher machine worked like magic. Radio-listening stations in Hawaii, Washington state, Virginia, and elsewhere forwarded Purple code intercepts to Magic for decryption. Duplicates were unavoidable. To streamline processing, Magic split the workload. The Army processed on even days of the month, and the Navy communications department took over on odd days.[6] Captain Stafford's Navy boys worked around the clock. The Army employed civilians, so processing on even days stopped at 4:30 PM weekdays and 1:00 PM on Saturdays.

Military leaders clamped down the lid on Magic. It was vital that the breaking of the Purple code remain secret so Japan wouldn't devise a new code or encryption machine. The command at Magic denied access to anyone who did not have an Ultra security clearance, which was higher than Top Secret. Only a handful of senior officers and Secretary of the Navy Frank Knox held the Ultra clearance. [7] President Roosevelt did not receive clearance until January of 1941 — 140 days after the replication of the Purple machine. [8] When FDR joined the Ultra list, the security-conscious team at Magic alternated months for the delivery of Purple intercepts to the White House. [9] The Army couriered dispatches one month and Navy the next.

Army and Navy aides carried the magic decrypts in locked cases to the Ultras and interrupted meetings if needed. The courier waited while the Ultra read the Purple decrypt. Then he snapped it back into his case and delivered it to the next Ultra on his list. Only the president and the secretary of state could retain a Magic decrypt for twenty-four hours. No copies were allowed. The Ultras had to rely on their memories for briefings and consultations.

The U.S. Navy and the Army at Magic controlled two Purple machines each — one for current traffic, the other for previous ciphers. London received one. Another was given to the commanders of the Philippines and set up in the caves of Corregidor.

Pearl Harbor received none.

Chapter 1

Purple Haze

14 October 1941 – Honolulu, Territory of Hawaii

George Street, district manager of Radio Corporation of America (RCA), walked into his office at 223 South King Street, Honolulu, to the sound of typewriters clacking, phones ringing, and ticker-tapes chattering. It was music to his ears. The smell of rubber, canvas, well-oiled metal, paper, and people enveloped him. He inhaled deeply. All was right in *this* world. It was familiar, logical, and easily tamed.

RCA-Honolulu Office in 1938
(George Street Archives)

He had grown up enthralled with the magic of radio, fascinated by the sounds that came out of the ether. At the age of thirteen, he ran an antenna wire along the top of his neighbor's fence and built his first radio. Now at the hub of a worldwide web of wireless networks that connected the United States to the Far East, he placed work above all else. He ran a tight ship, and he did not hesitate to speak his mind. He was the glue that held RCA-

Honolulu together. Employees respected him. So did the military and business communities.

He arrived in Honolulu with his two children and second wife in 1935, two years before Ito masterminded the J-97 "Purple" encryption machine. George had been in Japan expanding RCA's wireless network while the Red machine hammered out code. It was there he'd contracted polio. Leg braces and a cane were now part of his life. He respected the Japanese, made many contacts, and was comfortable with their culture. And he was well aware that Japan used RCA to transmit coded messages to facilitate the purple haze of politics he avoided.

His Honolulu office processed approximately fifty percent of America's wireless traffic to the Far East and sixty percent of the Far East's inbound traffic. RCA-Honolulu linked San Francisco and Japan wirelessly, as well as other locations throughout the Pacific. Stateside, RCA connected to Western Union and provided a direct connection to AT&T (American Telephone and Telegraph) in Dixon, California. Wireless radio technology surpassed the web of telegraph cables that crisscrossed the globe over land and under oceans.

RCA-Honolulu also routed transpacific radiophone calls that cost two dollars a minute, a hefty sum when typical wages were less than a dollar an hour. Once a phone call connected from the mainland to Hawaii, RCA patched it to the local Mutual Telephone Company. Three years earlier, George had facilitated the first radio phone call to Japan. According to the 25 March 1938 article in the *Honolulu Star-Bulletin,* which featured George's picture with the president   of   Mutual   Telephone,   the   "veil   of   radio telecommunications parted." Japan's Director General of Telecommunications K. Tamura, said, "We can now communicate by radiophone, and this achievement will strengthen the traditional friendship and lasting peace in the Pacific."[10]

An active participant in community organizations, George explained to the local Rotary Club that "Within these Hawaiian Islands, there is quite a unique and exceptionally complete radiotelegraph, radiotelephone, and ship-to-shore wireless service that ranks among the very first to be engaged in this interesting business ... Along with the rapid advancement made in the type of equipment employed, radiotelegraphy and telephony have equally made progress in overcoming atmospheric static, fading and distortion."[11]

RCA's cables and radiograms were like text messages — short, cryptic, and quick. They cost twelve to thirty cents per word. Night messages were sent at the reduced rate of one to two dollars for twenty-five words. Radiograms moved forward through complex routing links — radio transmitters and receivers, landlines, and undersea cables leased from a host of different companies.

The U.S. military on Oahu had separate wireless networks, but antiquated and unreliable equipment hindered their operation. The Army Signal Corps experienced sporadic connections to Washington, D.C., because of their low transmission power. Their inter-island communication links were not secure enough to transmit unencrypted messages classified as Secret or higher.[12] Static was common. The military often used RCA when they couldn't break through the atmospherics because RCA had the most powerful transmitter in the Pacific.

The Japanese consulate in Honolulu also used commercial carriers to transmit messages to Tokyo. They did not have the equipment necessary for transmission and could only *receive* messages.[13] Whether encrypted or in plain text romaji, romanized Japanese, companies like RCA sent their radiograms across the globe. Messengers facilitated deliveries and pickups.

George Jr. hustled as a messenger boy for RCA during his high school years, driving his father's car to make his deliveries. Other messenger boys rode motorbikes. All wore RCA company shirts emblazoned with RCA's red circular logo. RUSH and URGENT messages took priority and were delivered immediately. They had specific routes and knew their customers, sometimes too well as George Jr. was soon to learn.

Shorthanded one day, the office manager asked him to deliver a message to Tommie Tomlinson at the New Senator Hotel, a notorious brothel that wasn't on his usual route. George Jr. said, "No problem," and headed out the door.

"I'm here to deliver a telegram to Tommie Tomlinson," he told the madam when he arrived.

"She is in room seven, upstairs." The "she" gave him pause. He assumed Tommie was a man.

According to George Jr., "It was ratty-looking; there were a bunch of girls hanging out." He knocked on the door of room seven and announced, "Telegram for Tommie Tomlinson."

The door opened, and there stood Tommie, stark naked. George Jr. took a step back. He'd never seen a naked woman. Red-faced, he said, "I need you to sign here," and he pointed to the receipt. Tommie made no attempt to cover up and proceeded to explain that her *nom de guerre* was Tommie. She was Gilda, and she signed accordingly. George Jr. beat a hasty retreat as the girls offered him favors behind their snickers. He would make more runs to the New Senator Hotel and have coffee with girls, "but nothing more," he swore decades later.[14]

In addition to routine traffic and messages delivered with a lesson attached, numerous coded communications passed through RCA, including those in Red and Purple codes. Barbara Jean, George's daughter, who worked at RCA's service counter on holidays and after school, counted the random five or six-letter code clusters, confirmed that each group had a vowel, and included the letters in the address line when calculating the cost. Money was collected or billed to an account, and the message was time-stamped and placed in an outbox to await a free operator.

She and the other RCA personnel could only decrypt standard radio code used to reduce the word count, such as HU for Honolulu, S for George Street, or JIJAY for duly delivered. The one item on a commercial radiogram that needed full text was the address line which was critical for proper delivery and receipt.

Personnel at RCA keyed and delivered whatever was submitted — no questions asked. Employees could not reveal the contents of the message, the addressee, or the sender. George Street — the man with the cane — was responsible for compliance and the processing of each radiogram, cable, and money order that passed through the office. His reputation and livelihood depended upon it.

***

Two things happened in short order that changed George Street forever. The first affected his personal life. The second inserted him into the footnotes of history. Both had consequences he never dreamed of.

Stocky, forty-four years old, brown-eyed and dark-haired, George took pride in his success and boasted that he had accomplished much in spite of the fact that he never finished high school. He preferred to learn by experience which, as he wrote, "could only be obtained from actual work, and whatever study was needed or required to further one's own experience."[15]

George was the youngest in a household of four bullying brothers and three assertive sisters. His Victorian-era father swam the Alameda estuary daily. It was an every-man-for-himself kind of household, fine-tuned by a mother with little time for affection.

The Street clan hailed from Worcester, England, and their footfalls imprinted history. George's ancestors fought in the American Revolution, received a land grant in New Brunswick, Canada, and became bankers, mayors, lawyers, architects, and real estate tycoons — women included. They were listed in encyclopedias, received kingly honors, and sailed the world.[16]

They were *Streets*, not a Boulevard, Avenue, or Road, as he once quipped. "[We] were great individualists, hardly seeming to care or even wonder how one brother or sister might be getting along for better or worse, each having their own selfish interests to a very considerable extent." George wrote to his son years later that the Street genes remained strong through the generations and demanded success and respectability.[17]

On this October day, George Street took command of his domestic situation. The First Circuit Court was finalizing his divorce from Nina Mihalavan Lenzeva-Nevsorova, his once wild Russian mistress, who had accompanied him while he expanded radio in the Far East. He filed because of "cruel treatment, neglect, and personal indignities, a catch-all complaint that rarely needed proof."[18]

George Street
(George Street Archive)

George met Nina in Tsingtao. She was street smart and twenty-three, much younger than his thirty-five. RCA's former Shanghai manager warned him to "watch [your] step in playing with those Russians ... Get yourself a couple of good white mamas and leave the Slavs alone."[19] But Nina's charm proved too much for George. She cloaked her vulnerability with allure and played to his naiveté and conceit. She had survived the streets of Little Russia in Shanghai as an "entertainer" at the age of thirteen, when her parents put her on a train to escape the Red Army during the Bolshevik Revolution. Nina was a damsel in distress, waiting for a knight in shining armor to rescue her. She posed as his wife as he toured the Far East and nursed him through the worst of his polio. He eventually married her in Japan so she could assist him, as he returned to the States. In exchange for her ticket to citizenship, she provided him with physical happiness and companionship.

Her fiery temperament added to their passion, but her insecurity made for a tumultuous domestic life. She would not be tamed. She had disappeared the summer before his divorce — this time to San Francisco. Twice, she had bolted to Shanghai and left him to take care of his children while he worked twelve-to-fourteen hour days.

When Nina returned from San Francisco, she broke down the front door and demanded that George choose between her and his children. The children weren't hers, and she resented them. Nina considered them spoiled, and hated sharing George. She wanted him to live without them, as the two of them had done in the Far East.

What Nina failed to comprehend was his deep sense of obligation and respectability. His intense desire to prove his capability as a responsible man and father trumped her desire for happiness. He had divorced his children's mother, Kathryn Alberta Heunisch, because she did not live up to his Victorian expectations. He had no problem doing the same to Nina. Women were supposed to take care of house and home.

Life without Nina would be okay. His kids could take care of themselves. They had fended for themselves under their mother's care after the divorce, and then again when his family placed them in a boarding school without his knowledge while he was in Japan. He'd obtained custody of his kids when they were eleven and thirteen. Now, Barbara was a senior at Roosevelt High School. George Jr. worked full time while waiting to transfer from the University of Hawaii to the engineering program at the University of California, Berkeley, on an ROTC scholarship.[20] The three of them were survivors. They did not need Nina.

At six o'clock in the morning, George swung his emaciated legs to the floor, sat for a moment, and reflected on his pending divorce. Then he positioned his leg braces around his limbs, and winced as he cinched the leather straps tight. Pulling on his gray trousers, he pushed himself to a standing position — and stood tall.

Like President Roosevelt, George worked hard to hide his disability. He had met the president at Warm Springs, Georgia, while taking a cure, before RCA sent him to Honolulu. George learned to prop his cane behind his back for photographs and lean on furniture for support. He refused to take an arm, preferring the greater dignity of his cane.

Once dressed, George hobbled to the kitchen, next to the screened lanai, put the coffee on, and cooked breakfast. The sizzle and pop of bacon cooking worked better than an alarm clock. His daughter, Barbara Jean, still in her pajamas, grabbed a piece of bacon. George Jr. wandered in from the detached maid's quarters that served as his bedroom.

After breakfast on the lanai, George brushed his teeth, shaved, and combed his black hair, now blazed with silver. He smiled into the mirror. He cut a handsome figure despite his receding hairline. There would be no shortage of women after the divorce. Clutching his cane, he shuffled to the closet for his shirt and tie. He wore long sleeves to work, no matter how hot, to cover the scar of a tattoo gone wrong. Like countless drunken sailors, he had acquired it while sailing the Pacific as a steam-schooner radio operator.

George hitched a ride to work with his son before heading to the courthouse for his divorce proceedings. He preferred to be chauffeured, even though he had retrofitted the car to accommodate his disability. Cords tied to the frame helped him lift his braced legs inside.

Chapter 2

The Need to Know

14 October 1941
The White House

On the day of George's divorce, the second drama that altered George Street's life took shape in Washington, D.C., as David Sarnoff and President Franklin Delano Roosevelt met for lunch. Washington was five and a half hours ahead of Honolulu, so George was just starting his day when they met.

When Sarnoff arrived at the West Wing door at the White House, his shoes appeared dull compared to the spit-shined boots of the Marine guard standing as rigid as a flag pole. Sarnoff had no need for shoe polish, in order to command a room. His reputation and intellect did it for him. Compact as a tank, with wide-set blue eyes, he was president of Radio Corporation of America, RCA, one of the top communication networks in the world.

The Marine opened the door to the lobby, and Sarnoff walked down the corridor. More comfortable in street-side cafes than ritzy establishments, he stepped into the most exclusive one of all, the Oval Office.

President Roosevelt cut an imposing figure when Sarnoff entered. He sat at the Hoover desk, situated in front of three floor-to-ceiling windows, each framed with green velvet curtains and gold trimmed valances painted with winged eagles. The American flag and the presidential flag pierced the divide between the windows and bracketed Roosevelt's wheelchair. A miniature museum of gifts sat on his desktop like a battle line. Amid this band of clutter, RCA had invented and installed a hidden microphone system so the president could document overzealous journalists when they filed their news reports. A switch in Roosevelt's desk drawer activated a recorder hidden under the floor.[21]

Roosevelt greeted Sarnoff warmly. He held him in high regard and valued his insight, addressing him as "Dear David" in their correspondence. [22] Roosevelt appreciated the fact that Sarnoff learned by doing, having once lamented that "I took economic courses in college for four years, and everything I was taught was wrong."[23]

Sarnoff grew RCA from a small seedling into a multi-branched corporate tree of communications, broadcast radio, television, and manufacturing in less than thirty years — and he had done it without a high school diploma, because he possessed a rare ability. Sarnoff could imagine the future and make it a reality. He cut to the core of problems. Doubt and uncertainty did not linger in his mind. A reporter described him as "too subtle to be a glad-hander and too intelligent to be a back-slapper."[24]

Sarnoff epitomized the people who made America great. He was a rags-to-riches man who gave hope and inspiration to others. The only son in a household of nine children, Sarnoff sold newspapers on the streets of Hell's Kitchen to support his Russian immigrant family, before destiny tapped him on the shoulder as he walked into a telegraph office instead of a newspaper agency. By the time he was forty, Sarnoff was running RCA. Later, he would become a member of FDR's Fair Employment Practices Committee. After he received an endorsement from Prime Minister Winston Churchill, General Dwight Eisenhower, commander of the Allied Expeditionary Forces, asked him to be his communication czar for the D-day invasion.

During lunch, perhaps in the Fish Room across the hall from the Oval Office, the two men discussed a host of topics over a typical bland and meager meal selected by Eleanor. The president valued Sarnoff's opinion on such things as how to counter propaganda, how to prepare the nation for war, and how to use radio for military applications.[25]

He needed Sarnoff's help to figure out when and where the enemy was going to attack. FDR said, "When you see a rattlesnake poised to strike, you do not wait until he has struck to crush him," The Nazis were his rattlesnake.[26] FDR reasoned that if Russia fell, England would fall next, so he shared intelligence with Winston Churchill, and American factories and shipyards were in full-scale production supplying Britain under the lend-lease program.

Newspaper headlines that morning told of a world in crisis. The Battle of the Atlantic raged as German U-boats prowled the English Channel and the German Luftwaffe attempted to wipe the Royal Air Force from the sky during the Battle of Britain.

There would be no lag in the conversation between the two men as they dined. Temperatures and temperaments were well above normal in Washington. FDR was also worried about Japan because negotiations were at a stalemate. If America was pulled

into war they'd be fighting on two fronts, in the Atlantic against
the Germans, and in the Pacific against the Japanese. He could not
tell Sarnoff about Purple or the fact that he'd been cut off from
receiving Magic intercepts because of a careless aide — something
which angered him beyond measure. Back in June, Magic
intercepts were found in his aide's wastebasket, and delivery of
Magic intercepts to the White House had come to a screeching
halt.[27]

Meanwhile, the Allies cut off Japan's war material imports,
steel, scrap metal, and aviation fuel. Oil required applications and
licensing because he feared Japan would attack the Dutch East
Indies in a bid to obtain their reserves, if America cut off their
supply completely. When Japan advanced on Indochina,
Roosevelt's cabinet froze their American assets, rendering a
crippling blow to Japanese businessmen. Then, with the misplaced
stroke of a pen, the partial oil embargo became a full embargo and
over eighty percent of Japan's oil supply stopped overnight. FDR's
fear about Japan hunting for oil reserves became a reality.

What he and the intelligence community did not know was
that the commander in chief of the Imperial Japanese Navy,
Admiral Isoroku Yamamoto, was already busy planning a multi-
pronged attack which included an assault on Pearl Harbor.
Yamamoto shared his bold plan with just a handful of officers.
Two were aviators, Commander Minoru Genda and Mitsuo
Fuchida, who would lead the air group in the attack on Pearl
Harbor. It was their job to figure out how to drop torpedoes into
Pearl's shallow harbor.

Yamamoto's final hurdle in developing his attack on Pearl Harbor proved tougher than the torpedo problem. How would he ensure a surprise attack? Japan's entire fleet needed to sail halfway across the Pacific undetected. His solution was to sequester the entire attack force, in order to keep word from leaking out.

As an added precaution, Yamamoto ordered all existing fleet radio operators to work from various Japanese islands and transmit simulated radio traffic to make it appear as though they were in their home waters. He assigned new radiomen to the fleet, because radio operators keyed with a distinctive pattern called a "fist," which could then be associated with a particular location.[28] Some operators keyed ham-fisted and slow. Others were lightning fast and tapped out code at forty-five words per minute. As an added precaution, the Japanese did not list Pearl Harbor as a destination in their encrypted messages.

Cut off from Magic, desperate to figure out Japan's intentions, completely unaware of Yamamoto's plan, worried that the embargo had cocked the trigger, Roosevelt asked Sarnoff for a favor at lunch. He needed RCA's Honolulu office to turn over to the Navy all suspicious radiograms sent by the Japanese consulate, or by any other person who communicated with Tokyo.

Sarnoff's prior cooperation with the War Department had set a precedent. For six months in 1940, Army Signal Corpsman Lieutenant Earle Cook had "trained" at RCA. In actuality, Cook sniffed out intelligence that passed through RCA's New York office. Later Cook transferred to the RCA's Washington office, where he photocopied and delivered messages to Army Intelligence in the Munitions Building.[29]

The Oval Office became thick with acrid tobacco smoke on this hot, muggy day.[30] The two men discussed and dissected the war and the need for better intelligence — Roosevelt's cigarette holder punching the air when he emphasized a point. He reasoned that, since a British-owned company supplied bomb plot intercepts to Prime Minister Churchill, then RCA, a U.S. company, could provide him with bomb plot messages, too.[31]

The president's request was unusual, even illegal, as the U.S. was not at war. It meant that a civilian must agree to break the law and ignore privacy and nondisclosure regulations. Sarnoff was compelled to choose between his country's pragmatic needs and the law. Puffing on his pipe, Sarnoff concurred and agreed to convince George Street to become an unofficial spy.

Chapter 3

Sitting Duck

Captain Irving Hall Mayfield was probably the man who served up George Street at Sarnoff and Roosevelt's luncheon, undoubtedly having reported his unsuccessful attempt to recruit George. Mayfield, the senior officer of Admiral Husband Kimmel's counter espionage team, was a blistering man who would not take "no" for an answer.[32]

Mayfield followed Kimmel when he replaced Admiral James O. Richardson. Twice, Richardson had gone to Washington to protest the Pacific Fleet's relocation to Pearl Harbor, making his concerns known to Secretary of the Navy Frank Knox. When Knox brushed him off, Richardson told FDR to his face that he believed keeping the Pacific Fleet at Pearl Harbor was a disaster waiting to happen. The president thought otherwise. The Navy reassigned Richardson, and the fleet remained at Pearl Harbor.

Kimmel, tall, ramrod straight, and a stickler for detail, ran his command by the book and expected the same from his officers. He had been an aide to Secretary of the Navy, Franklin D. Roosevelt in 1915, a gunnery officer, and commander of two destroyer divisions, among other duties. Within a month after Kimmel's arrival, Hawaiian Command received the following synopsis from Washington war planners:

– Item (b) Summary of the Situation: In the past, Orange [code for Japan] never preceded hostile actions by a declaration of war.

– Item I Summary of the Situation: It appears possible that Orange submarines and/or an Orange fast raiding force might arrive in Hawaiian waters with no prior warning from our intelligence service.

– Item III of Possible Enemy Action section: A declaration of war might be preceded by:

    1. A surprise submarine attack on ships in the operating area.

    2. A surprise attack on Oahu, including ships and installations in Pearl Harbor.

    3. A combination of these two.[33]

Consequently, submarines became Kimmel's nightmare, and offensive drills and anti-submarine operations became routine at Pearl. Kimmel was notorious for walking aboard a ship unannounced to initiate a drill. Eight bells clanged from the quarterdeck, and "Pacific Fleet arriving" blared from the loudspeaker when he would roar up to the ship with his admiral's flag flying. Those onboard scrambled. Walking up the gangway, his staff in tow, Kimmel breathed in the sharp odor of tar, brine, oil, and men. The ship's duty officer logged him in. The commanding officer greeted him, and Kimmel began his inspection, marking time. On his command, switches were thrown, emergency generators stirred with a growl, and the sounds of a living fortress of metal and men rumbled. Most people under his command were grateful for his perfectionism — as long as they got it right. Mayfield was no exception.

Like Kimmel, Mayfield was a Naval Academy grad, a "ring knocker," a member of the elite fraternity that could climb above the rank of commander. His classmates called him "May" or "Ikey." Mayfield's naval academy yearbook described him as "Lord Chesterfield reincarnated ... a blue-eyed beauty from Louisiana." His soft southern drawl camouflaged his fiery temper. By the time George was introduced to him, his nickname had changed to "Hall."

Before Mayfield arrived in Honolulu, he had spent two weeks in Washington getting up to speed with naval intelligence. His previous duty in Chile, as a naval attaché, likely included an intelligence task along with his diplomatic and liaison duties.[34]

His new counterintelligence assignment meant he was to thwart enemy spies by intercepting their radio traffic, diplomatic traffic included. Mayfield's district had three offices on outlying islands and units on Oahu, Maui, and Midway.[35] His wife of thirty years, Juliet, accompanied him to Hawaii, and they settled in senior officers' quarters close to Kimmel. Kimmel left his wife stateside to avoid the complications of married life. For him, like George, work came first.

There were thirteen people at the Honolulu counterintelligence unit when Mayfield took command. He quickly recruited a select group of local businessmen, each of whom received a reserve commission. They had standing orders to put on their uniforms immediately in case of an emergency.

George Street fit the bill for this select group with one exception, his polio. His past experience in the Orient, when he was expanding RCA's radio network, gave him insights others lacked. He wrote, " I knew that foreign telegraph administrations in most foreign countries, owned, operated, or controlled by the government itself, abused and violated the International Telegraph and Radio regulations regarding the secrecy of telegrams ... and first hand, I knew it was the custom in China and Japan....."[36]

George had also figured out that the Japanese consulate in Honolulu alternated its transmission to Tokyo monthly.[37] They chose between his office and others in the city — Globe Wireless, British-owned Mackay Radio Telegraph Company, and old and slow Commercial Pacific, which did not have wireless capabilities. Its undersea cable line "joined up with the Japanese government cable at Bonin Island directly into Tokyo ... RCA-Communication was superior, having ample and the most up to date equipment and efficient operation of the lot," he explained later to author, Ladislas Farago.[38]

George requested a reinstatement of his reserve commission so he could join Mayfield's select group of reservists. He obtained the rank of lieutenant for communications duties at Special Services in 1927, but was discharged in 1935, when he contracted polio.[39] His request fell on deaf ears. "The Bureau regrets to inform you that, in view of your physical condition, favorable consideration cannot be given to your request for reappointment in the Naval Reserve."[40] Allowing a person with polio to join a well-run fighting navy was not in the book. Regulations were regulations.

Mayfield had suggested that George could help the war effort without a commission. He wanted copies of Japanese radiograms, knowing that Section 605 of the Federal Communications Act of 1934 barred George from disclosing the sender and receiver, much less the contents, without a court order.[41] Mayfield asked anyway.

George refused Mayfield's request. Instead, he asked Mayfield to hand him a court order, and then he would comply. "I did not want to violate the laws of the United States, but did feel strongly that our country was certainly headed for war with the Japanese ... and for months, I did think that the Japanese may well attack Hawaii; that the American Pacific fleet mostly lying at ease in Pearl Harbor was a sitting duck," George later explained.[42]

Mayfield, his captain's eagles pinned perfectly on his khaki uniform collar, insisted and threatened that "the Navy may take over operations of commercial radio companies: RCA Communications, Globe Wireless, and Mackay Radio Telegraph Company."[43] George did not take the bait. How could that not have rankled Mayfield? Aware that George once held the rank of lieutenant, three grades below his, he knew that in another time and place George would have faced severe consequences for his refusal.

Despite his refusal, George once again requested a reinstatement of his naval reserve commission. This time he explained in detail how he could help, and how his polio affliction would not hinder his work: "I ... formally requested the Commandant 14th Naval District Pearl Harbor to have my former Reserve Officer's Commission reinstated, so I might be in a morally better position to assist them in the never-ending quest for information." Again, the Navy rejected his request.

Suspecting much but knowing little, frustration drove Mayfield to George's office. He did not want to take "no" for an answer and finally quit beating around the bush. He demanded that George give him copies of messages sent by the Japanese consulate and Sumitomo Bank. If George complied, Mayfield could sort the wheat from the chaff and make life easier for his unit and Magic, although he could not tell George that. George refused. He would not jeopardize his career and risk imprisonment.

Wary and worried, and trying to stay within legal boundaries, George finally agreed to one of Mayfield's requests. He allowed him access to the Koko Head receiving station on the top of a volcanic crater on Oahu — for a price. There was nothing in the regulations that prevented him from doing so. He told Mayfield that "it would be solely experimental on the part of RCA to ascertain whether or not such a service may become commercial ..."[44]

Mayfield leased a pair of the telephone company's lines that ran from either Koko Head to his headquarters or to the Pearl Harbor Navy Yard. Mayfield assigned a receiving engineer to monitor incoming signals and radio transmissions of the Japanese fleet. Later, Mayfield admitted that the arrangement was beneficial.[45]

After a couple of weeks of access to the Koko Head station, George instructed his head office in New York to send a bill to the Navy for unilateral receiving service.

When naval headquarters questioned Mayfield about the invoice, George said that he "literally stormed into my office in a choleric manner, angry and enraged. He stood over my desk and pounded his fist on the desktop and shouted, 'Street, you have sabotaged me.'"[46] He undoubtedly rapped his academy ring on George's desk to remind him of his superiority in rank and authority.

George said of Mayfield, "[I] did not sabotage him; that it was also my country as much as his ... His manner was quite crude. I invited him to sit down and suggested he should cool off."

Mayfield retorted, "Now that Washington knows about this listening in, they won't let me use it."

Standing now, his cane in his hand, George told him "that the service was always immediately available for a reasonable price and that the military could not expect any commercial company to give them service without compensation."

George later wrote that he "really felt sorry for his unseemly outburst ... [It] was indeed poor thanks for our cooperation ... This made me wonder if Mayfield was not trying to make some sort of a personal hero out of himself."[47]

Mayfield abandoned the direct approach. It would take men more powerful than him to persuade George. Word probably got back to Roosevelt and prompted the turn-over request of RCA-Honolulu radiograms from George to the Navy.

In addition to Mayfield's naval counterintelligence unit and the fleet intelligence unit under Lieutenant Commander Edwin T. Layton, Op-20-G, the G section of the 20th naval communications division in D.C., set up Station "H" or HYPO, in Hawaii.[48] The station, referred to as a combat intelligence unit to conceal its communications identity, evaluated Japan's air and sea capabilities and movements. Daily information was supplied to Layton for Admiral Kimmel, Admiral Bloch, and sometimes the Army's intelligence division, known as G-2, under Colonel Fielder. Captain Mayfield received no information from HYPO.[49]

The men who worked at HYPO called it "the dungeon." Cloistered in a steamy, five-thousand square foot basement in the Pearl Harbor Naval District Administration Building, twenty officers and one hundred-twenty enlisted men worked in sweat-stained shirts, many stripped down to their t-shirts. Pencils poked from behind their ears. Desks abutted, so that the men faced each other in crowded bullpen conditions. Black oscillating fans affixed to shafts of steel riffled the men's decryption papers and stirred the locker-room smell.

The man in charge of the unit, Commander Joseph J. Rochefort Jr., sat between four traffic analysts and a double bank of linguists and translators. The cryptanalysts were on the other side of the room. A plot and map table separated them from two information desks.[50] They worked on decoding the Japanese naval operational JN-25 and flag officer codes, hunting for Japan's fleet, even though there was no declared war. Diplomatic traffic from the Red or Purple machines was off-limits to the HYPO team.[51]

Chapter 4

Mending Fences

George had a rare moment to himself. He sat at his desk, his cane hooked on the back of his low slung chair. Diffused light illuminated his work area. Sweat dampened his white long-sleeved shirt. He closed his eyes and listened to the music of machines and the hubbub of humanity and acknowledged that he was bone tired.

Then he reread the servicegram that advised him of David Sarnoff's upcoming visit to the Honolulu office. George was not sure of what to think. Sarnoff had never called on his office. Typically his mentor and manager, W.A. Winterbottom inspected the operation. Sarnoff's visit was most certainly not a ten-day vacation, as the newspapers professed.[52] His wife was not joining him.

Searching for a reason, George reflected that less than a year ago RCA honored him for his long service. Winterbottom lauded his work. Perhaps he should have denied Mayfield access to the Koko Head receiver. Maybe Sarnoff was coming to tell him the government was taking over RCA, as Mayfield had suggested. Perhaps he wanted to evaluate Oahu's communication readiness? Had his dysfunctional domestic situation raised rumors? Had he stepped on toes? On the bright side, maybe Sarnoff had talked the

Navy into reinstating his commission. He would know soon enough.

George followed the news stories and arranged a luncheon to honor Sarnoff. He buzzed his office manager, Sue Sharp, and asked her to handle the particulars. He jotted down a list of invitees, including the local top brass. His list stretched to over one hundred Army, Navy, and civic leaders.[53] He was sure to include Mayfield. Perhaps that would mend a fence or two.

Lieutenant General Walter C. Short, Admiral Kimmel's counterpart in the U.S. Army, received an invitation.[54] Short had distinguished himself in combat in WWI, rapidly rising in rank. He trained and taught others in the art of war. General George C. Marshall, the Army's chief of staff, in Washington, D.C., was an acquaintance. Short had recently replaced Major General Charles D. Herron at Fort Shafter, the command post for the U.S. Army's Pacific operation and the 25th Infantry Division. Short was in charge of defending the islands. Sabotage and lack of preparedness became his nightmare.

Short brought his wife, Isabel, and they moved into Quarters 5, on Palm Circle Drive, Fort Shafter. Despite the warm island weather, Isabel was not pleased with the transfer. She believed they deserved a position in Washington or at the Presidio in San Francisco, not one on a godforsaken island in the middle of the Pacific.[55] She preferred formals and furs to the muumuus and kimonos worn by the officers' wives in Hawaii.

Lieutenant Colonel George W. Bicknell would also attend George's luncheon. A giant of a man at six feet four inches, he staffed the Army's G-2 counterintelligence unit. Herron had hinted that Bicknell should head G-2, but Short, as the new commander, ignored his suggestion.

The FBI rounded out Hawaii's intelligence operations. The special agent in charge was Robert L. Shivers, who was surely on George's list of invitees. If he could not attend, he would send a representative. Shivers and his wife settled down the road from the Street family on Black Point.

Shivers had his feet on the ground when Kimmel and Short arrived. A coworker described him as "a small, soft-spoken man with an expression of utter guilelessness, the last person one would expect to be an agent of the Federal Bureau of Investigation."[56] J. Edgar Hoover thought otherwise. The Honolulu FBI office, shuttered for years, needed a full-time special agent in charge to reopen its doors. Shivers was his man. He had disarmed button-lipped gangsters, the Ku Klux Klan, and ordinary men under the influence of strong drink and a weak moral compass when Prohibition brewed gangs, moonshine, and speakeasies awash in booze.

Shivers rented an office in the Dillingham Building on Bishop Street in downtown Honolulu, within walking distance of the Iolani Palace and the RCA office. The building was Art Deco opulent. Gold metallic fans served as floor indicators above gleaming elevator doors, their pattern echoed in the tile floor and ceiling frescos. Light flooded the lobby through arched columns. Reflections danced across the room. Just entering the space lifted one's spirit.

Initially, Shivers staffed the second-story FBI office with a stenographer and just two agents. He reached out to the local community, including George, but the reception was cold. Hawaii did not want the FBI. Asian cultures avoided his office altogether.[57]

Within two weeks of his arrival, Hoover sent Shivers files of 125 worrisome individuals living in the Islands. Bernard Otto Kuehn and his family were at the top of the list. They were one of the reasons Hoover reopened the office. The FBI suspected that Kuehn spied for Germany because he was an ex-Nazi who lived high on the hog and had no visible means of support.

The Army and Navy handed Shivers a list of hundreds more. The task of investigating so many proved too much for his small staff, so Shivers analyzed the structure of the community instead. He did not want to fall into the trap of racial profiling in such a multicultural municipality.

Shivers learned the ins and outs of the Asian culture by taking in a Japanese student, Shizue (Sue) Kobotake, who attended the university. Sue helped him understand the complexities of the Chinese, Japanese, Korean, Philippine, and Hawaiian cultures, particularly those who lived on the islands. And she enabled him to appreciate the depth of their loyalty to the United States. Sue often invited students to their home, and Shivers and his wife, Corrine, welcomed them.

By the time Kimmel and Short arrived, Shivers' office had expanded to fourteen special agents, an assistant special agent in charge, a radio operator, eight clerical people, and a Japanese translator.

As the FBI expanded, the army and naval intelligence units on Hawaii tried their best to figure out what the Japanese were planning, so they could effect an appropriate response.[58] Where and when was Japan going to strike? Would Japanese, German, and Italian aliens remain loyal to the U.S., or would they turn if the wind shifted? Because of its location, Hawaii would become a launch-pad for U.S. forces when war broke out. If Japan captured the Hawaiian Islands, then they would become their gateway to the mainland. Was Hawaii prepared?

Answers drifted into the air like feathers in the wind, waiting to be caught by insightful interceptors and astute decoders. The intercepted data filtered up the ranks and was then forwarded to Magic for decoding. The higher and further away intercepts went, the less likely they were to grab the attention they warranted. Too much data overwhelmed these short-staffed, spartan offices.

The only consistent lateral movement of information in Hawaii occurred on Tuesdays. One Navy man, one Army man, and one FBI agent, Mayfield, Bicknell, and Shivers, met to compare notes.[59]

***

The head of fleet intelligence admitted that he never had any contact with G-2.[60] Because Hawaii did not have a Purple machine to decode diplomatic traffic, international developments filtered back to Hawaii's command from Washington. As a consequence, newspaper reports became Hawaii's primary source for world news. The man in charge of the Navy's long-distance air reconnaissance said, "my only information concerning our relation with Japan and the imminence of war came from the Honolulu newspapers...."[61] Communication was in a chaotic state, but Mayfield and Shivers assumed that George had answers at his fingertips. Shivers wanted specifics, but George only shared suspicions. The Army respected international and federal communications law and did not attempt to sway George to hand over radiograms, as did the Navy. As a result, no single clearinghouse existed to ensure that all services and relevant government officials received the same intelligence.[62] As Special Investigator Henry C. Clausen later pointed out, "We might have possessed the genius to break the Purple code, but in 1941, we did not have the brains to know what to do with it."[63]

Chapter 5

Preparing for War

General Short primed the islands for war, while G-2 and MS-5 scurried through code and intercepts like mice in a maze. Monitoring station MS-5, at Fort Shafter, was under the direction of Signal Officer Lieutenant Colonel Carroll A. Powell. It was part of Magic, even though it did not have a Purple machine. Consequently, it was subject to the same ultra-security protocols established in Washington. Even if Powell could decode Purple, he could not share the decrypts with his commanding officer, General Short, because Short did not have an Ultra clearance. Short could not even know that MS-5 was part of Magic![64]

Powell's task was to forward *relevant* intercepts to Magic for decoding, but how could he sift the wheat from the chaff without a Purple machine?[65] His unit only had a Red machine. Hamstrung and blindfolded, his only alternative was to send all un-coded messages to Magic, usually by airmail. Weather permitting, they arrived stateside in two weeks — too late for timely intelligence.

While Powell stumbled around in a cave with narrowing passageways, General Short began preparing the islands for war. Two months after his arrival on Army Day, 7 April 1941, Short stood in front of Honolulu's politicians and business leaders at a Chamber luncheon and lobbed a bombshell — war was coming, and Hawaii must be ready. Short told his shell-shocked audience that shipping lanes might close and that the islands could face bombardment. He did not mince words. Households needed to stockpile food — now. Honolulu had to develop a strategy for the evacuation of women and children, preventing the sabotage of utilities, and building bomb shelters near vital industries.[66]

Unable to ignore newspaper headlines and General Short's warning, the new mayor of Honolulu, Lester Petrie, appointed a committee to create a city disaster plan within two months of the luncheon. Petrie wanted the Islanders to take care of themselves in the event of an emergency but acknowledged the need to coordinate with the military so they would not be "hampered unnecessarily by civilian problems...."[67]

George supported the endeavor and encouraged readiness and unity during a weekly radio program, *The American Way.*[68] His years in China and Japan gave him a perspective a less traveled person wouldn't possess. He respected both Chinese and Japanese cultures and knew not to underestimate the Japanese in the run-up to war.

In response to Short and Petrie's call to readiness, the new plan established the Major Disaster Council, organized into twenty subcommittees based on a plan drawn up by the Army.[69] The Red Cross and the city raided their coffers to help fund the council. Businesses, the Young Men's Buddhist Association, and even the United Japanese Society, among others, loaned facilities and employees and held benefit ball games. The money raised purchased firefighting equipment, two-way radios, and medical supplies for first aid stations.

Even though no funds existed for air raid sirens, a committee to oversee early warnings was organized. Separate committees were formed to protect power, light and water supplies, animals and art, and to bury the dead. The transportation committee compiled a list of five thousand vehicles and their owners for use in an emergency. The engineering committee surveyed equipment, tools, repair shops, and machinery.

Organizers patterned fire wardens and block wardens after emergency preparedness systems already in place in Europe. Five thousand people were needed to cover all blocks in the city. Five hundred stepped up, including George's son.

George attended Businessmen's Military Training Corps (BMTC) meetings. Unable to man a checkpoint because of his disability, he nonetheless learned what to do if an attack or invasion occurred. It was vital for him to keep communication lines open to the mainland and inform the RCA chain of command if war broke out.

A food committee formed, in part because the islands relied on imports from the mainland. An inventory revealed that Oahu possessed a thirteen-day supply of rice, an eighteen-day supply of potatoes and onions, thirty-seven days' worth of meat, and a seventy-five-day supply of wheat and cereal.[70] A reduction in fresh-market fish became an unintended consequence when authorities impounded falsely registered alien fishing vessels. The seizure sprang out of the fear of espionage and the desire to reduce competition between Hawaiians and Americans, who trolled the same patch of ocean. The committee printed ration cards in July.[71]

Experiments to convert sugar cane and pineapple fields to vegetable gardens did not go well. Plantation owners, unfamiliar with other foodstuffs, planted seeds for crops that would not grow well in Hawaii. Sugar cane grew best in wet, soggy soil, pineapple in dry areas. Replacing them with vegetables not suited for those conditions resulted in disaster. Waterlogged and emaciated crops became hog feed. To make matters worse, Congress denied funds for additional food-storage refrigeration units. Surpluses, stored in inadequate facilities, turned into rat and mouse nirvana. A sea of vermin and worms carpeted the floors like something out of a horror movie, but the hogs loved it.

The food committee also created menus and recipes, so that a thousand volunteers could feed ten thousand people a day. School cafeterias would serve as distribution points. Later, the committee discovered they had forgotten to add baby food to their list.

The evacuation committee found over two million bags to fill with sand for making bomb shelters and to protect storefronts. The members drew up plans for three evacuation centers at Tantalus, Alewa Heights, and Moanalua Gardens, each of which could house fifteen thousand people. When no funds materialized to build the centers, the members went to the public and asked them to open their homes in the event of an emergency. The committee included a questionnaire with residential electric bills to assess capacity and willingness. As a block warden, George Jr. conducted door-to-door surveys for those who did not respond.

A medical committee organized forty-five hundred volunteers. The Red Cross trained one thousand of the most qualified for first aid, and scores of others for lesser duties. The committee identified locations for first aid stations, organized branches on the other islands, and drafted policies for the evacuation of hospitals. They planned to scatter patients, medical supplies, and medicine at specific schools around the Islands. Committee members fabricated bandages and dressings and stashed them in the basements of private homes, aid stations, and schools.

The Red Cross Women's Motor Corps supplemented the current transportation infrastructure. They even had uniforms. It was their job to transport the wounded, assist with evacuations, run errands, move blood and supplies, and do whatever else needed to be done. The women learned how to maintain a truck, deliver a baby, drive during blackout conditions, render first aid, and handle a gas attack.[72]

Police reservists trained once a week. Businessmen, professionals, and government officials made up this volunteer force and accompanied police officers on their shifts. They learned to perform all the duties of a police officer. One hundred twenty reservists received their commissions before 7 December. [73] Classes were offered to the island's ladies, so that they could learn how to shoot a pistol. The bomb squad designed an insignia.

✳ ✳ ✳

By late summer, military practice maneuvers occurred daily, including Sundays. A never-ending air show glided across the skies of Oahu. The drone of aircraft and the thunder of artillery became the new white noise of the islands. Searchlights streaked the night skies like flashlights in a darkened room.[74] The sound of Pan American seaplanes, called flying boats or Clippers, reverberated for miles as pilots throttled up to ease them onto the step of a wave for liftoff. Locals learned how to handle firebombs and deal with gas attacks, but most did not expect to use their newly acquired skills. They looked toward Asia for the fireworks of war.

By now, movies played a dominant role in the United States' propaganda machine. George and his kids went to see movies like *Wings of the Navy* with Olivia de Havilland. Barbara loved to listen to

Barbara Street ROTC Drill Team
(George Street Archive)

the Andrews Sisters harmonize eight to the bar. *Boogie Woogie Bugle Boy* was a favorite. She got caught up in the flurry of war preparedness and helped her dad stockpile food.

Barbara believed the United States would go to war, but, like most Oahu residents, she thought that Hawaii was too isolated to become a live target. How could the Japanese possibly attack over such a great distance?[75] Besides, the Pacific Fleet would protect them. Barbara's reality consisted of the simple joys of teenage life in paradise — beaches, girlfriends, palm trees, school, her boyfriend, sock hops, movies, and a dad who worked long hours. When Barbara started her senior year at Roosevelt High School, Oahu teemed with diversity. Cultures clashed as people jostled to make room for new arrivals, military and civilians alike. For the Street family, this meant more business for RCA and longer working hours for George. For Barbara, it meant more choices.

Her high school "Class of '42" anticipated a memorable year, according to senior class president Gene Rabe. He and class secretary, Muriel Moffitt, purchased a class banner to display at football games and dances. It hung above the orchestra at the Red and Gold dance. Goalposts decorated with ginger and ti leaves, welcomed the students. Gold football-shaped programs rounded out the theme. Multicolored globes hung from trees that encircled the school's patio. Light flickered across the dance floor as her class celebrated the Punahou-Roosevelt football game.

Girls wore long, short-sleeved Hawaiian print gowns, high heels, and leis draped around their necks by hopeful boyfriends. Boys sported coats, ties, and fashionable two-toned oxfords. A live band filled the night with the latest music. Conga lines wound through the trees, and rumbas emboldened sweaty hands on bare skin.

Barbara also joined the ROTC Sponsor Corps at her high school to answer the call to patriotism and war preparedness. Signing up brought her closer to her boyfriend, Billy Thoene, handsome, dark-haired, and tan. He was also one of the male cheerleaders for the Roosevelt football team. He captured her heart like no one had done before.

Roosevelt's Junior Reserve Officer Training Corps, in its eighth year, prepared students for further military training. Those who signed up could chart their own path rather than wait for their number to drop into the draft bingo wheel slot. Billy was a cadet-lieutenant, and Barbara was in the ROTC Sponsor Corps for Company D.[76] She could not join the regular program, because she was a woman. Instead, her corps hosted military balls, participated in uniformed parade drills, and became sharpshooters. Under the leadership of Lieutenant J.W. Jackson and his twelve cadet officers, she practiced close order drills and dry-work arms fire after school in preparation for qualification tests slated for mid-December. Affectionately called "Streetie" by her friends, Barbara and her classmates looked forward to their graduation, their rite of passage, come June.

"The future would take care of itself," Barbara said, "... even if my father refused to send me to nursing school with Peggy, and even if Mutt and I did not go on that tramp steamer excursion we dreamed about, or even if all I ended up doing was getting an office job somewhere." [77] The senior picnic, the fall drama presentation, *Ever Since Eve,* Class Day, and ROTC drills filled Barbara's fall calendar. War was not a serious concern; it was far away, on distant shores.

But that soon changed. FDR issued a proclamation that froze Japanese assets in the United States and its territories. Japanese importers and retailers had no choice but to close. Several hundred thousand dollars flew from Japanese banks, depressing the local economy. [78] General Short went to "half an alert" and placed guards on bridges and utilities. [79]

Suddenly, diplomatic tensions became real. Paranoia replaced trust. General Short feared Japanese-Americans would become turncoats and fill the ranks of an invading Japanese army. General Herron had predicted that five percent would hold firm to their American roots, five percent would turn, and that ninety percent would wait and see which way the wind blew. [80]

FBI Special Agent in Charge Shivers took a different tack. He put together a committee for inter-racial unity, made up of Chinese, Filipino, and Japanese volunteers because he feared massive arrests of non-whites, if war came to Hawaii. Committee members worked hard to encourage displays of loyalty and support for the United States among their communities.

Honolulu planned for war like people in earthquake country organize for the big one — be prepared, but put worry on the shelf. What were the chances? Volcanic explosions, tsunamis, and hurricanes happened in Hawaii, not war. George Jr. later wrote: "… the replacement … of Admiral Richardson and General Herron by Admiral Kimmel and General Short … did not mitigate our collective yawn … In Hawaii, we were too busy with our normal interests to give the ongoing war much thought."[81]

Chapter 6

Inside Outside

George now worked fourteen-hour days, six days a week. The inevitable boom that came when the Pacific Fleet relocated from San Diego increased military personnel to over forty-three thousand. They expected twenty-five thousand more. Men outnumbered women in the city by about a hundred to one. The boogie house hookers on Hotel Street and the New Senator Hotel did a hell of a business. Civilian contractors from the mainland, who camped in temporary housing units called cantonments, built the infrastructure to house and supply the ever-growing number of military men. Drab green army tents dotted Oahu while soldiers waited for barracks. RCA's staff was stressed to the limit as they tried to keep up with all the radiograms and money orders wired to the mainland by new arrivals. George ran "help wanted" ads almost continuously. Then the Japanese consulate ramped up its operation, and more work flowed through RCA's doors.

In March, Captain Kanji Ogawa, chief of the American section for Japanese Naval Intelligence in Tokyo, had appointed a new consul general to Honolulu. Ogawa was a career intelligence officer, a bright, diligent, and organized spymaster familiar with Americans and America because he had served as a naval attaché at the embassy in Washington. Ogawa chose a person who could do more than just run the consulate, Nagao Kita, a descendant of warriors.

With the support of influential Japanese naval officers, Kita obtained access to a secret fund that helped him live beyond his means at his new assignment.[82] Projecting the air of a social gentleman that belied his pug dog appearance, it wasn't long before he had the Honolulu consulate running like a well-oiled machine.[83]

Ogawa and Kita set up an "inside" and "outside" spy system in Honolulu.[84] The inside system consisted of consulate personnel and diplomats who reported activity legally obtained by ordinary observation. There were no covert James Bond tricks — the outside agents handled those. Ogawa sent selected men to Kita to operate quietly and effectively under assumed names.

One outside agent was a grocer, another, the proprietor of the Venice Café, a hotbed of information frequented by American servicemen. One was a chemist who made homebrew. Occasionally, the chemist enjoyed the fruits of his labor a little too much and boasted that he was in the Imperial Navy.[85] "Johnny-the-Jap," Yoshie Mikami, a scruffy cab driver with a fleet of one aged Oldsmobile, was also a member of Ogawa's spy ring. He pumped arriving sailors for information when he drove them to the pleasures that awaited them on Hotel Street. Unfortunately, this motley crew of outside agents contributed little to Ogawa's secret files.[86]

It was Kita's vice-consul, Otojiro Okuda, who accomplished most of the espionage work in Honolulu. He, like Kita, was a serious man, unjaded by Hawaii's aloha ways. Okuda used a small fund to pay hundreds of informants anywhere from five to fifty dollars for tidbits of information. An informant would go to a bar and get the skinny on all sorts of comings and goings from the loose lips of unaware service members, or they might get a haircut and hear gossip. They could climb a ridge or ascend Red Hill and observe military bases and the harbor. It was easy money for people looking to make a buck. Taxi drivers, agents planted at cable companies, and even a Buddhist priest contributed to Kita's network and supplied him with regular reports. Steamship passengers and crews provided him with additional information.

Hawaii was so wide open that any formal effort to obtain more intelligence was not necessary until Tokyo briefed Ogawa about the Pearl Harbor attack.[87] Once he was aware of the plan for a sneak attack, he needed a trained spy at the Honolulu consulate. Ensign Takeo Yoshikawa, a graduate of the Japanese Naval Academy who washed out because of tuberculosis, fit the bill. He spoke English well and was an expert on the U.S. fleet and the U.S. bases in Hawaii, Guam, and Manila.

Yoshikawa, code named Tadashi Morimura, was clean-cut, lean, and lantern-jawed. He booked first-class passage from Tokyo on the *Nitta Maru,* a luxury class ocean liner, for the record-breaking twelve-day crossing from Tokyo to Honolulu. Kita and Okuda welcomed him at the dock when he disembarked and drove him to the *Shincho-ro* tea house before heading to the consulate.[88]

When they walked into the tea house, Honolulu and Pearl Harbor's sweeping views overpowered the traditional Japanese décor. Yoshikawa stepped up to the telescope provided for the guests and turned the screw. Pearl Harbor snapped into focus.

Crews lashed down cargo, polished brass, and tended to their home on the water.

Yoshikawa exclaimed, "This job will be a cinch and lots of fun besides!"[89]

His comment did not inspire confidence in his two hosts. Kita already had one "money eater" bleeding him dry, sleeper agent Bernard Otto Kuehn. After the three men got acquainted over tea, they drove to the consulate. Kita assigned Yoshikawa a cottage on the grounds and a desk in Okuda's office, which connected to Kita's.[90]

Kita gave Yoshikawa free rein. Yoshikawa preferred working alone, especially when visiting the geisha girls at the *Shincho-ro*. The owner of the restaurant, Laurence Fujiwara Jr., disclosed that his "grandmother let him sleep in an upstairs room where we had a telescope. Unbeknownst to us, he was using it to watch the ship movements in Pearl Harbor."[91]

Yoshikawa quickly developed his cover as a playboy. His fellow office workers spurned him and called him a "goof-off." He showed up late for work, returned to work drunk, and regularly entertained women in his quarters overnight.[92] He was living the life in paradise for the good of his country and with Kita's blessing to boot.

Taxi driver "Johnny-the-Jap" drove him on sightseeing tours to military installations, hot spots, and vantage points where Pearl Harbor unfolded like an open book. Yoshikawa rented airplanes at John Rodgers Airport with a geisha girl in tow as a cover and flew over military airbases unchallenged. For a different view of Pearl, he dressed as a laborer and headed out to the cane fields. After ten observations from that vantage point, Yoshikawa ended the ruse. He did not want to push his luck. Disguised as a garbage collector, down to his bare feet, he sorted through dumpsters at Pearl.[93] He swam the harbor to report on marine conditions and to scope out torpedo nets. During a glass-bottom boat trip on Kaneohe Bay (K-Bay) with two maids from the consulate, he confirmed that it was too shallow for the Pacific Fleet to use as an alternative anchorage. He also determined that the carriers were usually in the harbor on Sundays.[94] Yoshikawa kept careful records of patrol flights, ship names, maneuvers, locations, and drills. Unknowingly, RCA transmitted his Purple coded messages to Tokyo when the consulate chose RCA for their monthly rotation.

After the blitzkrieg in Poland on 1 September 1941, FBI Special Agent in Charge Robert Shivers and his staff began to keep a closer eye on Japanese consulate personnel. Shivers liked to visit Kita and spar with him about spying around the island. His presence at the consulate made Yoshikawa nervous.[95] Shivers distrusted Yoshikawa but could not arrest him. How could he throw him in jail for flying around Oahu or taking girls on trips in glass-bottom boats? In short order, Shivers placed wiretaps at the consulate. Wisely, Yoshikawa never revealed even a hint of his espionage activities over the phone.[96]

On 24 September 1941 at 8 PM, Kimika Asakuru, Kita's maid, knocked on Yoshikawa's cottage door. He was to report to Kita immediately. Yoshikawa slipped on his shoes and walked over to Kita's house, just a short distance from his own. Opening the door to his knock, Kita handed him a decoded telegram delivered by Joe Hashida, a new delivery boy at McKay Telegraph. It was from Ogawa. He wanted Pearl Harbor mapped into a grid — a bomb plot — that identified the berths of the U.S. fleet. He also wanted weekly updates.

From: Tokyo (Toyoda)

To: Honolulu

September 24, 1941

#83 Strictly secret

Henceforth, we would like to have you make reports concerning vessels along the following lines insofar as possible:

1. The waters (of Pearl Harbor) are to be divided roughly into five sub-areas. (We have no objections to your abbreviating as much as you like.)

Area A. Waters between Ford Island and the Arsenal

Area B. Waters adjacent to the island south and west of Ford Island (This is on the opposite side of the island from Area A.)

Area C. East Loch

Area D. Middle Loch

Area E. West Loch and the communicating water routes

2. With regard to warships and aircraft carriers, we would like to have you report on those at anchor (these are not so important), tied up at wharves, buoys, and in the docks. (Designate types and classes briefly.) If possible, we would like to have you make mention of the fact when there are two or more vessels alongside the same wharf.[97]

Careful reconnaissance got underway. Yoshikawa and taxi driver Johnny-the-Jap headed to Aiea Heights just below Chester Clarke's residence to record the battleships in Area A. Next, they drove around the peninsula and observed the destroyers in Area C. At Pearl City, Yoshikawa dismissed Johnny, sat on a pile of lumber, and studied the cruisers and carriers in Area B and the mine layer in Area D. The submarines were in the Southeast Loch – Area A.[98]

Four days later, Yoshikawa completed the grid and coded it in Purple. He sent the bomb plot to Tokyo via RCA. It was his one hundred seventy-ninth report. Colonel Powell's MS-5 operation at Fort Shafter promptly intercepted it and sent it to D.C. since it was in Purple code. It hit the desk at Magic on 3 October, two months before the attack. Commander Kramer translated it from Japanese to English on 10 October. He believed the grid's abbreviations represented a cost-cutting measure initiated by Tokyo, similar to ones spotted before.[99]

Kramer and his Army counterpart, Colonel Bratton, delivered it, along with a gist sheet, to the Ultras on their respective lists.[100] Unfortunately, the president was no longer on the list.

Yoshikawa's grid message was discussed and rehashed, then finally dismissed as insignificant. No one informed the commanders in Hawaii about its contents.[101] Only Colonel Bratton believed it important enough to warrant a pin at Pearl Harbor on the National Geographic Society map he used to track hints of Japan's war plans.[102]

Meanwhile, America's embargo on Japan halted commercial shipping between the two countries. The U.S. permitted passenger vessels on a limited basis. The Japanese press announced that three passenger ships received their U. S. oil permits so they could refuel and sail. *Tatsuta Maru* would depart on 15 October for San Francisco with a stop in Honolulu, *Nitta Maru* would head to Seattle on 20 October, and *Taiyo Maru* would sail to Honolulu on 22 October. As the rumblings of war became a drumbeat, droves of Americans who lived in Japan headed home and sent radiograms to alert relatives of their arrival, increasing RCA's overwhelming workload.

Admiral Yamamoto, fine-tuning the details of the Pearl Harbor blitz, arranged for the captain of the *Taiyo Maru* to scout the proposed attack route to Pearl, when he sailed on 22 October. He asked the captain to sail north of the Kuril Islands and then head south and approach Oahu from the north.

The captain also carried sealed instructions to Hawaii's Consul General Nagao Kita about three spies on board *Taiyo Maru*. They were officers of the Imperial Navy. Commander Maejima Toshihide, staff officer for the battleships, cruisers, and submarines of Operation Z, code for the Pearl Harbor attack, posed as the ship's doctor. Commander Suzuki Suguru, a staff officer of the air fleet, impersonated the assistant purser. Lieutenant Matsuo Keiu, a midget submarine pilot, disguised himself in the uniform of a merchant seaman. En route, they recorded the weather, winds, and sea currents. Yamamoto also ordered the three spies to set up a backup communication channel from Oahu, in case the Americans suspended wireless transmissions through the commercial carriers.

***

Three days after FDR and Sarnoff's October lunch in Washington, and thousands of miles away, the emperor of Japan placed a call to General Hideki Tojo, the minister of war. He ordered him to appear at the Imperial Palace. Tojo expected a reprimand, as he had tried to dismantle Prime Minister Fumimaro Konoe's cabinet because of the worsening embargo.[103]

At 5 PM, Tojo stood before Emperor Hirohito. The emperor told him that he had nominated him to be prime minister! Surprised and tongue-tied, unable to give the ritual response, the emperor rescued him. "Let us give you a little while to think it over."[104] Tojo left and visited the Meiji Shrine, the Yasukuni Shrine, and the Shinto monuments to warriors and warlords. When he returned, his office buzzed with congratulations. Japan's destiny was now effectively in the hands of the military.

Americans were stunned and dismayed when they found out that anti-American Tojo and his extremist followers now controlled the government. FDR quickly met with Secretary of War Henry Stimson, Secretary of the Navy Frank Knox, Admiral Stark, Secretary of State Cordell Hull, and Harry Hopkins, a close advisor living in the White House. FDR warned that "if war did come … we should not be placed in the position of firing the first shot if this could be done without sacrificing our safety, but that Japan should appear in her true role as the real aggressor."[105]

Chapter 7

Signals in the Night

The sky wore gunmetal gray on the morning of Saturday, 25 October 1941, when Consul General Kita instructed Yoshikawa to activate Bernard Otto Kuehn, the bumbling German sleeper agent Ogawa had sent to Honolulu in 1935, the same year George and his family arrived. As war crept toward Hawaiian shores, Kita worked seven days a week to keep up with Tokyo's demands.

Kuehn, the spurned son of an aristocratic German family, used the moniker "Doctor," even though he was not one. In fact, he did not have a degree in anything. "Doctor" Kuehn married late in life. His wife, Freidel, came to their marriage with three children from two different liaisons. Her older son, an aide to Reich Minister of Propaganda Joseph Goebbels, remained in Germany. Her half-Jewish daughter, Ruth, joined the ranks of Goebbels' mistresses in her late teens. Friedel kept Ruth's ethnicity secret and married Kuehn to provide herself safe haven in a respected German household. At the time of their marriage, Freidel's younger son, Eberhard, did not get caught up in the Nazi furor. Bernard and Freidel's union produced a third son, Hans.

Friedel and Bernard were two peas in a pod. Both wanted an easy way to make a buck. Kuehn rode on his stepchildren's coattails, living high on the hog with no visible means of support when he settled in Honolulu. A blind bank account for a fake loan set up by Japanese intelligence at the Deutsche Bank funneled installment payments to him. Over time, as much as seventy thousand dollars, the equivalent of over a million dollars, flowed into his account. In return, Kuehn sent periodic observation reports to Tokyo through the Japanese consulate. He also purchased two strategically placed houses that overlooked military bases on Oahu.

Kuehn taught Hans the details of ships when they relocated to Honolulu to help with his clandestine work. Hans, dressed in a sailor suit, would stroll the Pearl Harbor docks with his dad and charm his way on board. He then reported his observations to his dad. How could a lonesome officer refuse to show off his ship to a cute, blond-haired boy in a sailor suit? Kuehn met with Kita frequently, and regularly gave him complete counts of the U.S. Navy vessels present in Hawaiian waters. But he made a pest of himself at the Japanese consulate and broke protocol often. He once suggested to Vice-consul Okuda that he could invigorate the consulate's espionage efforts, and then he demanded more money for the paltry bits of information he provided.[106]

Most Hawaiians figured that Kuehn spied for Germany. In January, a *Honolulu Sentinel* gossip columnist wrote that he would like to know "when the deportation of the local Nazi family ... is going to be announced officially. We hear their house, set up with the bar for the servicemen, to get them in the mood to talk, was a tip-off as to just what the little lady of the trio [Ruth] was up to in her playing around with the local gold braid boys...."[107]

Kuehn's boldness and lifestyle did not slip past the FBI. The San Francisco office had opened a file on him in 1939, thanks to an informer.[108]

Under orders from Washington, the FBI and Army intelligence produced a potential detainment list of local people based upon their heritage, alien status, and position in the community. They called it the ABC list.

"A" listed people were those most likely engaged in subversive activities, and Kuehn was at the top of the list. "B" listed people were classified as potential threats. The dragnet swung over Shinto and Buddhist priests, Japanese language school teachers, judo clubs, subscribers to particular magazines, donors to specific organizations, Japanese newspaper reporters, and students who studied in Japan. Those on the "C" list included people and organizations with ties to foreign nations — including their homeland — businessmen with ties to Japan, German and Italian aliens, and those who engaged in activities not in the United States' best interest. Merely attending a meeting or banquet could land a person on the ABC list.

When it came time to activate Kuehn, the consulate's official driver, Mr. Kotoshirodo, drove Yoshikawa and Okuda to Kailua.[109] They all dressed for a game of golf.[110] Yoshikawa wore blue slacks and an open-fronted shirt. Okuda put his golf clubs in the trunk. They traveled in silence and hoped the FBI would not spot them. The driver dropped Yoshikawa at the intersection of Kuulei and Malunui with a bag full of money from Yokohama Specie Bank.[111] Kotoshirodo drove the nervous Okuda down to the ocean and stopped at Kalama Road to wait for Yoshikawa's return.

It was about four in the afternoon when Yoshikawa trudged a half-mile to Kuehn's house carrying the thirty-one-pound bag of money. His arms ached. Sweaty and hot, he found Eberhard in the front yard, wrenching on his bicycle behind the ironwood trees that surrounded Kuehn's house. After a quick exchange, Eberhard directed Yoshikawa to the backyard, where Kuehn puttered in his garden.

Yoshikawa walked-up to Kuehn and asked, "Are you Otto Kuehn?"

"Yes," Kuehn replied. He recognized Yoshikawa as Tadashi Morimura from the Japanese consulate and became uncomfortable with the fact he had entered his yard.

Yoshikawa then said the prearranged password phrase, "I have something for you from Dr. Homberg."[112]

Confirming the official contact, Kuehn escorted Yoshikawa to his garden shed. Yoshikawa handed him instructions, and Kuehn learned that Tokyo wanted him to test his shortwave radio, which he did not have, and implement a signal system scheme. He previously described a system to Ogawa when he was in Tokyo to renew his visa and receive payment.

When Kuehn finished reading, Yoshikawa passed him a blank piece of paper and an envelope for his response. Panic raced through Kuehn. He explained that he could not test the radio as requested. He did not have the equipment. He had lied to Ogawa about the fact that he owned a shortwave set that would have allowed him to communicate directly with Tokyo in the event of an emergency. However, he wrote that he could perfect the signal system, now that it was needed.

Kuehn asked, "Do you know what is in the bag?"

Yoshikawa said, "No," even though he knew it was jammed with cash. He dropped the bag to the ground and left with Kuehn's reply to Ogawa.

Kuehn unzipped the bag sitting at his feet. Crisp New York Federal Reserve notes and twenty-dollar bills filled it to the brim. He counted fourteen thousand dollars. And it was all his. Kuehn was officially activated as a Japanese spy. He tossed the instructions into his trash fire and went to work on a signal system.[113]

He figured his attic window was perfect for flashing coded signals. It faced seaward. He could pull back the curtain and switch the light on and off in a coded pattern to signal the departure of the ships at Pearl. Sheets hung a certain way on the clothesline at his beach house could serve as his daytime code. Ads published in the local paper about a Chinese rug for sale, farm supplies, and a beauty operator position afforded a backup plan. During this time, Kuehn stopped at the Honolulu consulate three times, ostensibly to send money to his stepson in Germany. What he wanted was more cash for his work. Shivers took note of Kuehn's visits, confirming the FBI's suspicions that he was a spy. Okuda told Kuehn to stop coming.

Kuehn needed to test his system before Kita would send it to Tokyo. Yoshikawa rented a boat one night to find out if he could see the signals from the dormer window.[114] As it happened, Barbara spotted a light out in the dark sea. Then a light flashed from the shore. She tensed. "There was so much talk of war. Spies!"[115]

The next day, Barbara told her friends about the lights, and one agreed to join her in a foolhardy plan. They would see who answered the door when they offered magazine subscriptions for their school fundraiser. The two girls walked up to the house that flashed the lights out to sea. Barbara knocked on the door, her heart racing. A Japanese man opened the door.

She held out the subscription page of magazine options and asked, "Would you like to buy a magazine subscription?"

"No," he replied and slammed the door. Barbara and her friend eyed each other and beat a hasty retreat. They told no one about their suspicions. Barbara later admitted that they did not know what to expect, much less what they intended to do. When they checked the next night, the lights did not appear. Barbara admitted that "it was a dumb thing to do."[116] They could have gotten in trouble.

***

George Jr.'s muscles strained, his clenched jaw relaxed, and he smiled at the sound of sand scraping the bottom of his outrigger as he pushed it into the water off Hunakai Beach. Across the bay, turquoise ripples melted to deep blue, where the waves broke across the reef. His sister was selling magazine subscriptions, and his dad was at work, as usual. He had the house and the boat to himself and just enough time for a quick sail before his block warden meeting. George Jr. scanned the volcanic Koko Head crater to his left and Black Point to his right, a lava flow that formed Oahu's southernmost tip. When the boat floated free of the sand, he jumped in, shoved the boom to fill the sail, and forced the boat's bow away from the wind. He trimmed the sail to close-hauled and steered for the break in the reef, toward Koko Head. Offshore winds propelled his craft and his spirit forward. His thick blond hair whipped across his face, and the sun warmed his skin.

Rounding Koko Head, the wind snapped his sail, and he rocked with the surge. The boat ran faster, and spray misted over the bow, as he spied fishermen perched near the edge of the Halona blowhole, on the rocky shore. Water sucked and boomed in time with the waves, and a plume of white shot skyward. Avoiding the roiling sea, George Jr. came about and ducked under the boom. Now on a reach, the boat accelerated, and he raced toward home. His grin said it all.

He pulled his boat ashore, well above the high tide line, trotted home, and took a quick shower. Then he hoofed it two blocks to the wardens' meeting at 4459 Kahala Avenue, his unit's precinct headquarters, on the ocean side of the street. It was just two blocks east of his house at 4604 Kahala. He arrived right on time and opened the gate to the backyard. Once inside, he descended the stairs into the empty swimming pool and took a seat in what used to be the deep end of the pool. Boards placed across the pool kept out the sun. It was a perfect place to meet — the Royal Hawaiian of dugout shelters.

The members of Precinct 29, Section 15, Zone 3 gathered for a training meeting. George Jr. and his fellow wardens reviewed emergency procedures, received their rendezvous points in case a call to action should come, and undoubtedly discussed the news. It was no longer a matter of "if" America would go to war with the Axis powers — Germany, Italy and Japan — but *when*.

General Short ordered the Army and the block wardens to anticipate a Japanese invasion now that Tojo was in power. The Army readied itself for a fight on the beaches and sabotage to its aircraft. Admiral Kimmel prepared the fleet for offensive operations. PBY flying boats flew submarine patrols. The Army Air Forces also flew patrols, but their grids fell well short of the launch distance for enemy carrier planes, because they possessed no long-range surveillance aircraft or bombers. Radar stations positioned around Oahu scanned two hundred miles out to sea. The technology was new, so the men assigned to the mobile units trained in shifts.

George Jr. and Barbara Street
(George Street Archive)

The block wardens learned what to do in case of a gas attack —put on a gas mask and cloister in a trench or a depression below grade. They were issued gas masks, as were most of the population, He and the other wardens affixed gas-attack alarms to the telephone poles in their precincts. Before they ducked and covered, they had to implement the alarm — a metal clacker attached to an old automobile brake drum.

Chapter 8

The World Turns Gray

David Sarnoff left to meet with George within days of his luncheon with the president. He likely flew on a Douglas DC-3, a twenty-one passenger plane, from New York to San Francisco via Chicago rather than take the forty-nine-hour boat train that connected to the cruise line. His twelve-hour flight cost one hundred sixty dollars, one way. There was only one class of ticket — first class. Onboard lounges, game tables, and gourmet meals made the trip as comfortable as possible.

After a short stay in the "City by the Bay," Sarnoff boarded the ocean liner, SS *Lurline,* for the ten-day crossing. The Matson liner's white hull stood bright against the water. Black smoke billowed from her two stacks and smudged the sky gray like a gathering storm. Crowds of departing passengers lined the rails of her two decks and waved goodbye. Handkerchiefs flapped. A cacophony of shouts, cheers, and tears from well-wishers sent the ship on her way. Tugs jostled her past Alcatraz, and people lingered on the pier as *Lurline* left them in her wake.

Onboard, fresh flowers brightened Sarnoff's dressing table, and a fruit basket sat on the coffee table in his first-class cabin. After settling in, Sarnoff spent much of his time in the radio room.

He "got a kick out of this trip ... fiddling with the radio equipment" as he reminisced with the radio operators.[117]

While Sarnoff steamed to Hawaii, *Taiyo Maru* sailed the prearranged route Yamamoto had requested. No hula girls greeted the ship when she docked in Honolulu. Instead, customs officials, Shivers' G-men, and Colonel Bicknell's agents boarded and inspected the passengers' passports and baggage.[118] They found nothing out of the ordinary and cleared everyone to come ashore.

Kita greeted the three spies sent to scout Pearl Harbor when they debarked. One of them handed Kita instructions from Tokyo that ordered him to provide a detailed schematic of each military post and base location, size, and strength on Oahu. Combined with Yoshikawa's intel, the map completed the picture of Oahu's defenses. Kita went to the ship almost daily to pass information he'd written on slips of paper rolled in the morning newspaper. American inspectors at the gangplank didn't check the paper when he boarded.

The three spies did not have much time to reconnoiter. *Taiyo Maru* docked just long enough to pick up departing Japanese. Toshihide Maejima scrutinized the hangars at Hickam and Wheeler and picked up folded packets of postcards with aerial views of Pearl Harbor for one dollar each. Then he and Suzuki headed to the RCA building on King Street.

"Suzuki and Maejima [and] seven or eight alleged, uniformed (quite old and dirty uniforms) *Taiyo* 'radio operators,' trooped into the RCA central radio office," George recounted. "Normally, a ship the size of the *Taiyo* carried a staff of three radio operators, not seven or eight."[119] The group was detained at the public

counter while a clerk fetched George. Alerted, George tapped out
his steps with his cane as he approached the receiving window.

One of the Japanese men leaned across the counter, "Are you
the manager?" he asked George.

"Yes, I am the manager."

Looking George in the eye, the spokesman then asked,
"Would you please allow them to visit the large transmitter station,
located on the northeastern part of Oahu Island?"

"No, visitors are not allowed, but tell me why you would like
to visit the site," George queried.

"We are radio operators from the *Taiyo*."

"... since when did any passenger ship in the Pacific carry as
many as seven operators?" asked George of the crew.

"Well, not all are ship operators, but the others are interested
in radio."

Next, the spokesman asked to see RCA's large receiving
station located at Koko Head.

"Sorry, not possible," George replied curtly.

"Could they come into our control central behind the counter,
and could he explain the operations of your multiplex machines?"
the spokesman pleaded.

George thumped the floor with his cane and said, "Sorry, men,
no visitors allowed." [120] As the men eyed his bustling operation, he
remained rooted in place until they left the building, incredulous at
the audacity of their requests.

George railed that there weren't "any FBI agents, ONI or G-2
men following such a group of obvious spies around the town ... it

seemed to me there were far more spies than uniformed crewmen." [121]

The FBI, ONI, and G-2 men did not have their heads in the sand, as George surmised. They and customs inspectors questioned 238 alien Japanese and 210 AJAs (Americans of Japanese Ancestry) scheduled to depart for Japan. But they did not question Maejima about the packets of postcards he purchased. The only items of interest that Bicknell listed in his "Operation *Taiyo Maru*" report were obscene pictures found in the luggage of a Buddhist priest and an entry in the diary of a young man stating he intended to join the Imperial Army. [122] They found no special report from the spies who visited RCA and inspected the bases, and they found no evidence that Pearl Harbor was a target.

When October rolled into November, it was time for the Japanese consulate to switch commercial telegraph companies to transmit their diplomatic traffic to Tokyo. [123] Mackay Radio Telegraph Company drew the short straw.

***

Sarnoff arrived on 5 November 1941, within days of George's encounter with the supposed radiomen of *Taiyo Maru*. His ship eased to the docks below the Aloha Clock, a reflection of the San Francisco Ferry Building tower they had left behind. "Three men with ukuleles and guitars, directed by Sol Kamahele, swung off the tug, galloped to 'A' deck, and began warbling and plunking in front of the astonished Mr. Sarnoff," a newspaperman reported. [124] Palm trees crackled in the breeze. Carts and outdoor tables crowded the sidewalk, and messenger boys ran to the pursers' offices. When Sarnoff exited customs, women in hula skirts offered him flower leis for sale. His photograph in the *Star-Bulletin* the next day pictured him draped with plumeria leis. "*RADIO'S NO. 1 MAN IS HAWAII'S GUEST*," shouted the front-page headline.[125] George Street and a host of others welcomed Sarnoff at the pier before he headed for his room at the Royal Hawaiian Hotel.[126] That night, Sarnoff attended a luau given in his honor by the president of *The Honolulu Advertiser* newspaper, Lorrin P. Thurston. Thurston took him to the opening of the newly renovated Volcano House lodge and restaurant perched on the summit of the Kilauea caldera and escorted him through a lava tube. Sarnoff quipped that the tube was "an invention he had not suspected, in spite of his familiarity with [radio] tubes."[127]

A few days later, at 7:30 PM, *Taiyo Maru* slipped from Pier 8, without the usual fanfare. Three spies and four hundred fifty Japanese loyal to the emperor headed for home. No band played *Aloha*. The passengers carried whatever household goods they could take with them. The Imperial Japanese naval spies had their "goods" with them.

***

The farewell luncheon for Sarnoff, planned by George, took place on 12 November, the day before his departure. George later wrote, "I made a point of introducing the chief naval intelligence officer, Captain Mayfield, to Mr. Sarnoff."[128] Getting right to the point, Sarnoff conveyed the president's hand-over request. George reiterated the same objections and concerns he had discussed with

Mayfield about breaking the law without the protection of a naval commission:

> **Mr. Sarnoff told Mayfield my position in the matter was technically correct, but at the same time thought if the 14th Naval District Commanding Officer, Admiral Kimmel, would write me a letter giving assurances of protection ... that he (Sarnoff) thought perhaps I could comply. From this brief oral conversation, I made out:**
>
> **(a) That, of course, I would not receive any such letter from Kimmel and**
>
> **(b) That I might sub-rosa give naval intelligence what they wanted.**[129]

George sat with Sarnoff and General Short at the head table during the farewell luncheon. A *Honolulu Star-Bulletin* photographer captured the moment. General Short, in civilian dress with a Hawaiian print tie, sat on Sarnoff's right and twisted his body toward the featured guest. Sarnoff was the center of attention in his white jacket and dark tie. He gazed directly at the camera. Power radiated from his countenance.[130] George sat on Sarnoff's left sipping from an oversized martini glass, hunched as though he were sneaking a drink behind Sarnoff's back. The flash captured George's eyes. He looked like a man about to walk the plank. How could George not comply with a presidential request delivered by his boss?

The Great War and his time in the Naval Reserve had prepared him for the moment when he would put his country before all else. George later wrote, "A man cannot serve two masters successfully.

I chose to violate the message secrecy laws and regulations, since ... I believed it was amply evident during those times that the safety of our Nation must be the prime factor."[131] The exigencies of war demanded much of men, including compromising their convictions. George grudgingly accepted that he would not get recommissioned and that he must fully cooperate with his bosses and the president's request, without legal protection. If anything went wrong, he worried that he would end up as the scapegoat sacrificed on the altar of political expediency.

Sarnoff publicly assured the local military brass before he departed that "We're now co-operating fully with the Army, Navy, Federal Communications Commission (FCC), and all government agencies."[132]

Concerned, conflicted, and not too confident, George realized that he needed help to fulfill Sarnoff's request. He let a couple of his staff members know about his mission to supply communiques to Mayfield. Then he swore them to secrecy.

Chapter 9

East With The Wind

On the same day as Sarnoff's farewell luncheon, special envoy Saburo Kurusu arrived in Honolulu aboard a Pan American China Clipper from Tokyo. He was on his way to the Japanese Embassy in Washington, D.C., to assist Ambassador Admiral Kichisaburō Nomura with a last-ditch effort to preserve peace between Japan and the United States. Tokyo had set a deadline of 1 December 1941 to make it happen, and he had lost three days, due to a forced layover for repairs on Midway Island. When the Clipper finally departed on the next leg of his trip, he left with the impression that the Marines had a large detachment on Midway, thanks to a ruse pulled by Colonel Harold D. Shannon. A handful of soldiers, cooks and mess-men included, spaced themselves two yards apart and marched in a continuous loop, during his stay at the Pan Am Hotel. Small arms fire and anti-aircraft practice added to the display of force. Word made its way to Tokyo that there was a significant American force at Midway.

Lieutenant Colonel George Bicknell greeted Kurusu when his seaplane eased into Honolulu waters. Bicknell stood in for General Short, because the general was at Sarnoff's luncheon. Customs officials, the press, and other military officers swarmed Kurusu. A reporter wrote, "Undiscombobulated, suave Mr. Kurusu bowed, murmured, polished his glasses, and glanced hastily around for a sanctuary and mistakenly headed for the Ladies' Room." [133] Embarrassed silence fell. "Shall we join the ladies?" John Morris, Far Eastern manager of United Press, asked with a hint of chagrin. The reporters marched in after Kurusu and held a press conference in the bathroom. They christened themselves the "ladies room journalists."

Meanwhile, Tokyo cocked the hammer, ready to fire if diplomacy failed. Seven Japanese fleet submarines of the Second Submarine Group set out from Japan to swarm the waters off Hawaii and California. Five carried midget submarines.

General Marshall, U.S. Army chief of staff in D.C., invited seven select reporters from the Washington press corps to a secret, off-the-record briefing. He laid out his strategy: "We are preparing for an offensive war against Japan ... the Japs believe we are preparing only to defend the Philippines ... If war with the Japanese does come, we'll fight mercilessly. Flying fortresses will ... immediately set the paper cities of Japan on fire. There won't be any hesitation about bombing civilians — it will be all out."[134]

Sometime in November, thanks to a presidential order, FDR was back on the Ultra list and able to read Magic dispatches in the "raw" again, instead of having to rely on briefings. [135] On 1 November, Bratton chose to ignore the new order and did not deliver any Magic intel to Roosevelt. Seven days later, the president instructed his naval aide, Captain John R. Beardall to "settle this thing once and for all." For three days, the Navy and the Army haggled over delivery protocols. Angry, FDR told Beardall to "pay no attention to those dunderheads in the Army and Navy" and bring him the intercepts as soon as they were processed.[136] From then on, only Beardall would courier Magic intel to the president and the other Navy men on the Ultra list. The Army delivered to the state department, Secretary of War Stimson, Secretary of State Hull, General Marshall, and the generals and colonels on their list. New protocols established that the War Department could retain one copy of a Purple intercept and the Department of the Navy could retain one copy, also.

***

While Japan positioned itself, and Roosevelt fought for reinstatement of his Ultra clearance, Sarnoff steamed back to the mainland. George established handover protocols to cover up RCA's noncompliance with FCC regulations. Working with his employees now sworn to secrecy, George later confessed that "I [had] our office prepare copies of scores of messages to and from the Japanese consulate for a period backdating several, if not many months, right up to Dec. 7, 1941."[137] George's crew redacted the information about the sender and receiver and kept no written record or communique receipts. They typed the body of the dispatch on plain paper, not RCA letterhead, then stamped it with the RCA message number and sealed it in an unmarked envelope. Mayfield's unit would then match the radiogram's number with the Japanese secret message serial number.[138] George placed a phone call to Captain Mayfield and arranged for a pickup when they finished preparing the messages. He insisted that only Mayfield come to his office and that only he would hand him the envelopes. There were stacks of them.

When Mayfield arrived, George asked "if his department had any people schooled in cryptanalysis or any who could read romaji, a system of writing Japanese in the Latin alphabet."

Mayfield asked, "Are they not in English?"

Surprised, George recalled, "Maybe he was pulling my leg, but I do not think so. I then told Mayfield that I thought the best thing he could do would be to have all these messages re-transmitted to Washington via the efficient naval radio circuits promptly. Airmail was at most one or two flights weekly."[139] Mayfield left with the packet. George continued to "tab incoming and outgoing messages to and from the Japanese consulate, Honolulu, from as far back as early October, if not as far back as August or September 1941."[140]

On 17 November, two days after Marshall's press briefing and about the time of George's first handover, Bernard Otto Kuehn delivered his proposed signaling system to the Japanese consulate for transmission to Tokyo. His plan involved lights flashed from his dormer window, automobile headlamps pointed out to sea, sheets hung from a line, flags on a boat, radio ad broadcasts, newspaper ads keyed to several items, including the sale of his chicken farm, a bonfire set on Maui, and shortwave radio calls. It was so convoluted that the vice-consul sent him back to the drawing board.

Then, on 19 November, Consul General Kita received a radiogram from Tokyo. American listening posts snapped it off the airwaves. It was in J-19 code. Days passed before it was decoded and distributed to the Ultras, because Magic had designated J-19 as a low-priority code. The message alerted all Japanese points about a planned radio broadcast updating prospects of war, keyed to a weather forecast. The Navy translated the following on 28 November:

From: Tokyo
To: Washington
19 November 1941
(J19)
Circular # 2353

Regarding the broadcast of a special message in an emergency.

In case of emergency (danger of cutting off our diplomatic relations), and the cutting off of international communications, the following warning will be added in the middle of the daily Japanese language shortwave news broadcast.

In case of Japan-U.S. relations danger; HIGASHI NO KAZEAME (East wind rain)

Japan-USSR relations: KITANOKAZE KUMOEI (Northwind cloudy)

Japan-British relations: NISHI NO KAZE HARE (West wind clear)

This signal will be given in the middle, and at the end as a weather forecast, and each sentence will be repeated twice. When this is heard, please destroy all code papers, etc. This is as yet to be a completely secret arrangement.[141]

Tokyo sent six variations of the same message over the next few days, and they captured the imagination of Washington. They dubbed it the Winds code. Command ordered listening stations throughout the Pacific to hunt for those illusive words.

***

Meanwhile, military activity on Oahu animated island life. George Jr. said there were "tanks and troops … on the roads, aircraft practicing dogfights, 8" howitzers located in the mountains behind the city firing their shells out to sea … Sunday, November 23, was my nineteenth birthday. Dad, Barbara, and I drove to Lanikai on the windward side of Oahu for dinner at the Fehlmans and joined the celebration of my Cousin Leo's birthday two weeks off … We could hear shells whistling overhead at dinnertime…."[142]

Two days later, at 6 AM, 25 November (26 November Japanese time), thick clouds diffused the light of the rising sun at Hitokappu Bay, on Iturup Island in the Kuril Practice for the attack on Pearl Harbor had now been concluded. The Japanese task force, led by three submarines, cruised into the rough waters of the Pacific. Commander Gishiro Miura, at the con of the carrier *Akagi,* did not broadcast his usual jokes. He set a course of east-southeast under radio silence, and the helmsman turned the bow toward Pearl Harbor.

***

Colonel Bratton studied his wall map, now full of pins. He was sure there would be war by the end of November. Japan and the United States had not reached a compromise in their diplomatic talks in Washington. On 27 November, Roosevelt, General Marshall, and Admiral Stark agreed to issue a war warning message to CINCPAC and CINCAF, the commanders in chief of the Pacific and Asiatic Fleets. It stated in part:

> **Japanese future action unpredictable but hostile action possible at any moment." The Navy added, "This dispatch is to be considered a war warning. Negotiations with Japan looking toward stabilization of conditions in the Pacific have ceased, and an aggressive move by Japan is expected within the next few days....**[143]

In response to this warning message, General Short ordered his troops in Hawaii to Alert Level One. In Hawaii, Alert Level One was the lowest of the three alert levels. Oahu's Army installations prepared for acts of sabotage and uprising. Admiral Kimmel continued to view submarines as his primary threat.

Washington was unaware of the fact that General Short had reversed the order of Hawaii's alert levels. Now Alert Level One was the lowest and three was the highest in the Islands, and it no longer agreed with the Navy's standard operating procedure.[144] In Washington, Alert Level One still meant that all field units would prepare for the maximum defense of Oahu and the outlying islands.[145] Short's revised *Standing Operating Procedures,* which included the reversal of the alert levels, had been printed and distributed on Oahu, while it made its way to Washington for final approval. Hawaii was at Alert Level One, while Washington thought it was at Alert Level Three.

Mayfield alerted Special Agent in Charge Shivers of the alert-level order. He also told Shivers about Japan's anticipated Winds code warning, and instructed, "if I suddenly call you and say I am moving to the East side of the island (Oahu) or north, south or west sides, it will mean that Japan is moving against the countries which lie in those directions from Japan."[146]

Shivers and the police held arrest rehearsals for those on the ABC detention list. They readied internment camps. He and the Committee for Inter-Racial Unity and Oahu's Citizen Committee for Home Defense worked hard to sway doubtful Japanese to take the American side. Shivers lamented, "I cannot send someone like Sue and hundreds of them like Sue to concentration camps, because it would ruin their lives."[147] Nonetheless, he did his job and prepared for the worst.

George Jr. received word of the Alert Level One security status at a block warden meeting. Personnel manned strategic intersections and bridges. The Army positioned aircraft wing tip to wing tip at Hickam, Wheeler, and Bellows fields to make them easier to monitor for sabotage. The *Hilo Tribune-Herald* and *The Honolulu Advertiser* headlined that the Japanese might attack that weekend.[148] But where? And how?

November careened into December, but Japan did not attack the Allied positions in the Pacific. General Marshall would not receive Short's revised operating procedures until after 7 December.[149] None of the listening stations heard the Winds code.

Alert Level One remained in place on Oahu. After the rush and fury of late November, the island exhaled. Civilians let down their guard and went back to their aloha ways. Christmas was coming!

Chapter 10

Messages in the Wind

Monday, 1 December 1941

It was the first of the month, time for the Japanese consulate in Honolulu to switch cable companies for the transmission of their messages to Tokyo. RCA's was the short straw.[150] Mayfield now had access to all their traffic, thanks to the arrangement facilitated by Sarnoff.

Refueling at sea one last time, the Japanese First Air Fleet steamed to its launch point north of Oahu. They received the GO order — *Hinode Yamagata 1208* — code for "Climb Mount Niitaka" on 8 December, which meant attack Pearl Harbor on 7 December, Hawaii time.[151] Ambassador Nomura and Special Envoy Kurusu's continued efforts to avoid war with America had failed. Tokyo instructed Nomura to use the transpacific telephone instead of cables, as Operation Z's execution on X-day approached. Tokyo established code names. FDR was "Miss Kimiko," and Secretary Hull was "Miss Umeko," The code word for "war" was "child."[152]

Tokyo instructed Japanese consular offices to evacuate and return home. The London, Hong Kong, Singapore, and Manila consulates destroyed their Purple machines, as well as all their codes and any incriminating papers. The embassy in D.C. received an order to destroy all but one Purple machine for last minute instructions.[153] Details on how to disassemble the machine came over the wire.[154] Tokyo retransmitted tons of old messages in an effort to hide the code-destroying directive from American interceptors, but U.S. radio interceptors found it anyway and alerted the president. FDR cut short his Thanksgiving break at Warm Springs and headed back to Washington.[155]

Tuesday, 2 December 1941

Americans awoke to a quiet news day. It was business as usual on the mainland. First Lady Eleanor Roosevelt advised women not to be "too practical" when selecting Christmas gifts. Stockings were hung for the White House staff. An all-white tree glowed at the White House among the holly, poinsettias, and mistletoe. The much-debated movie, *Citizen Kane,* debuted in Birmingham, Alabama. Columnists took potshots at Sinatra, disparaging his screeching teenage fans. Tallulah Bankhead and John Barrymore, both famous movie stars, were in the hospital.

In Honolulu, Bernard Kuehn drove his brown roadster to the Japanese consulate and delivered his *simplified* signal light system to Kita while Friedel waited in the car.[156] This time Kita found it acceptable. Kuehn also handed Kita an envelope with five hundred dollars for his stepson in Germany. Kita sent Kuehn's plan to Tokyo via RCA in PA-K2 code. Fort Shafter intercepted it and sent the message to Magic by surface mail. It arrived on 23 December.[157]

Once the Kita/Kuehn signal light radiogram was transmitted, George called Navy Captain Mayfield for a pickup. When

Mayfield showed up, George handed him a large envelope with a bundle of radiograms, including Kuehn's. Returning to his office, Mayfield broke protocol and sent them by courier to HYPO in a different envelope stamped "SECRET" from a "confidential source."[158] Mayfield did not want to send them by Clipper to D.C. It would take too long.

At HYPO, chief cryptanalyst, Lieutenant Commander Dyer, assigned the decoding of Mayfield's packet to Petty Officer Farnsley C. Woodward. Working sixteen hours straight, Woodward deciphered the ones in the low-grade LA code system first. They proved uninformative. He then went to work on the PA-K2 coded RCA cables, including the Kita/Kuehn signal light message to Tokyo.[159] Among the dispatches George handed over to Mayfield was Yoshikawa's information about American warships at Pearl Harbor, anti-torpedo nets, and observation balloons.

Woodward had never worked on PA-K2 code before. He had to start from scratch, because he could not ask Washington for the key without creating a flap, since HYPO was not supposed to decode diplomatic traffic. Unfortunately, he made a time-consuming error which took him days to unsnarl. As a result, the valuable Kita/Kuehn and Yoshikawa messages were not decoded in time to avert disaster.

That same day, a Honolulu Mutual Telephone Company employee found wiretaps on the Japanese consulate phone lines placed there illegally by Mayfield's unit. The telephone repairman promptly disabled them.[160] Fortunately, the FBI tap on the Japanese consulate's kitchen phone was not discovered. Shivers's telephone tap revealed that the staff was burning its secret files and codes. Shivers later testified, "About noon ... I immediately gave this information to Captain Mayfield and Colonel Bicknell ... Bicknell informed me that he personally gave this information to General Short's staff at a meeting on 6 December 1941."[161]

Wednesday, 3 December 1941

Once Mayfield's wiretaps were disabled, George Street's handoffs became the primary source for the diplomatic traffic between Tokyo and the Hawaiian consulate.[162] Neither the Army nor the Navy in Washington expedited RCA handoffs, because prior decoded dispatches from RCA had revealed only administrative-type instructions between Tokyo and the consulate. Consequently, they completely missed a series of RCA radiograms that described U.S. ship departures and arrivals occurring on the 3rd and 4th of December, which would have clearly pointed to Pearl Harbor as Japan's target.

A message sent by Chief of Naval Operations Admiral Stark advised Hawaii command that "Highly reliable information has been received that categoric and urgent instructions were sent yesterday to Japanese diplomatic and consular posts ... to destroy most of their codes and ciphers ... Circular Twenty Four Forty Four from Tokyo one December ordered London, Hong Kong, Singapore and Manila to destroy Purple machine."[163]

After reading Stark's dispatch, Admiral Kimmel turned to his Intelligence officer, Lieutenant Commander Layton, and asked him if he knew what a Purple machine was. Neither man knew of its existence. Then Layton told Kimmel HYPO had not cracked Japan's recently changed flag officer's code that would locate the Japanese fleet.[164]

Kimmel retorted, "Do you mean to say they could be rounding Diamond Head, and you wouldn't know it?

Layton replied, "They would be sighted before that."[165]

That night, an intelligence officer at the British consulate in Honolulu forwarded to Bicknell, Mayfield, and FBI Special Agent in Charge Shivers an urgent message from their Far East operative. It specified that Japan had accelerated its airfield preparations and deployed 100,000 troops, fighter planes, medium bombers, tanks, and guns to Southeast Asia.

Thursday, 4 December 1941

"FDR WAR PLANS!" shouted the headline on the front page of the *Chicago Tribune*. The news story exposed a confidential report for total war.[166] Congress exploded. FDR had some explaining to do. He won the election on the promise of no war unless attacked, and according to at least one newspaper, here he was planning for war. The White House scheduled a press conference for the next day. Secretary Stimson would do the talking.

Distracted by the leak but not disengaged, FDR read his Magic dispatches that morning, including the one confirming that the Japanese were destroying their codes and machines, and wondered aloud to his aid, Captain John R. Beardall, about when the war would break out. He was certain war was on the Allies' doorstep. Command drafted another war-warning message and then tore it up. They figured that the 27 November war-warning message was sufficient.[167]

In addition to FDR's war plan exposé, newspapers featured opinion pieces about the probability of Thailand being Japan's intended target. Other news included a report about a man in San Jose, California, who filed for divorce because his wife was addicted to listening to the radio. He claimed she did not clean, cook, or care for the children because all she did was to sit in front of the radio. The judge granted his divorce but gave his wife the radio.[168] They reported on Eleanor Roosevelt's speech in New York, where she reassured her audience that "aliens with good records ... need have no anxiety about being placed in United States concentration camps."[169]

At ten o'clock that night, while the revolving dance floor on the sixty-fifth floor of Rockefeller Center's Rainbow Room was in full swing, the FCC said they had intercepted the Winds code, suggesting a break in relations between Japan and Great Britain.[170]

Friday, 5 December 1941

Command ordered all U.S. naval radio stations to institute special watches to listen for the elusive Winds code broadcast, which had apparently been heard the previous night. After a flood of false reports, translation cards were issued to the already overworked and understaffed OP-20-G department in D.C. The War and Navy departments both debated whether the FCC's intercept was fact or fake. Colonel Bratton believed it a backup code for Japanese embassies and consulates to alert them that war had broken out.[171]

Meanwhile, Secretary of War Henry Stimson declared war on the *Chicago Tribune* for publishing secret military plans leaked from unknown sources. Stimson questioned their loyalty and patriotism and lectured them about the importance of keeping secrets. He went so far as to disclose his own plans, including the need for more men, more training, and more bases, turning the leak into a call for preparedness. Newspapers in Japan pounced on the news report like a cat on a mouse. It exposed an unprepared America and its deepest fears in anticipation of war.[172]

Yet the nation lived on. A warm rain dampened Capitol Hill. The First Lady directed final preparations for a one hundred-twelve guest Christmas party. While Eleanor's guests dined in comfort, the Japanese attack fleet crept within seven hundred miles of Hawaii, in stormy seas. The Pacific was a cauldron. Ships rolled forty-five degrees. Commander Mitsuo Fuchida prayed for the seas to calm, so the sneak attack could be launched as planned. The storm that pitched the Japanese fleet flung remnants of white waves onto the shores of Hawaii. Rain tramped across the ocean like a herd of elephants when an urgent radiogram from Ogawa roused Yoshikawa from the cocoon of his slumber: "Please report comprehensively on the American fleet."[173] He quickly hitched a ride to John Rodgers airport and rented a Piper Cub. After the flight, he strolled Pearl City and scanned the airfield on Ford Island. Then he sent a radiogram to Tokyo via RCA that summarized his sightings.

At RCA, the staff braced themselves for "boat day." SS *Lurline* was departing with a record number of passengers — seven hundred thirty-eight — which translated to a record number of radiograms that would fly across the airwaves as passengers let relatives and friends know that they were on their way.

In the middle of this beehive of activity, Mrs. Ishiko Mori, a medical doctor and the daughter-in-law of the renowned Dr. Iga Mori, approached the RCA counter. She wanted assurances that the radiogram she had filed the day before had made it to Tokyo. Mori explained that she was a correspondent for the *Yomiuri Shimbun,* with over ten million subscribers, and she could not afford to miss her deadline. She insisted on speaking only to the manager — in his office.

The counter clerk buzzed George's intercom and reiterated Mrs. Mori's request. Street's mental alarm bells went off. She and her husband, Dr. Motokazu Mori, had been on his "spy radar" for quite a while. He had turned their names into the FBI because they frequently sent long radiograms to Tokyo. When shown to his office, Mrs. Mori asked George if there were "interruptions on our path to Tokyo between Honolulu and San Francisco and then directly from San Francisco to Tokyo."[174]

George examined a copy of Mrs. Mori's radiogram sent on Thursday, 4 December 1941, at 9:46 PM. He reassured her that there were no delay reports. As soon as she left, he took a second look. Her entire transmission was in romaji, romanized Japanese. He recognized a few words. "I made out ... Christmas shopping was active in the new Mitsukoshi department store in Honolulu, the mention of *Tatsuta Maru* and *Taiyo Maru*, the mention of a machine, and even 'sigararet' ... Perhaps this was a paraphrased 'tip off' message confirming the Fleet is in," George later wrote.[175]

He was certain it was a critical message that confirmed the Japanese navy planned to attack Pearl Harbor.

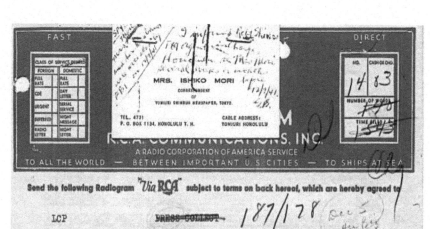

Send the following Radiogram *Via RCA* subject to terms on back hereof, which are hereby agreed to

LCP   PRESS COLLECT   187/178

YOMIURI   TOKIO

1941 DEC 4 PM 9

TEKITOONAHITOWO ERAREZU HENJIGAOKURETA KITASORYOJINIMO
ICHIYOATATTE MITAGA NICHIBEIKAIDANGA IMACHODO NAMIGASIRANO
YOONATOKORONI ARUNODETOKUNI DELICATENA KOKOROZUKAIWO YOOSURU
YAMUHAKUHIKISAGATTA KONNAKOTOGA ARASIMOMAEWO OMOWASERUTO
IYEBAIYERUGA KAKKOKUJINNO YUUWASITEIRU SAMAWAGAIJODEWA
HAINICHITOYUU KEHAIMO KANJIRARENU HODODA CHRISTMASMO
SEMATTASAKKON HONOLULUWA REINENYORI NIBAIIJONIMO BOCHOSITARASII
JINKOOYA GUNJUKEIKIDE MACHINONEONGA HONOLULU HAJIMATTE
IRAINOAKARUSA MIRUWAREWARENO MUNENIWA SHUJUNO KANGAEOYOBU
SONONIGIYAKASA AKARUSANOUCHINI WAKAI SUIHEITACHIGA MASSIROHI
ARUITEIRU TOKINIWAREINO MITSUKOSHINIMO HAITTENISEINO URIKOKARA
NIKONIKOTO KOKYONIOKURASII CHRISTMAS PRESENTWO KATTEIRU
TADASHIKAIGUN JOSOBUNO KINCHOWA SIZENDARO TATUTAMARU
TAIYOMARUGA KITEKAETTAATO NIPPONNI KAERUMONOWA KAERI HONOLULUNI
KAERUMONOWAKITE ZAIRYUDOHOWA TONIKAKU GYOMURI OCHITSUITE GYOMUNI
HAGENDEIRU NICHIBEIKAIDANNO NARIYUKIWO KINCHOSITE MIMAMOTTE
IRUNOWAWAREWARE NIPPONJINBAKARIDEWA NAIRASII WAREWAREMO

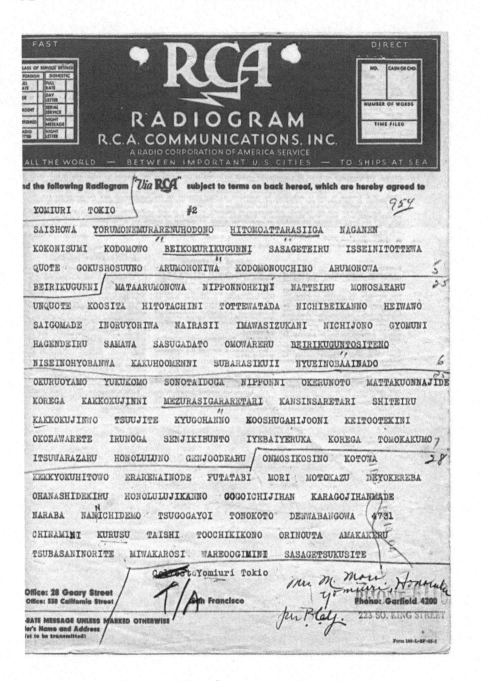

Two-page Mori radiogram (George Street Archive)

George phoned Captain Mayfield and asked him if he had anyone who could read romaji. "I felt quite sure I had an important message and that he should come by at once and pick it up. He never showed up. I phoned Mayfield's office (1 to 1.5 short blocks away from RCA) again Saturday, 6 December, but was informed he was very busy or was not available, so I left word for him to call me as soon as possible. He did not call...."[176] Mrs. Mori's article appeared in the paper the following day.

After he placed the call to Mayfield, George began preparations for training he was to complete the next day at Fort Shafter. RCA and the other commercial cable companies in Hawaii tried for years to facilitate deliveries to the Fort by installing a telex tic-line. Messages keyed into one telex machine would automatically appear on the receiving telex machine at Fort Shafter. For whatever reason, the military always refused. Now, finally, the tie-line was installed, hardwired, and machines at both ends were tested. RCA personnel were trained and ready to go. All that remained, in order to activate the line, was the training of Fort Shafter personnel. According to George it was a simple process dealing with "clerical details for interchanging messages to and from commercial carriers telegraphically."[177]

Until the tie-line was activated, a messenger on a motorbike was the fastest way to deliver messages to the fort. George later wrote, "When this job was ready to GO on 6 December 1941, Powell, by phone, informed me their civilian printer-operating personnel did not generally work on Saturdays or Sundays ... and that the available army personnel under Sergeant Thompson was too limited to undertake opening this new line for their first telegraphic connection with a commercial telegraph office. Colonel Powell … suggested that I delay the matter until Monday, Dec 8 … So, here was a "go" facility that remained unmanned and inoperative only because of the "do it next week" attitude of the … Signal Corps."[178]

That Friday afternoon, the FBI intercepted and translated a telephone call between Mrs. Mori's husband and Mr. Ogawa, a newspaper reporter. [179] The call cost two hundred dollars and grabbed the attention of the FBI, especially because the Moris were on their watch list.[180] They recorded the conversation. Unknown to the FBI, Mrs. Mori had received a telegram from Ogawa asking her to set up interviews with prominent Japanese living in Oahu, for another news article. She asked General Kita of the Japanese consulate, but he declined. Others she contacted were unavailable, so she talked her husband into doing the interview.

"Are airplanes flying daily?" Ogawa asked.

"Are they large planes? Are they flying from morning till night? What about searchlights? Do you know anything about the United States fleet?"[181]

Ogawa's questions were peculiar for an article about Japanese life in Hawaii. Was intelligence officer Captain Kanji Ogawa posing as the reporter?

Listening in on the illegal wiretap, Agent Shivers became convinced that the call contained code words of military significance. He arranged to deliver the transcript to Mayfield the following afternoon.

Chapter 11

"Why Don't You Run Along ..."

Saturday, 6 December 1941
Washington, D.C.

Roosevelt's meeting with Budget Director Harold Smith started ten minutes late. They were interrupted by an urgent phone call from Secretary of the Navy Knox. The British had just sent a triple-priority message about Japanese convoys moving south toward Bangkok and Malaya. The British army and air force in the Dutch East Indies had been mobilized. FDR pulled out his map of the Malay Peninsula and the South China Sea and penciled in the reported location and the Japanese ship type identified in the communique. As recalled by Smith in his diary, FDR remarked that "'we might be at war with Japan,' although no one knew."[182] Despite the apparent threat to Allied territories in the Pacific, FDR was convinced the Japanese were stalling for time.[183]

The budget meeting was not a typical government review of operations. Smith and FDR's talks included the development of a critical new weapons system. Before Smith departed, Roosevelt authorized the funding for an atomic bomb, and he set the Manhattan Project in motion. In August of 1939, physicist Albert Einstein warned FDR that Germany might construct an atomic bomb.[184] FDR was cautious about this new and exciting technology but reasoned that if Germany had an atomic bomb, America needed one too. It could be a game-changer. The Council of National Defense had scientists identified, costs nailed down, and the project ready to launch. In order to fund the Manhattan Project, FDR cut the Navy's request for forty thousand additional Marines, and then he broke for lunch.

Sometime between nine and ten on Saturday morning, Navy Station M, in Cheltenham, Maryland, intercepted two radiograms and teletyped them to Magic for decryption. Navy Lieutenant Brown input the second one through the Purple machine and then remembered it was the Army's day to decrypt; so he stopped.[185] The two intercepts revealed that Ambassador Nomura should expect a fourteen-page message. Tokyo wired that the situation was "extremely delicate ... Be most extremely cautious in preserving secrecy."[186] Tokyo also ordered Nomura *not* to use a typist from the typing pool to transcribe the fourteen-part message.

On the opposite coast, in the early morning hours of an otherwise quiet shift, Navy Station "S" at Bainbridge Island, Washington, intercepted a thirteen-part message. Station "S" was secreted in a defunct post exchange at Fort Ward, amid towering cedars. Oyster-colored beaches necklaced the blue-green waters of the sound separating it from the mainland. Bainbridge waited until five minutes to noon local time to teletype the intercepts to Magic.

In Washington, D.C., the hunt for the Winds code had died down. Army intelligence headed home at noon, because it was Saturday, and left the Navy to babysit the Purple machine that sat idly in its cage.[187] For the first time in a long time, the six translators had no top priority messages to transcribe. They had processed over seventeen hundred intercepts since 1 November. Now, there were only seventy-eight low-priority intercepts remaining in the in-basket.[188]

Translator Dorothy Edgers had no assignments that Saturday morning but wanted to prove herself. She had lived in Japan for thirty years and was fluent in the language. Hired three weeks earlier, thanks to her brother, Fred Woodrough, a leading Japanese linguist, the Navy had offered her beginner's pay. She convinced them that she was worth more and deserved compensation on a par with other translators. With no Purple intercepts to translate, she paged through the low priority messages in her in-basket.

One of the messages she perused was from Honolulu. It was the longest one, and it was three days old. She later remembered, "At first glance, this seemed to be more interesting than some of the other messages I had in my basket."[189] She went to work on it and kicked it back to a "crippie," as decoders were called, to clarify garbled letters. By 12:30 PM — a half-hour after others left for the day — her translation revealed a plan to communicate the Pacific Fleet's movements with "signal lights" flashed from the shores of Oahu.

She passed the document around to those who remained. The chief petty officer in the section said it could wait until Monday, but she could not put it down. By the end of the day, she had teased out these specifics:

If the above signals and wireless messages cannot be made from Oahu, then on Maui Island, six miles to the north of Kula Sanatorium ... at a point halfway between

Lower Kula Road and Haleakala Road ... visible from seaward to the southeast and southwest of Maui Island the following signal bonfires will be made daily....[190]

Edgers hurried down to the office of her boss, Commander Kramer. He chastised her for working past noon on low priority intercepts. A stickler for detail, Kramer marked up her translation, ignoring the content. He eyed Edgers and said, "Why don't you run along now? We'll finish editing this next week."[191]

***

By the time the thirteen-part radiogram intercepted by Bainbridge Island hit Magic, only Captain Robert E. Schukraft remained in the office. Since the Army crew had gone home for the day, it was given to the Navy side of Magic. Schukraft sensed the importance of the messages and called Major Harold Doud, who rushed back to the office. By now, it was 1 PM on Saturday. Doud received permission to call back his staff to assist the Navy, since it was the Navy's assigned day to decode and decrypt.

Then an inexperienced naval officer made a critical error. He did not set the key correctly on the Purple machine; so the entire device failed. His commanding officer, Captain Stafford, did not know how to reset the key; so he called the senior watch officer, Lieutenant George Lynn, and asked him to come in on his day off to fix it. Lynn arrived at about 4 PM to unsnarl the machine. A half-hour later, Stafford told Lynn, "There is nothing I can do but get in your way and make you nervous, George. I'm going home."[192]

While Lynn struggled to fix the Purple machine, more intelligence streamed in, this time from the British. They reported that the Japanese convoy, observed by both the British and the Dutch, was hours from launch points in Southeast Asia. President Roosevelt sent a message to the emperor of Japan, saying, in part:

"I address myself to Your Majesty at this moment in the fervent hope that Your Majesty may, as I am doing, give thought in this definite emergency to ways of dispelling the dark clouds."[193]

After he proofread the final copy of his plea for cooperation, a little before 7 PM (9AM Tokyo time), FDR attached a note to Cordell Hull, who would see that it was delivered to the emperor: "Dear Cordell: Shoot this to Grew [American ambassador to Japan in Tokyo] — I think it can go in gray code — saves time — I don't mind if it gets picked up."[194]

Once received in Tokyo, President Roosevelt's radiogram went through the Japanese post office, as did all cable and wireless telegraphs sent to Japan. In response to a request from their army, the Japanese censorship office delayed incoming messages from foreigners four hours on one day and ten hours the next. Since it was a ten-hour day, Ambassador Grew received the message at the American embassy in Tokyo at 10:30 that night.[195] He immediately called the Japanese foreign minister to arrange a meeting with the emperor.

The minister denied his request. When Prime Minister Tojo was informed about FDR's plea, he asked if there was "anything new" in the message.

"No," came the reply.

"Well then, nothing can be done, can it?" Tojo told the foreign minister.

"It seems a pity to go around disturbing people in the middle of the night," the foreign minister replied. [196]

Tojo said, "It's a good thing the telegram arrived late. If it had come a day or two earlier, we would have more of a to-do."[197] According to author Leonard Mosely, Tojo presented FDR's message to Emperor Hirohito at 3 AM (Tokyo time), twenty minutes before the attack on Pearl Harbor.[198]

Meanwhile, Lynn finally got Magic's Purple machine running. It was 5 PM in Washington. Two hours later, the Navy completed decoding the long message. It was in English and did not need translation. He asked the Army to lend him a typist because the Navy had not called back their civilians. Miss Ray Cave, a civil servant employee, sat down and typed the three thousand-word message. It was ready for delivery by 9 PM local time.[199]

While Commander Kramer waited for his wife to pick him up, he examined his six copies of the fourteen-part message's first thirteen pages to make sure they were perfect and ready for the Navy's Ultra distribution list. Shortly after nine that evening, his wife put their Chevy in gear, and they headed down Constitution Avenue — first stop, the White House. Hours later, he completed his last delivery.

Before Colonel Bratton headed out to deliver his six copies of the first thirteen pages of the fourteen-part message to the Army's Ultra-list recipients, he called Doud to ask him if he had seen the fourteenth part.

"I don't know, sir," Doud said, "either the Navy missed it, or the Japs haven't sent it yet."[200]

Dog-tired, Bratton instructed his assistant to wait for the fourteenth part. On his way home, he made his deliveries. He left a locked attaché case with the night duty officer to give to Secretary Hull in the morning. General Sherman Miles, assistant chief of G-2, attending Captain Wilkinson's dinner party, reviewed his copy. He told Bratton not to bother General Marshall until Magic received the fourteenth part. When it hadn't arrived by midnight, Bratton's assistant went home.

***

Just as the Japanese fleet entered the patrol range of American PBY flying boats stationed in Oahu, the Japanese embassy staff in D.C. buzzed with anticipation. A fourteen-part radiogram was on its way. In an unusual move, Tokyo sent it through two commercial carriers, RCA and Mackay. Senior Telegraph Officer Horiuchi and five other decoders completed eight of the thirteen parts on their J-97 (Purple) machine. Then they took a break to attend a going-away party for Secretary Terasaki. The men returned an hour and a half later with several rounds of saké and a good dinner under their belts and went to work again. They finished around midnight and delivered the message to Ambassador Nomura. He instructed Horiuchi to have his staff wait for the fourteenth part. He sent all but one clerk home when it hadn't arrived by 3 AM.

Chapter 12

One Last Day in Paradise

Saturday, 6 December 1941
Oahu, Territory of Hawaii

As the Japanese attack force steamed toward Oahu, Kimmel's nightmare arrived. Twenty-one Japanese attack submarines positioned themselves under Hawaii's water. Six task forces had cruised different routes to their joint destination, and each carried the world's most advanced torpedo, Type 95.[201] It could cruise at fifty-six miles an hour and deliver over one thousand pounds of explosive within a five-mile range. A few of the subs even carried a folded-up seaplane in a hangar attached to the deck. Five motherships transported miniature submarines strapped to their hulls.[202]

The sub commanders found little shipping traffic around Oahu, and the two hundred sampans that usually fished Oahu's tuna-rich waters were either tied up at the dock or steering for the North Shore village of Haleiwa to attend a wedding luau.[203]

While the waters of Oahu teemed with submarines, the most anticipated football game of the year was about to begin at Honolulu Stadium. A record twenty-four thousand fans filled the stands to watch the Shriners benefit game, which was always held on 6 December. Pregame activities started at 1:15 PM. Fourteen bands from high schools, service organizations, and the university played their hearts out, oblivious to the menace that cruised their waters.

At 2:30 PM the Willamette University Bearcats from Oregon and the University of Hawaii Rainbow football teams lined up on the gridiron for the kickoff. The Bearcats did better than expected and outplayed the Rainbows in the first quarter, with a six-point lead. Halftime activities kept spectators glued to their seats. Rockets, bands, batons, and bubbles delighted the crowd. During the second half, the Rainbows roared. *"UNIVERSITY OF HAWAII DOWNS WILLAMETTE 20 – 6,"* read the sports headline in the *Honolulu Star-Advertiser* the next morning. It was a hell of a game, with a classic comeback by the home team.[204]

For those not at the game, it was a typical Saturday in downtown Honolulu. More men than women crowded the streets, sidewalks, and bars. Swing music vibrated the moist Hawaiian air, as it slipped through the doorways of honky tonks and bars. The Royal Hawaiian and Ala Moana hotels featured live bands. On base at the Bloch Arena, battleship bands blared. Dressed in formal whites, pilots from Hickam and Wheeler air bases whirled their dates around officers' club dance floors.

Agent Shivers' secretary, Ruth Flynn, attended an anniversary party thrown by a lieutenant from the USS *Arizona* (BB-39). She proclaimed the party to be "the gayest yet." Young officers and their ladies jammed into the small cottage on the Halekulani Hotel campus.

Schofield Barracks hosted the annual Ann Etzler's Cabaret. Lava rock columns surrounded by ferns welcomed the guests onto the officers' club dance floor. This year's dinner, dance, and show was especially lively because the 24th and 25th Infantry Divisions had just come off a hard week of maneuvers.

General Short arrived late for the cabaret. He and his wife had invited intelligence officer Lieutenant Colonel Kendall "Wooch" Fielder and his wife, May, for cocktails at their quarters on Palm Circle at Fort Shafter. "Wooch," known for his magic tricks, likely entertained the general and his wife over drinks. Just as the couples settled into their car to make the fifteen-mile drive to Anne's Cabaret, Short's aide called the general to the phone. Lieutenant Colonel Bicknell was on the line. Bicknell asked the general to wait there for a few minutes. He wanted to show him a transcript. It was 6:30 PM.

Bicknell hustled over to Short's quarters. They retired to the lanai while their wives, dressed to the nines, waited in the car. Bicknell showed them the transcript of the Mori telephone tap. The phone call's high cost made it suspicious. Questions about air traffic, searchlights, and ship movements made it more so. The three men could not make sense of it. If the Moris were spies, why would they use the telephone?

Isabel and May sat in the car for an hour, undoubtedly displeased about being late for the show. Finally, General Short concluded that Colonel Bicknell was too "intelligence conscious" and, dismissing any urgency, suggested that they take up the matter in the morning.[205]

Over on Nuuanu Street, the Japanese consul hosted a stag party. Colonel Bicknell described such affairs as "really wet parties, a bottle of scotch at each place with a geisha girl pouring it out."[206] Bicknell and Admiral Kimmel declined their invitations. Instead, Kimmel went to a dinner party at the Halekulani Hotel.

At 9 PM, Agent Yoshikawa filed his last intelligence report before the attack. Most of the consulate personnel were still at the stag party. Yoshikawa had spent the day checking out the Pacific fleet, only to discover that the carriers were gone. His final report read:

The following ships were observed at anchor on the sixth: nine battleships, three light cruisers, three submarine tenders, seventeen destroyers. In addition, there were four light cruisers and two destroyers lying at docks. It appears that no air reconnaissance is being conducted by the fleet air arm.[207]

***

At sea, north of Oahu, a growing sense of *bushidō* spread among the men of Japan's First Air Fleet. A message read over the intercom said it all: "The fate of Imperial Japan depends upon this one battle. Everyone must fulfill his duties with the utmost dedication."[208]

Ships hoisted the Z-flag, symbolizing that the fate of Japan rested in their hands. Admiral Nagumo announced over the loudspeaker Yoshikawa's final count of American ships at Pearl Harbor, which updated Kuehn's report of 2 December, "At present, there are no signs the enemy anticipates an attack."[209]

Carriers crammed with planes pitched and rolled as the wind picked up and seas rose. Men carted black torpedoes and bombs across the heaving deck and mounted them to the bellies and wings of the Nakajima B5N "Kate" and Aichi D3A "Val" aircraft. Ground crews struggled to maintain their footing as they hefted the 20-millimeter cannon shells and 7.7-millimeter machine gun rounds aboard the Mitsubishi A6M Zeros. Like many of his squadron mates, aviator Iyozo Fujita believed he would die the next day. He was the leader of the first flight, an officer in the Imperial Navy, and, therefore, a samurai. He must act with honor and fairness and do his best to achieve victory. Fujita wrote a note to remind himself to triumph with dignity and honor. Then he drank six beers. By nightfall, the first of two waves of aircraft was ready to be launched.

Aboard aircraft carrier *Soryu* — the Green Dragon — Petty Officer Juzu Mori sat down to dinner at 5 PM and mused. "With each tick of the clock war drew closer ... It was now Saturday — the American sailors were most likely ashore, probably dancing the hula in the shade of a coconut palm."[210]

Juzu Mori hit the nail on the head. In downtown Honolulu, sailors and soldiers on liberty began their prowl at the Army-Navy YMCA on Hotel Street, across from the Black Cat Café. Three sailors — Clifford Olds, Jack Miller, and Jack Kosa — spent their evening at the Monkey Bar. The barmaid snapped a picture of them and offered to sell them a print. "What a scam," one said, but they bought it anyway.[211]

Men lined up in a river of white uniforms for a turn with a lady of the night. Others had their pictures taken with hula girls, or dropped some coins on Skeeball, played pinball, or tried to smack down milk cans with a baseball. Taxi-dancers swung with sailors on over varnished floors, collecting their fee after each dance. Others grabbed a bite to eat at the New Emma Café downtown and braved a tattoo. *Honky Tonk* with Clark Gable played at the Hickam Post Theater.

Before the night ended, the MPs rounded up thirty-eight soldiers, and the shore patrol threw four sailors in the brig. A sailor from USS *California* (BB-44) used a mate's liberty card; so he would surely suffer a captain's mast disciplinary hearing. The police flung thirty-nine civilians into jail. Not a bad count when there were eleven thousand liberty passes issued for the seventy-five thousand men stationed in the area that night.[212] Shortly before midnight, men with "Cinderella" liberty passes returned to their ships and bases.

At the Street household, George and his family stayed home and listened to the radio. They had not gone to the Shriners game, even though George was a member. It was tough for him to navigate through crowds. Barbara was interested in football but only when Billy was cheerleading. George Jr. never got into the sport. According to George Jr., "the evening of December sixth was not out of the ordinary. We heard, over the radio, the status of negotiations with the Japanese ambassador in Washington, D.C. There was a sense that things were not ready to unravel — yet. My father may have had a conscious view, but the average citizen would not have given it too much thought."[213]

Chapter 13

The Rising Sun

Sunday, 7 December 1941
Washington, D.C.

In the early morning hours of 7 December 1941, Magic decoded the long-awaited fourteenth part of the message sent the previous day. It stated that the Japanese government was breaking off negotiations with the United States.

Then Lieutenant Alfred V. Pering rushed in with two additional decoded intercepts that contained instructions for the Japanese ambassador. The first read, **"Please submit to the United States Government (if possible to the secretary of state) our reply to the United States at 1:00 PM on the 7th your time."**[214]

The second decrypt ordered Nomura to destroy the remaining Purple machine and all secret documents.

Colonel Bratton was convinced Japan was going to attack America somewhere in the Pacific. He ran down the hall to the office of Brigadier General Miles, assistant chief of staff for intelligence. Miles wasn't in. Next, he called General Marshall's home at Fort Myers. Sergeant Aguirre, the general's orderly, answered and told Bratton that the general was out for his customary Sunday horseback ride.

"Do you think you can get a hold of him?" Bratton asked, the urgency in his voice evident.

"Yes, sir. I think I can find him."

"Please go at once, get assistance if necessary, and find General Marshall. Tell him who I am and ask him to go to the nearest telephone, that it is vitally important that I communicate with him at the earliest practicable moment."[215]

While the Army alerted the Ultras on their list, Kramer delivered the decrypts to recipients on the Navy list. He walked down 16th Street to Pennsylvania Avenue and the White House. Captain Beardall, the president's aide, took the decrypts upstairs to Roosevelt, who was in bed perusing his daily stack of newspapers. After reading the decrypts, Roosevelt made a remark about the Japanese breaking off negotiation. Beardall would later testify that Roosevelt did not seem overly concerned, and he did not take further action. Beardall also testified that he did not recall telling the president about the one o'clock deadline or Kramer's remark indicating that the Japanese were about to strike somewhere.[216]

Meanwhile, Bratton dialed the phone again and called General Miles' home. He brought him up to date and added with great urgency, "You better come down here at once."[217]

Chief of Naval Operations Admiral Stark, studied the latest decrypts. He had read the first thirteen parts the night before, around eleven-thirty. As he discussed the fourteenth part and the one o'clock deadline with Captain Wilkinson and Commander McCollum, word spread, and his staff streamed into his office. They worried over the threat to Singapore, Thailand, and the Dutch East Indies. Initially, they did not consider an attack on Hawaii, but soon the possibility of a threat to Pearl Harbor did cross their minds. Apprehension took hold. A staff member suggested, "Why don't you pick up the telephone and call Admiral Kimmel?"[218]

Stark hesitated. According to a letter he sent to Kimmel on 17 October, he did not think the Japanese would attack the U.S. Besides, the five-and-a-half hour time difference between Washington and Hawaii meant it was around 4:30 AM in Hawaii. He disliked telling field commanders how to do their jobs, so he returned the telephone receiver to its cradle. He had warned Kimmel on 27 November. To do so again would show disrespect.

On this day, of all days, General George Marshall took a different route on his horseback ride. His orderly did not find him until he returned home. As requested, Marshall called Bratton, who volunteered to come to the general's house. He did not want to discuss the secret intercept over the phone. Marshall told him, "No, I'm coming to the office. You can give it to me there."[219]

Twenty minutes after Marshall hung up, Commander Mitsuo Fuchida went down to *Akagi's* ready room, which overflowed with pilots. After their briefing, just as the sun lit the sky, the aviators headed to the flight deck. When the first man opened the door to the flight deck, wind forced him back. The aviators plowed forward, as waves pounded the hull and spray spewed across the deck. The ship rolled ten degrees, and men broke their stride to catch themselves. Aircrews mounted planes that bucked like wild horses. Flight deck crews braced themselves against their aircraft and waited for the order to take off. A sailor raised, lowered, and raised the battle flag again to signal the other carriers to launch their planes. The aircraft strained in their tethers, as *Akagi* turned into the wind.

"Start your engines," the loudspeaker blared, and salt-laden air vibrated with the thunder of radial pistons. The deck crew scrambled and removed wheel chocks, timing their pull to the pitch of the bounding carrier.[220] A green signal light swung in a circle at the end of the flight deck. The first pilot eased his plane into takeoff position. Just as he revved his engine to full throttle, the carrier's deck plunged toward the sea. The deck crew held their breath. Then the bow rose, and the plane sprang into the sky. All hands waved hats and scarves and yelled, "*Banzai!*" When the attack force formed up, they were three airplanes short. One went into the drink on takeoff. The other two had mechanical issues and turned back. Shadow clouds scudded across the sky, diminishing the purple-orange rays of the rising sun.

***

In D.C., Bratton expected General Marshall to arrive within fifteen minutes of his phone call. A half-hour came and went. Bratton had missed seeing Marshall when he arrived. He found him in his office reading the entire fourteen-part message. Bratton tried to interrupt him to give him the two most recent intercepts, but the general waved him off. Bratton waited as instructed with a time bomb in his hand—the message that specified the one o'clock deadline.

After he read Bratton's intercepts, Marshall polled his staff. They agreed that the Japanese were likely to attack somewhere around 1 PM. Marshall picked up a pen and scrawled:

The Japanese are presenting at 1:00 PM Eastern Standard Time today what amounts to an ultimatum. Also, they are under orders to destroy their codes immediately. Just what significance the hour set may have, we do not know but be alert accordingly.[221]

The general grabbed the phone and dialed Admiral Stark to ask him if he wanted to add his signature. Stark said he did not think an additional warning was necessary because of the 27 November dispatch. Stark called back in less than a minute and asked Marshall to include in the message: "Inform the Navy."[222]

Marshall added those three words and turned to Bratton. "Take it to the message center and see to it that it gets dispatched at once by the fastest, safest means. If there is a question of priority, give it first to the Philippines."[223]

Just before noon, Bratton charged through the war department signal center's door and handed Marshall's message to the officer in charge, Lieutenant Colonel Edward French. Glancing at the dispatch, French told Bratton he could not read Marshall's handwriting. French had never seen Bratton that agitated. Bratton snatched back the message and hustled over to a typist in the outer office. He dictated Marshall's message to the typist and then handed the typewritten copy to French. French checked his watch. It was two minutes before noon Eastern Standard Time — just an hour before the one o'clock deadline.

French coded and then transmitted Marshall's message on Army circuits to all the destinations on his list, but he could not reach Fort Shafter. Atmospherics over the Pacific were acting up—

the ionosphere interrupting radio waves as morning approached Hawaii. Honolulu's Army circuit was down. [224] French had a decision to make. He considered three options:

1) Use the Army relay facilities from Washington to San Francisco and then San Francisco to Fort Shafter. French indicated that "the atmospheric condition was so bad that to transmit the message to San Francisco would mean ... slow speed and then recopied and retransmitted ... to Honolulu."[225]

2) Give it to the Navy to transmit to the Naval radio station on Oahu, who would then forward it to Fort Shafter.[226]

3) Send it by teletype cable to Western Union and have them forward it to RCA-San Francisco for wireless transmission to Honolulu.

Six Western Union teletype machines were right in his room. French assumed RCA-Honolulu would link it to the tie-line at Fort Shafter, the connection that was supposed to have been activated the day before.[227]

Without knowing that the RCA tie-line to Fort Shafter was not yet operational, French decided on option three. Waiting for the atmospherics to settle down, so that he could send it on the Army's low-powered transmitter, would take too long, and he wasn't sure how quickly the Navy would deliver it to Fort Shafter. He sent Marshall's message to Western Union/RCA at 12:01 PM EST (6:31 AM Hawaii time).[228] Meanwhile, Army circuits cabled the message to the other Pacific outposts. The Caribbean Defense Command received it at 6:30 AM, the Philippines at 6:36 AM, and the Presidio in San Francisco at 6:41 AM Hawaii time.

General Marshall had Bratton ask French how long it would take for the message to get to its destinations. French did some calculations and said it would be in the recipients' hands in thirty to forty minutes. That satisfied Marshall. The outposts would get it before the one o'clock deadline.

French telegraphed the message to Western Union in San Francisco, using the Western Union equipment in his office. WU-San Francisco typed the final warning message destined for Fort Shafter, on paper tape, at 9:18 AM Pacific Coast time — 6:48 AM Hawaii time — then rolled it up, put it into a pneumatic tube, closed the end, and shot it over to the RCA office across the street.

The RCA operator opened the tube and stamped it with the originator's time zone, 12:18 EST. However, RCA-SF was not connected to Honolulu yet. What French had overlooked, or maybe did not know when he chose option three, was that the Honolulu office opened an hour later on Sundays, 7 AM instead of 6 AM. The San Francisco operator waited twelve minutes for Honolulu to power up for the day.

Colonel French then picked up the telephone and placed a call to Colonel Powell at Fort Shafter to confirm that he had received the warning message. The operator who answered said that Powell was out in the field. French told the operator it was urgent to check. No one did.

At 7 AM, the operator on duty at RCA-Honolulu turned on the line receivers and the telegraph and printing equipment. He contacted the operator at the transmitter station at Kahuku and the receiving station at Koko Head to make sure they powered up. Then he reestablished a link with San Francisco. The RCA operators exchanged several call-and-responses in their shorthand lingo: ACK RQ/ACK BQ — ACKnowlege ReQuest responded to by an ACKnowldege Back reQuest with any corrections. It took a quarter of an hour. Finally, at 7:17 AM Hawaii time — just thirteen minutes before the 1 EST deadline — RCA-Honolulu was operational.

The first wave of Japanese planes was bearing down on Oahu when Japan's First Air Fleet carriers turned into the wind again and launched the second wave at 7:05 AM Hawaii time. At 7:15, the second flight formed up and banked toward Oahu.

The San Francisco operator did not phase in the MUX (multiplexing) channel that allowed several messages to be sent at once in Baudot code, because it took too long. Instead, he transmitted messages in Morse code on a Boehme recorder— not unusual at the beginning of the day. Marshall's final warning message, now Radiogram 1549, was the first one sent from San Francisco to Honolulu on 7 December.[229]

The Koko Head antenna caught the radio wave. Converted to electrons, the final warning message traveled from Koko Head over copper lines to RCA's printer on King Street. The Boehme machine's pen plotted Radiogram 1549 by drawing a short square pulse for each dot and a long pulse for each dash of Morse code.

General Marshall's coded radiogram (George Street Archive)

The address line reads as follows:

1549 = Number of radiogram

WS = Operators initials – William Steed

SCDE Washington, D.C. = Sender – Signal Corps, Washington, D.C.

74 = Number of words in the contents

73 = Number of billable words

RCA = via RCA

USGETAT = Government Message Routine Priority

7 = 7th day of the month

12:18P = 12:18 PM – time Western Union transmitted it to RCA-SF.

1941 DEC 7 AM 7:33 = timestamp that 1549 was received at RCA-Honolulu.

The receipt stapled in the upper left-hand corner reads as follows:

1549 = radiogram number

MH = Filer's initials – May Hobart

C G HAWAIIAN DEPT = addressee

Handwritten "S" = handwritten initial of Corporal Stevens who received the radiogram

Messenger Number 9 = Tadao Fuchikami's messenger boy number

1941DEC 7:00 AM 7:34 = Timestamp of when the message was placed in the envelope for delivery.[230]

George Street's notes are penciled across the upper right hand corner.

At 7:25 AM Hawaii time, RCA night manager William (Bill) Steed sat down at a typewriter and rolled in an RCA Radiogram half-page form. He typed message number 1549, added his initials, and pounded out the code letters in Morse code in "seven to eight minutes," George later wrote.[231] "Marshall" was the only plain text word other than the address line.

Steed zipped the form out of the typewriter and time-stamped it, "1941 DEC 7 AM 7:33," three minutes after the one o'clock deadline. He had never seen "C G" in the address line before. He asked the switchboard operator if she recognized "C G." She drew a blank, too. Because the tie-line was not activated, their only option was to have a messenger deliver Radiogram 1549 to the Signal Corps' office at Fort Shafter and have them locate "C G." The word Marshall was anyone's guess. It could have been a code word or anyone's name. It did not occur to them that it was General Marshall, the Army's chief of staff.

There was no indication that the message was a "RUSH" or "URGENT" communique, so Steed handed it to May Hobart. If the message had been designated as such, a messenger would have made a special run and delivered it immediately. Instead, Hobart typed out a receipt, added her initials, time-stamped the envelope — now a minute later — sealed it, and put Radiogram 1549 in the slot for the messenger boy to take on his morning rounds. "Forty-five minutes had elapsed from the official filing time in Washington to the official time of receipt in Honolulu." [232] French's anticipated delivery time was off by five minutes — and it still had to be transported by a boy on a motorbike.

The first of two messenger boys arrived at RCA at 7 AM. Their Sunday schedule started an hour later than normal, because "Many complaints had been received by the RCA office because messages were delivered too early, and experience showed that starting out between 8:30 and 9:00 AM was satisfactory," a justifiable nod to island living according to George.[233] Over the next hour, the first messenger organized the radiograms into delivery routes. Those marked "RUSH" or "URGENT" were placed at the top for priority delivery. By the time the second delivery boy arrived, they were both ready to go. Radiogram 1549 was prepped for delivery twenty-two minutes before the official time of the attack, and fourteen minutes after the Opana Mobile Radar Unit called in a large flight of aircraft approaching from the north. But Marshall's final warning message was too late. Nineteen minutes after Radiogram 1549 hit the delivery slot, Japan's flight leader, Mitsuo Fuchida instructed his radioman to key a repeating two-character code back to *Akagi:* "*tora tora tora,*" confirming that a surprise attack had been achieved.[234]

***

The party at the Japanese Embassy in D.C. that interrupted the decoding and typing of the fourteen-part message had raised the roof the night before. The directive to use staff rather than a regular typist to pound out the fourteen-part message left Ambassador Nomura with only one aide who "could operate a typewriter at all decently." [235] Embassy Secretary Katsuzo Okumura hunted and pecked his way through the message and made mistakes, line after line. His torturous typing was so bad that he threw his first attempt away and started again.

At 12:30 PM EST, Okumura finished, but a proofreader found errors. Okumura slowly retyped the fourteen-part message for the third time. There was no way he would have it finished for the one o'clock meeting between Ambassador Nomura and Secretary Hull. The ambassador's staff called Hull's office and requested a delay until 1:30 PM. John Stone checked with Hull and returned to the phone with a conciliatory response, "the Secretary will expect the ambassadors as soon as their preparations are ready."[236] Japan's attempt to give the United States a thirty-minute warning that they were going to war against the Allies failed. Marshall's attempt to warn Hawaiian command to expect "something" at 1 PM EST also failed.

Twenty-two minutes after May Hobart placed the final warning message in its delivery slot, the Rising Sun streamed in from the northeast, and all hell broke loose at Pearl Harbor.

Chapter 14

Lost in the Rising Sun

Sunday, 7 December 1941
Street Household

George Street tried to ignore the sounds of military maneuvers that wove their way through the venetian blinds in his bedroom, early on Sunday morning. He could not even hear the birds. What a way to start the day. He lay sprawled on his bed and relished the sea breeze that caressed his bare chest. Mornings were the time when he missed Nina the most. She liked to wake him with a kiss before she got up to fetch the newspaper and make coffee. They would have read the paper together in bed, propped up with pillows.

Then the phone rang. George listened as Barbara ran to grab it before it rang a third time. She'd catch hell if her friends called and disturbed "the sleeping tiger" on his day off.

"Street residence," she spoke into the handset.

"Get your dad on the line," George's right-hand man, Bill Steed, said with an urgency she had never heard before. Usually, they chit-chatted when he called.

"It's an emergency," he added.

Barbara padded across the oriental carpets in the living room and rapped on the wood-paneled door of her dad's bedroom. "Dad, Bill Steed is on the phone, and he says it's an emergency."[237]

George knew that it must be, as his staff did an excellent job of respecting his privacy on his only day off.

Barbara put down the handset and returned to the bathroom sandwiched between her dad's bedroom and hers. The call had interrupted her toilette. She needed to finish bobby-pinning her hair for the final dress rehearsal of the Roosevelt High School a cappella choir's upcoming Christmas program. They were going to perform the first live broadcast to the mainland, thanks to her dad. She was proud of him for arranging it, and she could not be more excited. She was certain the two-hundred-member choir would blow the roof off, and they'd look great in the white robes that director Hedvig Finkenbinder had acquired. Photographers were sure to be there. The performance meant the world to her.

Barbara widened and stretched her mouth, as she colored her lips with a tube of Revlon red lipstick. Bold, bright, and fashionable, red was her favorite. She smiled at herself in the mirror, then curled her tongue over her front teeth, and wiped away a smudge. Now she was ready.

Cocking an ear to make sure her dad was getting up, Barbara returned to the phone and told Bill that he was on his way. She dropped the handset and left it to dangle from its cord. The smack of the screen door announced her departure. Only two buses ran on Sundays and she couldn't afford to miss this one.

When Barbara stepped outside, moist, salty air, scented with the fragrance of a Hawaiian morning, bathed her face like a warm washcloth. The bus stop was directly in front of her house at the corner of Kahala and Hunakai Avenues. Inhaling the day, she paid no attention to the ear-splitting noise from the planes flying overhead. Sunday church bells tolled eight times, and she hopped aboard the twelve-passenger jitney packed with sailors and soldiers. Her deep brown eyes flashed. More than one man offered her a seat.

***

As her bus departed, Takeo Yoshikawa and Consul General Kita were sitting down to breakfast at the Japanese consulate. The sound of military maneuvers was louder than usual for a Sunday, but they did not pay much attention to them. As usual, they tuned the radio to the morning news. From the other side of the ocean, the radio announcer of NHK Radio Tokyo gave the weather report: "East Wind Rain." It was the Winds code! Negotiations with the United States had failed. Yoshikawa jumped up, scooted to Kita's office, and started burning codebooks and secret papers.[238]

***

Hearing the screen door slam, George swung his feet out of bed, strapped on his braces, steadied himself with his cane, and hobbled to the kitchen. He picked up the handset dangling from the wall phone. How many times had he told Barbara not to let it hang? Doing so stretched the cord. He glanced at the wall clock. It was 8:03 AM—no lazy morning for him.

Without preamble, Bill Steed uttered words that George had hoped never to hear, "Pearl Harbor is under attack."[239] The sound of explosions punctuated his words. George braced himself against the door jamb, hooked the crook of his cane into his pajama pocket, and heard the rumble of Barbara's bus pulling away from the curb.

Fear slammed him between the eyes like a thunderbolt. His daughter was headed to the Iolani Palace, downtown. It was under fire! His son? Where was his son? George Jr. lived in a detached maid's quarters in the corner of their yard. He hoped his son wasn't sailing as planned. Now he let the phone dangle and made his way to George Jr.'s quarters. He was gone. George had never felt more disabled in his life. There was nothing he could do for his children. Anxiety gripped his body. He was aware of how ruthless the Japanese military could be because he'd been in Japan during the Manchurian Incident, a weak prelude to the rape of Nanking in 1937. Brutal images flashed through his mind.

Breathing deeply, he shuffled back into the house and focused his attention. He knew from the meetings he attended, that the Businessmen's Military Training Corps would post sentries at roadblocks. To get downtown he would need a pass, which he did not have because, due to his disability, he was not an official member. His first decision in a long day of decisions was to stay put. His kids would head for home when and if they could. He could run operations from home, as long as phone lines held. For now, he would help the people at RCA keep communications open to the mainland, if they were willing to hold down the fort. He had a plan, even if just for a moment.

He told Steed to keep their line open when Steed advised him that all five incoming lines were jammed with callers trying to confirm the attack. "I told Steed … to try to get through to the police station for verification … it was two or three stories high with a cupola, and from the roof, Pearl Harbor could be seen."[240] Steed went outside, and George was startled to hear the blast of another explosion. Steed returned a minute or two later to report that a shell had landed on a nearby building. There was no doubt that Honolulu was under attack. The next day, they discovered that a U.S. anti-aircraft shell had damaged the rear of the Bishop Bank Building, just down the street from RCA. In the meantime, the RCA switchboard operator got through to the police, and verified the situation.

Street then dictated an XQ, an urgent intra-company servicegram, to RCA San Francisco: **"Japanese planes are bombing our Naval ships in Pearl Harbor. Suggest advising all broadcast networks and forward this XQ on to Supervisors in New York and Washington."**

George later explained that the San Francisco office had a "direct wire-line on their patch-over board to Columbia, National, and Mutual Broadcasting companies. I believe I also included in the original XQ to also notify ASSdPx [Associated Press] and Unipress as SF also had direct lines to those organizations." It was 8:11 AM.[241]

***

A bit after 8:00 that morning, George Jr. opened his sea-blue eyes and brushed back his blonde hair. He had been startled awake by a tremendous boom, which he later attributed to the explosion of USS *Arizona*. Eight o'clock was a late start for him. He'd had a busy week at work and wanted to savor his last few days in Oahu before shipping out to the prestigious engineering school at the

University of California, Berkeley. Working during the summer and fall, he now had just enough money to make the transfer.

Large screened windows in his one-room quarters ushered in the scent and sounds of the ocean—perfect for a nineteen-year-old who loved the sea. He kept his quarters in ship shape. The battleship gray floors just needed a sweep, and a sink made it easy for a fellow to be on his own. It was so much better than the cramped rooms he and Barbara had shared in San Francisco with their mother. They had existed on macaroni, cheese, and beans during the Great Depression until his dad negotiated their custody and moved them to Oahu. Now, with good food in his belly and the occasional thump of a falling coconut on his roof, even the constant noise from the joint Army and Navy practice drills that morning did not bother him.

George Street, Jr.
(George Street Archive)

Today, he planned to sail his twenty-one-foot, self-built outrigger canoe, forever grateful that his dad had introduced him to sailing. George had handed him woodworking tools with instructions to build a boat, when he and his sister first arrived in Hawaii six years ago. He researched designs at the public library. With each hammered blow, he drove his past into obscurity and built a seaworthy boat. He and his pal down the street, Norman Ives, had anchored his canoe at Hunakai Beach in anticipation of a day on the water.

George Jr. pulled on his swim trunks, his usual weekend uniform, and, "elected not to eat breakfast in order to not awaken my father."[242] As he headed to the toilet located in the carport, he overheard the little boy next door, "Mom, are we at war?" "No," thought George Jr., it was just "practice fire maneuvers" that had been going on for weeks.[243]

The sand was cool on his bare feet as he picked his way down the eight-foot-wide footpath to the beach to check on his boat and the sea. He kept his eyes aloft and scanned for falling coconuts — a hazard he'd learned to avoid the hard way. Gazing ahead, he was awed by the vastness of the sea welded to the sky along the horizon. Waves inhaled and exhaled the timeless rhythms of life at his feet. The swells were easy, and the sky was dotted with low, early morning clouds. Northeasterly trade winds riffled his hair and the turquoise-blue water. It promised to be another stunning Hawaiian day — perfect for sailing.

Anxious to be on the water, he hoofed it back to Kahala Avenue and Norman's house, on the next corner. Two Army tanks and several trucks raced from Fort Ruger toward Koko Head as he was about to cross the street. Their rumble overwhelmed the background noise of military maneuvers reverberating from the other side of Diamond Head.

George Jr. said out loud to no one, "Wow, these are some maneuvers."[244]

When he walked into Norman's driveway, a Jeep with three Marines careened into the yard. They jumped out, pounded on the back door, and were quickly admitted. A minute later, Norman stuck his head out the door and said, "I won't be able to sail with you today," and then disappeared with no further explanation.[245]

Taken aback, George Jr. reflected, "Well, it was a great day, and I proceeded back to the beach and walked to where my canoe was anchored. I thought it was possible to go for a single-handed sail as I had done previously on quiet days."[246] There were no other people on the beach. The sun's shimmer on the quicksilver water called to him.

He meandered along the empty stretch of beach, mentally planning his day on the water. Overhead, the growl of engines caught his attention. "I watched a dogfight between two fighter planes, and I believed they were in mock practice."[247] Coarse golden sand, speckled with white bits of coral, crawled away from his sinking feet as he stood and marveled at his own private air show.

The dogfight he witnessed was probably between First Lieutenant Lew Sanders and a Zero, waylaid on its approach to the Japanese attack forces' agreed-upon rendezvous point. As the two-plane contest drifted across the sky, George Jr. marveled at how realistically they fought.[248]

When the planes were long gone, George Jr. retraced his steps back to his house. He hoped his dad was frying bacon for breakfast. When he entered the front door, he was surprised to see his dad on the phone, braced against the wall and still in his pajamas, the crook of his cane jammed into a pocket. His dad caught his eye, put his hand over the mouthpiece, and said, "Japs are trying to shoot down the antenna at our Wahiawa Maritime

Radio Station [used for ship to shore communications], and one of their operators has been injured by a fifty-caliber slug."[249]

Stunned beyond words, George Jr. hurried into the living room and switched on the radio. Turning the dial to KGU, a local radio station, he sought confirmation, while his mind struggled to process this new reality. Certainty flashed. The dogfight he had witnessed was a real fight between enemy combatants. The red "meatball," as American sailors called it, on the wing of the Japanese aircraft had been lost in the rays of the rising sun.

Chapter 15

"I'm no Jap; I'm an American"

Sunday, 7 December, 1941
Oahu, Territory of Hawaii

Three minutes before the official time of the start of the attack, Admiral Kimmel ran out to his front yard, then over to Lalor Earle's yard because she had a grandstand view of Pearl Harbor. When USS *Oklahoma* (BB-37) rolled upside-down, Lalor stated matter-of-factly, "Looks like they've got *Oklahoma*."

"Yes, I see they have," replied Kimmel.[250]

Kimmel flinched when USS *Arizona* exploded and lifted out of the water.[251] Black smoke roiled into the blue Hawaiian sky. USS *West Virginia* (BB-48) capsized about the time Kimmel's command car swerved into his drive. He jumped in, and Captain Freeland Daubin, commander of Submarine Four, hopped onto the running board. They sped to headquarters, trying to outpace the planes flying overhead.

Downhill from Kimmel's quarters, Juliet Mayfield wrapped her pillow around her ears to muffle the noise. It was so loud and close that she imagined it was dynamite used to blast a hole in the lava to install her mailbox.[252] She gave up trying to sleep, tossed the pillow from her head, and was startled to see her Japanese maid, Fumiyo, grasping the door frame to her bedroom. Over the noise, Fumiyo said, "Oh, Mrs. Mayfield, Pearl Harbor is on fire!"[253]

Juliet scrambled out of bed and ran to the window. Her husband, Hall, was standing in the yard in his pajamas, looking toward the harbor with binoculars. She and her maid ran to join him. Juliet took one look at her husband and said, "Hall, go right back inside and put in your teeth." He mumbled that it might be a drill. At the same moment, two planes with red circles on their wings flew low over their yard, and they ran for the house. Mayfield pulled apart his closet to get his Navy uniform. Juliet threw on her clothes and asked, "Why don't the Navy planes do something?" Turning to her with a glare, Hall yelled, "Why doesn't the Army do something?"[254] Teeth in and uniform on, Mayfield hauled out and left Juliet and Fumiyo. The two women went next door to Lalor's house to ride out the attack. They turned a bamboo couch upside down and piled cushions on it for shelter. Huddled under the couch, Fumiyo asked, "Mrs. Mayfield, is it — is it the Japanese who are attacking us?" Juliet had to tell her, "Yes."[255]

Corrine Shivers and Sue Isonaga were cooking breakfast for the emergency services committee meeting when the phone rang. Sue answered it and passed it to FBI Special Agent in Charge Robert Shivers. He took the handset, listened in silence, and then exclaimed, "What? I'll be right down!" He hung up the phone and said, "Turn the radio on."[256]

Then Shivers turned to his wife, "Don't let Sue out of your sight. You take her wherever you go."[257] He feared Sue would soon be in danger of retaliation because she was Japanese.

As he hustled to the door, he added, "When the men come, give them breakfast and then send them to the office."[258] But, when they arrived, they skipped breakfast and got right back in the car.

A while later, Sue and Corrine spotted a plane with a red circle on each wing. That is when Sue realized "it was all real."[259]

Shivers sent a car to collect Corrine and Sue to take them inland to a house in the Manoa District, home of the University of Hawaii and its surrounding residences. When they arrived, they walked into a crowded living room. Women wept. Hysteria electrified the air. As their driver pulled away, a man walked in and passed out guns. He instructed the collected residents, "At the sight of a Jap, shoot to kill,"[260]

Fearing for her life, Sue quietly walked out to the front yard, and Corrine followed. They sat on a retaining wall together, away from the agitated gathering. Corrine and Sue's self-imposed exile from the gun-filled house ended when an understanding person, concerned about Sue's heritage, offered to take them to another home further up the valley. There, a family welcomed them, and they stayed for several days.

In her dressing room on the opposite side of the island, Friedel Kuehn stood in front of the mirror, with the radio playing full blast. The hot jazz she was enjoying stopped. The announcer shouted, "They are attacking! They are attacking!" Friedel gazed out her window that faced K-Bay. Planes dove and came back again. She said, "They looked like hornets buzzing the sky." When jazz played on the air again, she "couldn't believe anyone would play jazz while the fleet was being ripped to pieces, while thousands died."[261]

Upon hearing the news, Bernard Otto Kuehn raced out the door and jumped into his roadster. Hans was at Reverend Van Harbin's Sunday school. Kuehn roared up to the Methodist Church in record time. "Hans, Hans," he called as he raced across the yard. He grabbed his son's hand, and they ran to the car without a word.

Despite Kuehn's sympathies, twelve people ended up at his house to shelter from flying bullets and falling bombs. Friedel and her daughter, Ruth, went to the Red Cross station to help however they could.

* * *

After what seemed like endless minutes of communication with the RCA office, George let the phone's handset yo-yo on its cord again and got dressed, while Bill Steed talked to the staff. George had instructed him to keep the Honolulu-San Francisco circuit "in operation and to continue all other activities unless there were physical interruptions and that the messengers were to go out, if possible, on their delivery routes." George was worried about his personnel's safety and the possibility of sabotage to RCA's radio facilities and Oahu's power grid. Both he and George Jr. were anxious about Barbara. They hoped she would make her way to RCA.

At 8:15 AM, the second RCA messenger, twenty-six-year-old Japanese American, Tadao Fuchikami — Messenger Boy #9 —

rumbled to a stop on his Indian Scout motorbike to begin his regular deliveries. RCA was about a half-hour ride from his house at 2533 Namauu Drive, where he had just bid goodbye to his mother, Chie.[262] Like so many others, he assumed that routine maneuvers blazoned the sky as he made his way to the office. He learned otherwise as soon as he stepped into the office. He would later say, "Hey! It can't be Japan. Those Jap warlords are all cuckoo, like Hitler, but they're not strong enough to beat the old USA."[263]

When Steed asked Fuchikami if he wanted to make his run, Fuchikami did not understand why he was even asked. It was his job. He hurried to the pigeon-hole board and grabbed the radiograms from the slot marked *Kalihi*. He arranged the radiograms by street. Fort Shafter, his most distant stop, would be at the end of his run since none of the radiograms were marked "URGENT" or "RUSH" or "PRIORITY." Radiogram 1549, Marshall's final warning message, specified ETAT, radio shorthand for "Government Radiogram without priority."[264]

He fired up his Scout at 8:40 AM and entered the danger zone. Fuchikami was ten minutes into his route, when Japanese Ambassador Nomura presented the fourteen-part telegram — Tojo's version of a declaration of war — to Secretary Hall at 8:50 AM Hawaii time (2:20 PM EST). Nomura missed the one o'clock deadline by an hour and twenty minutes. He had failed the emperor, who had wanted to do the honorable thing and give the United States a half-hour warning. The attack was scheduled for 8 AM Hawaii time, 1:30 PM EST. It started at 7:55 AM Hawaii time, five minutes ahead of the planned time, with no warning from either Japan or Washington.

While diplomacy fizzled in D.C., messenger Tadao Fuchikami was dodging flack, while worming his way to Fort Shafter on his motorbike. Sirens wailed. He raced into the clamor, unmindful of the fact that when the first bomb dropped, his heritage labeled him as a possible saboteur. Anti-aircraft explosions, congested traffic, and blockades forced him to find alternate routes. Fire drove people out of the buildings at King and McCully Streets, two miles east of the RCA office. Terrified people blocked his way. Walls had blown out at Kamehameha School, shrapnel sliced through a pedestrian across the street from the governor's home, and anti-aircraft guns blasted anything that resembled a Japanese fighter.

Fuchikami later wrote that he traveled to "Beretania near River … went Mauka (toward mountains) on River St. to Doctor Takahashi's office on Vineyard about 9:05 AM." He jotted number #9 on the receipt and retained a copy in his pocket. Then, he had trouble finding one address "because of the funny nickname on the message and the excitement." He made a stop at Akepo Lane and then "headed Ewa [west toward the water] on Dillingham Blvd to Mokauea St., Mauka to King St, Ewa on King to Kopkie." Then "went to Pinkham," delivered a message, then "up Gulick to School St., Ewa to Kam 4th almost to Kalihiuke Rd. delivered message." Then, "Kam 4th to School St to Middle Street."[265] It was a circuitous route, as he delivered message after message on the way to Fort Shafter.

All the cars were being turned around at Middle Street by the police, so he went around — a ten to twenty-minute detour. Guards at two roadblocks stopped him and demanded to know where he was going. His uniform shirt with a red circle over the pocket made him a target: "I nearly got shot. They thought I was an enemy paratrooper."[266]

A lieutenant detained him at one checkpoint for his own protection, even after he explained who he was and whose uniform he wore. Minutes ticked by. The lieutenant warned him to be careful, because he could be mistaken for a "Jap." Back on his bike, Fuchikami "went Ewa on King St and [finally] to the Fort Shafter message center."[267]

George later wrote, "Familiar with the neighborhood, he circumvented the blockades by some side streets … and was admitted into Fort Shafter to deliver the messages to the Signal Corps message center sometime between 9:30 and 10:15 (at the latest)."[268] Fuchikami lowered the kickstand of his bike and raced into the Signal Corps office to deliver five radiograms, including Radiogram 1549. The receiving clerk wasn't at his desk. According to Fuchikami, he was out on the balcony with "many other army personnel who were looking down the hill at Pearl Harbor and adjoining Hickam Army Airfield destruction." [269] Fuchikami spotted Corporal Stevens in the group and handed him the packet of messages. Stevens initialed each RCA receipt with an "S" but did not go inside to date them under the electric timestamp, which was standard operating procedure.[270]

Fuchikami later told George that he "asked the men if we were to keep on delivering messages to them. They said yes, keep bringing them."[271] Fuchikami mounted his bike and delivered the rest of his messages to the naval cantonment near Pearl Harbor, and naval housing. George would later write that "Fuchikami went on his way without thinking of the perils of his journey. He was no 'Jap.' He was an American."[272]

***

At 8:50 AM, First Lieutenant Lew Sanders returned to Wheeler Air Base to refuel and rearm. He had lost the flying contest that George Jr. had witnessed from the beach. A P-36 was no match for a Zero. Gassed up, armed, and pumped with adrenaline, along with Lieutenants John M. Thacker, Phillip M. Rasmussen, and Gordon Sterling, Sanders' flight was off within minutes. Sterling had grabbed the first airplane he saw. It was that of Lieutenant Othneil Norris, who had left his plane to get a parachute.

The flight of four P-36s flew east toward Bellows Air Base, spotting the second wave of Japanese aircraft over Kaneohe. Sterling got on a bomber's six and opened fire, as the two barreled toward the water. A Japanese fighter appeared behind Sterling. Sanders swept onto the tail of the Japanese plane dogging Sterling, just as Mary Stuppy and Terry Chapman stepped onto the beach in front of the house they rented from Bernard Kuehn. Their husbands had just left to report for duty. Mary Stuppy said, "It was amazing … more like a newsreel than the real thing," as they stood struggling to identify which planes were American and which were Japanese.[273] She and Terry ran into the house to get a camera but couldn't find the film. Returning to the beach, they continued to watch.

Mary said a "plane flying very low went in front of us with three after it … Then plane number three dropped a bomb and we saw it hit the water. The second plane went lower and lower and I finally saw it hit the water at the shoreline … at least it seemed to."[274] Sterling shot down the bomber he pursued but hit the deck and drowned. Sanders lit up the fighter behind Sterling but did not see it crash. Lieutenant Rasmussen, who had jumped into his plane wearing purple pajamas, witnessed the air battle but was unable to participate. His guns had started firing spontaneously after he charged them. As luck would have it, an enemy plane crossed into his clearing burst and blew up.[275]

By 9 AM (2:30 PM EST), news of the attack reached the mainland. Major networks simultaneously broadcast bulletins. CBS announced: "The Japanese have attacked Pearl Harbor, Hawaii by air, President Roosevelt has just announced. Attacks made on all naval and military activities on the principal island of ō-hah-hoo [Oahu]."[276]

Instead of enjoying Danny Kaye's *Sunday Serenade*, Americans pulled out maps and globes to locate Oahu and Pearl Harbor. Children snuggled near radiators, wondering what was happening.[277] As the day wore on, around eighty million people, more than half of America's adult population, were glued to their radios. Doubtful listeners supposed that the broadcast was just another radio drama, like Orson Wells' 1938 *War of the Worlds,* which many misinterpreted as factual. Skeptics wanted hard information on how a country with no money, no oil, and a navy made of bathtubs, could cause such harm.[278]

Before the first raid ended, the locals responded. The howl of sirens wailed in concert with the high-pitched whine of dive bombers, as they delivered death blows along Battleship Row. Boy Scouts fought fires and served as messengers for emergency services. The American Legion and trained plantation staff turned out as guards. Forty-five trucks owned by local businesses were driven to Hickam and converted to ambulances.

At the university, a lecture on "The Treatment of Deep Trauma Wounds" was scheduled for 9 AM.[279] Twenty doctors who planned to attend the lecture got hands-on experience instead, when the call went out for all doctors to report to Tripler Hospital. The nursing staff was already there. Seventeen surgical teams formed up, each including an operating surgeon, assisting nurses, and an anesthetist, as planned by the Major Disaster Council.

The Red Cross Canteen Corps showed up to feed whoever needed food. The Women's Motor Corps dispatched ambulances and trucks that volunteered to serve as ambulances. The Surgical Dressing Corps, organized by the Red Cross, delivered supplies, called their volunteers, and told them to make more. The Chamber of Commerce blood bank found itself overwhelmed by five hundred donors within minutes of the last attack. They ran out of serum bags and used sterilized Coke bottles instead.

A corpsman from the seaplane tender, USS *Swan* (AVP-7), known as "Doc" to his shipmates, ended up at the Navy hospital. He remembered women helping wounded sailors in the showers scrub their oil-covered bodies. He later learned that they were prostitutes.[280] They were not shy around naked men like some of the young nurses.

Then the first damage reports rolled in: a bomb hit a supply building, another killed a woman in Nuuanu Valley, fire broke out at Lunalilo School, between Diamond Head and Pearl Harbor, and Japanese aircraft strafed pedestrians and cars. Fire, noise, and the smell of death shattered the world that was Hawaii. A question loomed in the air like thunder clouds, "How did it happen?" The atmosphere was electrified with anger.

George Jr., riveted to the radio, awaited instructions for the block wardens. Standard programming ceased. The announcer relayed general guidelines for the civilian population and specific directions to people in agricultural areas on how to discourage possible landings of hostile aircraft. Japanese paratroopers had reportedly landed in the mountains behind Honolulu.[281] At 9:30 AM, about ninety minutes after the attack began, the KGU radio station announcer barked orders like a drill sergeant:

1. **Calling all doctors, nurses, and aides.**
2. **Block wardens to report to assembly points.[282]**
3. **The United States Army Intelligence has ordered all civilians to stay off the streets. Do not use the telephone ... Keep your radio turned on for further news.**
4. **Get off the street. Drive on the lawn if necessary, just so you get off the street.**
5. **Fill water buckets and tubs with water, to be ready for possible fire. Attach garden hoses.**
6. **Here is a warning to all people throughout the Territory of Hawaii and especially on the island of**

Oahu. In the event of air raid, stay under cover. Many of the wounded have been hurt by falling shrapnel from anti-aircraft guns.[283]

George Jr. left as soon as he heard the announcement for all block wardens to report for duty. His dad was still on the phone with RCA. George Jr. forgot about his boat and headed to his assigned rendezvous point, the high school on the slopes north of Diamond Head in Kaimuki. Numbed by the shock of the news, yet invigorated by the call to action, he never expected to have to use his block warden training. He took his family's car and picked up a fellow warden en route. They were stopped and questioned at almost every other intersection by members of the BMTC, mobilized to keep civilians off the streets.

Once at the school, George Jr. stared at the billows of hot, black smoke that roiled from Pearl Harbor. A muddle of anger, apprehension, and an instinct to help ignited his visceral call to retaliate. Adrenaline surged among the several hundred wardens assembled in the auditorium. A three-star general quieted the room and told them that Japan had sunk three battleships, and he did not know if they intended to invade the island. They were told, "Further attacks may be expected, with strong possibilities of gas attacks on the city and residential areas."[284]

General Short then began to issue orders in anticipation of an invasion. According to George Jr., the block wardens were to "mobilize all families in your respective blocks to prepare slit trenches with berms large enough to stop a fifty-caliber round and to protect against strafing attacks, organize food and water supplies, set up ladders to roofs, connect water hoses, fill buckets of sand to fight fire, and prep for blackouts." Additionally, the wardens were to make floor plan sketches of each house, identify access points, locate service shut-off valves, and list the occupants' names. He also advised them to expect firebombs. As soon as the briefing ended, George Jr. hurried home and contacted each family in his ward. By the afternoon, George Jr. reported that "a good part of the population of Honolulu dug their slit trenches and prepared for further possible attacks."[285]

While the block wardens received their instructions, hundreds of people made their way to the top of the Punchbowl, near Roosevelt High School, to witness their once robin egg blue sky smolder to battleship gray.[286] Gossip fed the panic that raced below the surface. By now, all commercial radio broadcasts had ceased operations for fear the Japanese would home-in on the signal. Emergency personnel instructed the populace to tune into the police broadcast frequencies for announcements.

Before Naval Reserve censors arrived to take control of communications, RCA's switchboard operator brought to George's attention that "the overseas radiotelephone between Honolulu and Tokyo was in use ... with one call that lasted forty to forty-five minutes. Who was talking to whom, probably giving a ringside blow by blow account, [George did] not know."[287]

Around 10 AM, when the Japanese aircraft of the second wave had returned to their carriers, Governor Joseph Poindexter created the Hawaii Territorial Guard to defend the territory, as the Hawaii National Guard had been federalized the previous year and mobilized for national defense. The governor issued the ROTC's stock of antiquated 1903 Springfield rifles so that the Territorial Guard could defend Hawaii in the event of an invasion by Japanese paratroops. Later, one of the guardsmen remarked that, although most of them had Japanese "faces, names, and heritages, they were marched out, to fight their own kind."[288]

Military jeeps, fire trucks, and people clogged the debris-covered streets of Honolulu, while folks battened down the hatches of their homes, and their lives, to prepare for a land invasion that never came. George continued to direct operations at RCA from home. Barbara had not called, and she had not shown up at RCA. Meanwhile, war casualties flooded into local hospitals like a tsunami.

Chapter 16

JIJAY, Duly Delivered

Sunday, 7 December 1941
Island of Oahu, Territory of Hawaii

When the first wave of the surprise attack barreled across Pearl Harbor, Lieutenant Commander Charles Coe's wife and their two children, Charlotte and Chuckie, took shelter inside the foundation of Admiral Patrick Bellinger's quarters. It did double duty as a bomb shelter. In the months leading up to the attack, neighborhood kids used to sneak into the concrete bunker during their make-believe games. They called it "the dungeon." The Coes had practiced running to the shelter with their two kids in tow. Either way, as a bomb shelter or the dungeon, it was a scary place.

On the day of the attack, Dante's Inferno entered the dungeon. Men burnt to a crisp wandered in, naked and withering in pain. Their skin melted off their bodies, and fear took form. Mothers tried to shelter their children from the sight, but overwhelming numbers made their efforts useless. They rendered aid — gave up their blankets and bathrobes — and told their kids to be brave, while they lived the horror show that unfolded around them. A couple of women risked a sprint back to their quarters for water while waiting for ambulances to arrive.

Warned about the possible brutality they might receive at the hands of Japanese invaders, Mrs. Coe approached the Marine who guarded the bomb shelter's entrance. She asked him to save three bullets if the Japanese came — one for each of her children and one for her. "When I am sure that my children are dead, then you will shoot me," she ordered.[289]

***

Students in Barbara's high school ROTC unit were placed as guards throughout the city, forced to transition from boys to men in a matter of hours. They armed themselves with the school's rifle team's .22-caliber rifles and 12 and 16-gauge shotguns, as the Hawaii Territorial Guard had appropriated their drill weapons.[290] Eligible cadets, the University of Hawaii ROTC, and the American Legion were quickly appointed to the guard. Barbara admitted that the high school ROTC was called upon to help "get bodies out of the waters; bodies and parts of bodies."[291]

The Honolulu Star-Bulletin's second extra edition soon hit the streets. Eight pages reported: "Deaths over 400 on Oahu ... Tokyo Announces 'State of War' with U.S. ... Japanese Raids on Guam, Panama Are Reported ... Four Waves, Start at 7:55 ... Two Japanese Fliers Captured ... Water is O.K. ... Blood Donors Called In ... All Sampans Ordered Detained ... Sabotage Reported In Waikiki Area ... investigating a report that Japanese at a tea house at Alewa Heights had been using high powered telescopes."[292]

Loudspeakers mounted on cars barked instructions for the evacuation of families from Hickam and Pearl Harbor housing. How does one choose what to pack at a moment's notice? Toiletries, medication, undies for sure. But what else? How do you pack a lifetime into a small carryall? Pictures? Mementos? A teddy bear? What would become of the pets? Did it matter? Wives and children hustled into buses and cars and rode to the homes of strangers, to schools, the YMCA, and the University of Hawaii.[293]

***

About that same time, two police detectives burst into the Japanese consulate on Nuuanu Avenue. "The building is under guard," they shouted as they elbowed their way past the staff. They found Yoshikawa and consulate personnel burning papers in a back room and pulled a half-completed sketch of Pearl Harbor out of the trashcan fire.[294] Other incriminating evidence had already gone up in flames.[295] Consul General Kita, casually dressed with his golf clubs in tow, tried to walk out the front door. The FBI escorted him back into the consulate.[296]

Static crackled the airwaves, and the police radio band turned into a gossip mill. Concerns about Japanese parachutists invading the island became fact, as rumors spread to fill the vacuum left by radio stations being off the air, jammed telephone lines, and the lag inherent in newspaper reporting.

Colonel Bicknell wrote in his official counter-intelligence assessment: "Rumors … ran through the population like a brush fire before the wind."

Stories spread about the water supply being poisoned; the Japanese fleet was offshore within shelling range; hundreds of gliders filled with Japanese soldiers had been landing in the cane fields; hills and fields were filled with snipers....[297]

The American public, military, and government clamored for answers. How had the Japanese gotten the jump on the Pacific Fleet? At 11:19 AM Hawaii time (4:39 PM EST), the RCA office received an internal servicegram that asked for clarification about Radiogram 1549:

"1941 DEC 7 AM 11 19." Addressed to "A251 FTSHAFTER WASHDC 9" "1549 C G HAWAIIAN DEPT JOKID AND TO WHOM."

Servicegram series (George Street Archive)

Using standard radiotelegraph five-letter code, the servicegram read, "give time received and time delivered for Radiogram 1549 addressed to C G Hawaiian Department."[298] The inquiry was handed to the office manager, Sue Sharp, whom George Jr. teasingly referred to as a mother hen. She pulled the original carbon copy of Radiogram 1549 and its receipt stapled to the upper left-hand corner. She recognized Corporal Stevens' "S" but realized that it wasn't time-stamped. Sharp would have to call him to comply with the request. A second servicegram came over the wire: "Waiting for reply to our service request" and "Please reply urgently." Then more servicegrams poured in from RCA-New York, RCA-San Francisco, the War Department, and Western Union. All wanted specific details about the delivery of Radiogram 1549.

It took until 2:40 PM for Sharp to reach Stevens to confirm the delivery time, which was at least an hour after the attack began. Not knowing what Radiogram 1549 said because it was in code, there wasn't much more she could find out. At 2:43 PM (8:13 PM EST), Sharp wired: "JIJAY [duly delivered] 9:00 AM signed by Stevens at the message center." She time-stamped her servicegram "1941 DEC 7 pm 2 43" and hand wrote her initials "SS" on the RCA copy.[299]

It is stated in the *Congressional Record* that Radiogram 1549 — General Marshall's final warning message — was delivered to the signal officer at Fort Shafter at 11:45 AM Hawaii time. Fuchikami's handwritten testimony indicated he delivered the radiogram to Fort Shafter at 10:15 AM. His oral testimony established the delivery time as 9:40 AM. George wrote: "Stevens admitted to me on December 9th that he failed to time-stamp the RCA receipt as usual but that he believed our messenger was there at Shafter between 9 and 9:30 AM."[300] Without a timestamp, people were forced to rely on their memories, which often warp under stress.

Sue Sharp's phone call must have concerned Corporal Stevens. How long had he kept the radiograms in his pocket before he remembered them? Once Stevens turned in Radiogram 1549 for decryption, it took about an hour to run it through a cipher machine, probably an ECM Mark II or SIGABA machine, and play it back to make sure it was accurate. Radiogram 1549 was decoded and delivered to the adjutant general, Colonel Dunlop, at 2:58 PM Hawaii time, seven hours and three minutes after the attack.[301] When Dunlop read it, he "suppressed a bark of laughter" and said, "The damn thing won't do any good now."[302] He passed the message to Colonel Powell and told him to get it to General Short right away.

Powell said, "[I've] had a couple of run-ins with the general … General Short would probably go through the roof and land all over [me] … [Major Robert J.] Fleming would be safer from the flak.[303]

Fleming delivered the message to General Short at 4 PM. Hawaii time (9:30 PM EST), almost eight hours after the attack. As predicted, Short exploded. When Admiral Kimmel received his copy, thanks to the "inform the Navy" addition, he crumpled it, threw it in the wastebasket, and shook his head in baffled fury. He said later that he "considered the incident a prime example of fumbling vital intelligence."[304]

While America fumbled and fumed, Japan celebrated. Shortly after RCA received the first servicegram inquiry about Radiogram 1549, NHK Radio Tokyo reported the news:

The Naval Department of Imperial Headquarters announced that … the Imperial Navy, during predawn hours, initiated hostilities with the British and American navies in the Western Pacific.[305]

***

In the aftermath of the blitz, Tripler Hospital, the Pearl Harbor Navy hospital, first aid stations, and medical facilities all over Oahu burst at the seams. The madams on Hotel Street opened their doors and offered their beds to the injured. The walking wounded now replaced the white rivers of uniforms that had lined up for their turns.[306]

By then, General Short and his staff had retired to an underground bunker in Aliamanu Crater to prepare for the expected invasion. Soldiers dug foxholes and strung barbed wire. Sandbag barriers fronted doorways and first-story windows.

Governor Poindexter called the White House. The Honolulu Mutual Telephone switchboard operator, with a Navy censor at her side, insisted that the governor tell her what he planned to discuss on the call.[307] She had her orders. She did not care who was calling whom. Governor, president — it did not matter. The censor overrode her and allowed the call. The governor told the president that he wanted martial law declared. General Short, also on the line, said that for all he knew, "landing parties were on their way … the raid was probably a prelude to an all-out attack."[308]

By 3:45 that afternoon, Short stated to the press that Poindexter had proclaimed martial law, prompted by fears of an invasion and by concerns over the loyalty of the more than seventy-five thousand people of Japanese ancestry who lived on Oahu.[309] Short then assumed the office of military governor of Hawaii. The third extra addition of the *Honolulu Star-Bulletin* laid out the conditions of martial law, which included in part:

All citizens are warned to watch their actions carefully, for any infraction of military rules and regulations will bring swift and harsh reprisals.

1. **Information regarding suspicious persons will be telephoned to the provost marshal at Honolulu 1948.**

2. **A complete blackout of the entire territory will go into effect at nightfall tonight.**

3. **Avoid the slightest appearance of hostility either in words or in act.**

4. **All civilian traffic except in case of dire emergency will cease at dark.**[310]

Censors inspected all outgoing mail for military information. Habeas corpus was suspended, as well as all civil court matters. Trial by jury was abandoned. In its place, justice was meted out by military tribunals. Japanese aliens were not allowed to move or change occupations without the approval of the provost marshal.

Meanwhile, the thirty households in George Jr.'s ward, along with the rest of Oahu, prepared for an invasion. George Jr. grabbed a shovel and dug a trench in his yard. It did not take long. Pumped with adrenaline and strong as an ox, he plowed through the sand in the Streets' yard, and then he headed over to a neighbor's house and dug another, while Washington began its hunt for a scapegoat.

Chapter 17

Roundup

Sunday, 7 December 1941

In San Francisco at 4 PM PST (1 PM Hawaii time), military guards secured the Golden Gate Bridge. A call to arms went out, and the clamor for justice rang throughout America, from shore to shore. The military ordered all personnel in every duty station, every port, every city, and every town to report for duty. Secretary Knox put out a call for radiomen, lowered physical standards for military service, and offered higher ranks to induce recruits to fill the communication void.[311]

Shopkeepers pulled food grown by Japanese farmers off the grocery shelves out of fear of poisoning.[312] Reports of Japanese parachute troops over San Francisco Bay, hostile forces swimming ashore, and Japanese landing at Waikiki prompted a frantic rush to grocery stores.[313] Authorities demanded that Japanese nationals remain off California streets until they could confirm their loyalty. The Japanese were banned from all communication, licenses, and indirect commerce, which soon bankrupted many. Reports of false sightings of Japanese ships and aircraft off both of the mainland coasts ran wild.

The Pan American Coffee Bureau Series radio broadcast, "Current Events," aired on the mainland at 6:45 PM EST. Eleanor Roosevelt spoke:

For months now, the knowledge that something like this might happen has been hanging over our heads ... there is no more uncertainty. We know what we have to face, and we know we are ready to face it.

I should like to say just a word to the women in the country tonight. I have a boy at sea on a destroyer ... Many of you all over the country have boys in the services who will now be called upon to go into action ... You cannot escape the anxiety. You cannot escape the clutch of fear in your heart.

Yet I hope ... you will rise above these fears ... Whatever is asked of us, I am sure we can accomplish it. We are the free and unconquerable people of the United States of America....[314]

A message from J. Edgar Hoover arrived at Honolulu's FBI office at 4 PM Hawaii time (9:30 PM EST), authorizing the arrest of "all Japanese aliens listed for custodial detention."[315] The ABC list protocols were activated. A presidential proclamation, which invoked the 1918 Enemy Aliens Act and part of the 1798 Alien and Sedition Act, stated that naturalized Japanese-American citizens who lived in the United States and its territories could be "apprehended, restrained, secured, and removed as alien enemies."[316]

Under consideration by the authorities was the possibility that the entire Japanese population on the Hawaiian islands — 155,000 to 158,000 people — would be incarcerated on a separate island. Authorities, prompted by Shivers, recognized the impossibility of such an endeavor.

Police Lieutenant John A. Burns, Colonel Bicknell, and most likely Mayfield pulled out the index cards of Hawaii's ABC list. It named hundreds of Japanese Americans, three hundred Germans, and fifty Italians as possibly dangerous aliens. The Kuehns and the Moris were at the top of the FBI's list. Japanese aliens not under arrest nor on the list were ordered to turn over their cameras and radio transmission equipment.

The three men went through the index cards one at a time and announced each name out loud. If two voted for detention, the person's name went into the arrest pile. The review took three hours. Thirteen squads received cards for those in the dragnet. FBI agents, MPs, police officers, and deputized civilians, which included the visiting San Jose, California football team, spread across the islands and arrested A-listed people.

The FBI picked up Friedel and Ruth Kuehn at the first aid station where they worked. Bernard Otto Kuehn was arrested at his home. The FBI tore into Kuehn's house at 1476 Kailua Avenue on Lanikai beach. Agents interviewed his neighbors for four days. Mr. R. C. Waldron, who lived in the second house from the intersection of Lanikai and Kailua, said he'd seen a Japanese man carrying a fishing pole run toward Kailua during the attack. Then he spotted a red flare. He did not know who fired the flare but wanted to mention it. None of his other neighbors witnessed any suspicious activity.

Doctor Motokazu Mori and his wife, Ishiko, claimed they were unaware of the attack when police placed them under arrest at their house on 702 Wyllie Street in the Waolani Valley. The FBI suspected them of helping to plan the attack because of the phone call and radiogram sent to Tokyo just days before. The police also grabbed their nineteen-year-old son, Jiro. Mori's aged father, Dr. Iga Mori, who lived next door, was picked up later.[317]

The police kept the younger Doctor Mori, his wife, and son in solitary confinement at the police station. Police and FBI agents questioned Doctor Mori until midnight, denying him food and water. After the grilling, the interrogators cleared him of any wrongdoing. The police confirmed that his wife was a news correspondent who filed reports about Japanese life on the islands. Weeks later, both were sent to a detention center in California, where they put their medical skills to good use, for the duration of the war.

A car with blue lights pulled up to sixty-eight-year-old Yasutaro Soga's house as the setting sun turned the sky blood red. As the editor of Honolulu's largest Japanese language newspaper, he was a pillar of the Japanese community. So he was certain he would be on the ABC list. Unlike the Moris, he wasn't surprised to see the car. He had eaten dinner by himself because he wanted to finish before dark. Three young men, each six feet tall with an "MP" band on his arm, banged on the door, and his son answered. Soga went to his bedroom to gather the items he had laid out in anticipation. The MPs barged in and followed him. His children went silent. Soga's wife helped him put on his vest and coat. She whispered in his ear as he was hustled out of the house, "Please be careful not to catch a cold."[318]

The MPs shepherded Soga to their car, then sped to other houses, pounding on doors in the darkness. It was hours before Soga and four other prisoners arrived at the rear door of the Immigration Building. Guards manhandled them on the way to the basement and searched them. They took their identification papers and money. Soga was allowed his pen, watch, and the three handkerchiefs he had grabbed. Then the MPs gripped him by the arm, led him up a narrow stairway, and shoved him into a darkened room. The rank smell of too many men in too small a space hit him like a sledgehammer. There were one hundred sixty-four men in a room meant for half that number.[319] Two people occupied each bunk bed, stacked three high. A stranger offered to share his bunk with Soga. In the dark, Doctor Iga Mori recognized him and whispered, "Mr. Soga?"

Then the faint voice of the old gentleman who owned the Komeya Hotel added, "I am here too."

The military detained Yasutaro Soga for two days before they drove him to Pier 5 and herded him onto a scow for the short trip to the Sand Island Detention Center. After debarking, Soga walked for half an hour and then lined up with the others in front of the barracks — his new home. Captain John Coughlin of the 11th Military Police Company addressed him and his new bunkmates:

The United States and Japan are at war ... you are now detainees. In due time, you will get a hearing. Some of

**you will be released, while others may be detained for the
duration of the war. You are not criminals but prisoners
of war. Thus we will treat you equally in accordance with
military rules.** [320]

Soga wondered what prisoner of war meant.

Authorities also took into custody Alfred Preis, the future
architect of the Arizona Memorial. He was an Austrian who had
fled Vienna to escape the Nazis. The FBI wanted him to keep a
suicide watch on Kuehn while he awaited his hearing. For weeks,
Preis listened to Kuehn's unconvincing pleas of innocence. He
marveled at the ironies of war. Here he was, a man who had fled
the Nazis, now having to guard the life of the only Nazi spy in
Hawaii.

Before 7 December rolled into 8 December, authorities
rounded up two hundred people on the ABC.[321]

Chapter 18

"When It's Time to Panic, Don't"

Sunday, 7 December 1941

Just as the sky faded to darkness, George Jr. went home to check in with his father and grab some grub. Streetlights went dark. The night turned blacker than the night before. Smoke choked the air.

When he walked through the door, he found his dad, "under considerable stress. He lay in bed and appeared to be experiencing a heart attack."[322]

George mumbled to his son that he had to go back to RCA to black out the two big picture windows and that Barbara had still not called.[323]

George Jr. cringed as his father's "attack apparently deepened, and he could [only] whisper instructions. His final act before he totally ran out of energy was to write out a note regarding the disposition of his estate in the event he died. Then, he shooed me on my way," George Jr. recounted. [324]

Not wanting to disobey him and add to his stress, knowing there were no doctors available, George Jr. rummaged around the carport shed and found paintbrushes, rags, and two-thirds of a gallon of paint. He checked on his dad again. George breathed easier now and had stopped sweating. Hoping for the best, George

Jr. loaded the car and struck out for the RCA office, about seven miles away.[325]

George Jr. wrote: "It was dark, and I was violating the newly imposed curfew, but a lot of things had happened today, and I wasn't going to worry about that." The moon could not light his way. A veil of smoke and haze blocked its shine. "I didn't turn on the car headlights, so I limited my speed. Fortunately, as I drove around Diamond Head, a car with suitably blacked-out lights passed in front of me and provided a faint blue halo to follow — at seventy miles-per-hour...." he confessed.[326] George Jr. careened his way through the streets of Honolulu on the tail of the blacked-out car ahead, his knuckles white as he hung on to the wheel. He broke off near King Street and eased into a parking place two to three blocks from the office.

When he walked up to the RCA office, buckets and brushes in hand, a guard barked, "Halt and identify." The first thing George Jr. spotted was his ancient rifle. The cadets carried 1903 thirty-caliber rifles that would accidentally discharge as they made their rounds, scaring the hell out of the cadet and public.[327] After a brief argument with their rifles pointed skyward, the sentries let him pass.

When he went into the office, he found about eight people from both the day and night shifts. Most of them had ridden the bus to work and were stuck there because of the curfew. He then explained to the crew, "Dad wants us to paint the windows...to provide blackout protection." They grabbed brushes and rags, divided the paint into small containers, and went to work. Within minutes, the main door from the street burst open, and an officer with a squad of soldiers entered.

"What the hell are you doing here?" the officer demanded.

George Jr. explained that they were to maintain twenty-four-hour operations, so they were blacking out the windows. He was cut short.

"Out. Out," the officer shouted.[328]

They made a hasty exit and piled into George Jr.'s car and one other vehicle — curfew be damned. George Jr. crawled around Honolulu with no lights, returning the staff to their homes one by one, as tanks raced past, aware that the Japanese invasion might happen at any time.[329]

People hid in the dark. Some sheltered with others; some hid in old concrete bunkers. Most retreated to interior rooms in their unlit homes. Police shot out lights. Small fires flared. Soldiers and volunteers dug trenches, strung barbed wire entanglements, and created artillery and weapon dugouts to repel invaders. One soldier remarked, "The exhaust of gigantic tractors barked like gunfire, and the rumble of large-caliber weapon carriers shook the foundations of homes," putting nerves on edge.[330]

Radio listeners were glued to the police band as they sat in their darkened rooms, thanks to the blackout. Rumors ran wild. A dropped flashlight became an oscillating flare. A man sheltering under a tree was reported as an armed enemy. A car's uncovered red tail light became an enemy signal. As blackness shrouded Honolulu, in less than twenty minutes, the police desk sergeant logged:

7:34 PM - At 1037 Ilima Drive; suspicious car.

7:35 PM - At 1417 7th Ave.; a prowler; 1744 Kamehameha IV Rd., see complainant; on Mott-Smith Drive, lights.

7:40 PM - 1006 9th Ave., somebody has a light burning; Kalihi dump, lights burning; also check 1045 5th Ave., supposed to be a prowler there.

7:45 PM - Go right over to the MacDonald Hotel; [Find out] what all the shooting is about.

7:52 PM - Kahala; find out who's shooting those rifles around there.[331]

A report from one caller said in all earnest that "a dog had been heard barking in code." Whether it was English or Japanese code, he could not say.[332]

George Jr. and Mac, his last passenger, headed down Kaimuki Avenue to Mac's home shortly after 9 PM.

"HALT!" barked a BMTC volunteer, and he pointed his rifle at the car. He ordered them to park and exit the vehicle. The sentry kept his gun pointed toward their chests. Hearts pounding, they explained what they were doing. Then, "It appeared Pearl Harbor was under attack again. Tracers from AA guns were visible with blasts of shells at altitude," George later explained.[333] The three stood and stared. Was this the expected Japanese invasion? Unbeknownst to them, they were witnessing a flight from USS *Enterprise* (CV-6) taking friendly fire. Six F4F Wildcats were ordered to land at Ford Island after failing to locate an enemy carrier reported south of Oahu.

Admiral William "Bull" Halsey, Jr., commanding officer of USS *Enterprise*, fearful of a repeat of the friendly fire a flight of bombers had encountered earlier, radioed Ford Island to make sure word got out: do not shoot down his fighters. Lieutenant Commander Howard L. Young, called "Brig" by his friends, had survived the gauntlet that morning and now was in the control tower to make sure Halsey's fighters landed without incident.

The flight of F4Fs missed their approach because of the blackout and winged past the east end of the island. When they realized their mistake, they approached Ford Island from the south, over Hickam. It was a tragic mistake.

Flight leader Lieutenant (Junior Grade) Francis "Fritz" Hebel radioed the tower to indicate they would circle the island. Brig told him to make a straight-in approach. Hebel repeated that he was going around.

In the confusion, shots rang out. Word that the flight was American had only reached a few of the guards. Then the night sky lit up.[334] Anti-aircraft fire hit Lieutenant (Junior Grade) Eric Allen Jr.'s F4F. When he tried to bail out, his chute tangled, and he went down with his plane.

Flight leader Hebel and his wingman, Ensign Herbert H. Menges, broke off to land at Wheeler. The AA gunners did their job and brought down both planes. Hebel died the next day. His wingman crashed into the Palms Hotel and died instantly.

Ensign Gayle Hermann's plane took eighteen bullets from machine gunfire. Then a five-inch shell hit his engine and separated it from the fuselage. For a moment, his Wildcat hovered like a butterfly, then smashed tail first onto a golf course. The impact crumpled only the rear of the aircraft. Hermann crawled out of the cockpit, shaken but unhurt. He grabbed his parachute and walked to the squadron hangar, happy to be alive.

Ensign David R. Flynn was hit as he banked toward Barbers Point. He bailed out and landed in a cane field. Soldiers of the 15th Infantry spotted the canopy and raced to the spot where he landed. They fired at the "paratrooper," mistaking him for a Japanese invader. Infuriated, Flynn let out a string of American swear words that would have made a sailor blush. The men held their fire, convinced he was an American.[335]

The last of the six in the air, Ensign James G. Daniels III, flipped off his exterior lights and hugged the water as he sped past Ford Island. He would later say, "Every anti-aircraft gun, machine gun, rifle, pistol, rock, wrench and piece of metal pipe that was available was fired or thrown at the aircraft."[336] Low on fuel, he circled away from the fireworks that enveloped the other five aircraft in his squadron. He called the tower, trying to figure out if the Japanese had captured Oahu.

Brig demanded, "Who is there?"

Daniels gave him his aircraft identification — "Six Fox Five," VF-6, aircraft 5.

"What is your name?"

Daniels recognized Brig's voice and gave him his name.

Still unsure, Brig asked, "What is my nickname?"

"Brigham," Daniels responded.

Brig asked, "What is your middle name?"

Exasperated and flying on fumes, Daniels fired back, "I am your godchild's father. You tell *me* my middle name."

"Ganson," said Brig.[337]

Both men breathed a sigh of relief. As luck would have it, Daniels and Brig were friends. "Come in as low as possible, as fast as possible with no lights," Brig instructed.

Daniels cranked down his landing gear and raced past the mast of the beached USS *Nevada* (BB-36). Tracers blazed across the night sky as he did an S-turn to bleed off speed. He hit the deck at around one hundred sixty knots, stomped on the brakes, and careened toward barrels and trucks parked on the runway to discourage enemy landings. Daniels whipped his plane left and right to avoid them, then ground-looped at the end of the runway.[338] Dirt flew as his wheels dug in, and he braced himself against the torque of the twisting plane. Jolted to a stop, Daniels thanked his lucky stars and taxied toward the hangar. Then a Marine stitched a burst of fifty caliber bullets above Daniels' head. Ensign Hermann, having arrived at the hangar, grabbed a rifle and hit the Marine with its butt. The three were never more thankful to be alive.

When the night finally turned quiet again, George Jr. explained to the BMTC volunteer that they wanted to check on their families. The sentry would not let them drive after curfew, so they abandoned their car and hiked uphill a mile or so to Mac's house, situated next to Fort Ruger.

Mac's mother, father, and siblings were huddled around the radio when they trudged through the front door. George Jr. called home to check on his dad. He reported that he felt better now, especially since Barbara had called to say she was okay. George figured that he had had a panic attack made worse by his polio.

Relieved that his family was secure, George Jr. collapsed on Mac's double bed and slept an exhausted sleep.

Too tired to think, too dedicated to quit, doctors, nurses, and attendants worked by rote and treated 2,344 soldiers and civilians by the time the clock struck midnight. Time in Hawaii was now marked by before and after the attack.

The final toll from Japan's two-hour attack and America's friendly fire incidents was:

- 2,008 Navy personnel killed, 710 wounded.

- 218 Army personnel killed, 364 wounded.

- 109 Marines killed, 69 wounded.

- 68 Civilians killed, 35 wounded.

- Total killed – 2,403. Total wounded – 1,178. Total casualties – 3,581

- 2 Battleships destroyed, 6 damaged.

- 3 Cruisers damaged.

- 3 Destroyers damaged.

- 1 Auxiliary ship destroyed, 4 damaged.[339]

Chapter 19

The Morning After

Boom! Boom! Boom! Compressed air rattled windows and shook the house. The staccato of heavy gunfire startled George Jr. and Mac awake from their deep sleep. It was five in the morning. They put on their shoes and ran outside to the chain-link fence surrounding Fort Ruger, which was just across the street from Mac's house. According to George Jr., he saw, "a 40 mm anti-aircraft gun firing away at B-17s flying in from the coast."[340] The Army's radar system detected the flight but failed to inform the Navy. Friendly fire assaulted the B-17s. Fortunately, it missed.

Once the barrage ended, Mac called several RCA operators and organized a carpool to the office. George Jr. headed home to grab a bite to eat. He recalled: "On reaching my car, I found I had a flat tire, but under the circumstances drove home on the rim some four miles away."[341] Rubber slapped the pavement as he limped to a stop in their carport. When he walked into the house, he found his dad making breakfast. "I realized I hadn't had a meal all the previous day. While he was busy cooking, I replaced the tire."[342] Barbara hadn't made her way home yet and hadn't called again. After breakfast, he and his dad drove downtown, each buried in his own thoughts.

George Jr. dropped off George Sr. at RCA and proceeded to Hawaiian Electric, which was practically next door to RCA. "All activity had been suspended, and personnel were discussing the impact of the December 7th attack. They listened to President Roosevelt's "Day of Infamy" speech to Congress and his Declaration of War," George Jr. later wrote.[343] Roosevelt's midday speech at the nation's capital was heard at 7 AM in Hawaii. Sixty million other radio listeners also tuned in to FDR's speech. War was no longer at America's threshold. It had broken down her back door and shattered Honolulu with a single, lethal kick. When FDR's speech ended, George Jr. listened to the engineers and draftsmen as they speculated that Roosevelt had ordered a sneak attack by U.S. forces, and then boasted that it would take only six months to lick the Japs.[344]

George Jr. decided to see if his dad could use him at RCA, because at Hawaiian Electric people were just standing around talking. He and his dad agreed that he should assist the two RCA engineers and three radiomen who were flying in on the first Pan American Clipper sent from the mainland after the attack. It was packed with high-ranking Army and Navy personnel.[345]

The RCA men were coming because the Army Corps of Engineers wanted RCA to relocate its transmitter station at Kahuku to make way for an airfield. J.S. Philbrick and crew were to select a site for the relocated transmitter. The group began by mapping the locations of Oahu's existing commercial radio transmitters and receiving stations.[346]

RCA-Honolulu counter (George Street Archive)

News reports from the Navy, late in the day on 8 December, announced that "three battleships had been sunk and that several thousand personnel had been killed." Within hours of the declaration of war, the ONI was monitoring all radio and telephone traffic from the island so that casualty numbers could be contained. They didn't want false reports flying across the airwaves and creating panic. The military ordered soldiers and sailors to write their home addresses on postcards with a brief "I'm alive and well" message. As hard as they tried to get the word out, one postcard did not make it home until February.

Meanwhile, the military suspended wireless transmissions, except for servicegrams and military traffic. Still, RCA was in for a heck of a day. Aid workers arrived with armloads of messages that needed processing. Delivery boys brought back satchels full of messages, as well. RCA held the flood of "I'm okay" messages until they received permission to reopen commercial transmissions to the mainland.[347] Workers ignored their sore feet, tense muscles, and aching backs to get the job done.

Legionnaires were deployed to collect explosives from businesses that used them for work. A Japanese interpreter and an expert powder man from Red Hill, the underground fuel depot still under construction, accompanied them to two hundred fifty separate locations, all over the island.

Donors continued to overwhelm blood banks. They drew blood from fifty people an hour for ten hours straight. Welders, sailors, dock workers, plantation crews, mothers, and friends rolled up their sleeves. Strangers held babies when it was time for a mother to give blood. When they ran out of containers, chemical and industrial companies supplied sterilized bottles as a substitute. Volunteers with no prior training showed up to roll bandages, under the blue light of blacked-out lamps.

Exhausted troops fired on returning fishermen who were unaware of the attack. Sampans were hard hit, and six fishermen were killed. When word reached the other islands, civilians armed with cane knives, war clubs, and guns — some swiped from museum walls — manned bridges and crossroads. Boy Scouts fanned out and assisted with blacking out windows, acted as messengers, and did what needed to be done.[348] The Red Cross and Salvation Army offered food, coffee, and juice to police officers, workers, and volunteers.

Barbara's much anticipated live broadcast to the mainland never happened. Instead, Oahu secured its island paradise. By night's end, three hundred seventy Japanese, ninety-eight Germans, and fourteen Italians were in detention. People on the second tier of the ABC list were under surveillance, as the evening sky darkened to a bruised purple, devoid of stars.[349]

On the morning of 9 December, George Street arrived at work at zero-dark hundred. He often went in early to handle paperwork before the day crew arrived. He knew it would be a hell of a day because RCA had received permission to transmit commercially. It was all hands on deck, all day long; the "I'm okay" messages needed to fly. As fast as the RCA workers toiled, it would be days before word got to George Jr. and Barbara's mother that the two of them were safe.

In Washington, FDR received letters, cables, and radiograms that rang with support: "… may God give you strength, health and the always great courage to lead us to the greatest victory these United States ever achieved.…" wrote Frank Adelman of Adelman Bag & Burlap Co. Members of the International Association of Machinists promised to "roll up their sleeves and give everything they have for full speed ahead."[350] David Sarnoff had offered RCA's assistance even before war was declared. "All our facilities and personnel are ready and at your instant service. We await your commands," he wired to the president.[351] Sarnoff asserted that "Radio is more than a strong arm of defense … It is a powerful weapon of offense … it guides … protects the fleet, and is the ear and voice of the fighter plane and the tanks. It helps to carry the war to the enemy's territory."[352]

Americans were on the move. In New York, forty thousand people showed up to volunteer as air spotters. Lookouts manned forest stations on the West coast around the clock. Now they scanned for enemy aircraft, balloons, and ships, instead of forest fires. Even Hollywood lent a hand. The Motion Picture Association made its studio trucks available to the California State Guard.

The White House turned into a fortress. FDR's study and bedroom housed emergency backup generators, and soldiers manned anti-aircraft guns on the roof. [353]Roosevelt met with the Supplies, Priorities, and Allocations Board (SPAB) and ignited America's military-industrial might. Then he braced himself for the battles ahead.

Congress was up in arms. They had before them an Army request that would allow the government to confiscate factory machinery and equipment essential to the war effort. Before they signed away rights, they wanted answers.

Senator Charles W. Tobey demanded that the American people "be informed of the true situation." [354] How had the Japanese penetrated Hawaiian defenses? How did this happen to the Navy? Why were the planes lined up wing-tip to wing-tip? What happened to the radar system?

Secretary Knox and General Stark attended a secret session of the House Naval Affairs Committee to answer those questions. They released a statement about the losses at Pearl: "fifteen hundred dead and an equal number wounded; a destroyer was blown up; small ships and numerous planes were out of commission; two hundred Marines were captured in China."[355] The press secretary told the United Press that "the president had checked his official dispatches with the newspaper stories on the battle of the Pacific and had found that the newspapers had most of the facts that the government had at this time."[356] Then they released the good news — Americans had destroyed several Japanese planes and submarines.

At 4:10 in the afternoon, FDR held his first war press conference, in the Diplomatic Reception Room. He wore a somber gray suit, white shirt, black tie, and a black armband to commemorate his mother, who had died in September. Bulbs flashed, and newsreel cameras rolled. One reporter among the crush of newsmen had a note pinned to his lapel, "Chinese reporter — not Japanese — please."[357]

FDR smoked a cigarette in his ivory holder, chatted, and smiled with reporters to project an air of confidence and perfect health, even though he had seen his doctor three times that day. Dark circles under his eyes gave his failing health away.

Roosevelt cautioned the press that it was going to be a long, hard war. "I urge my countrymen to reject all rumors," he said. "These ugly little hints of complete disaster fly thick and fast in wartime." Then he warned newspaper and radio stations:

You have a most grave responsibility to the nation now, and for the duration of the war ... you have no right in the ethics of patriotism to deal out unconfirmed reports in such a way as to make people believe they are the gospel truth. The lives of our soldiers and sailors — the whole future of this nation — depend upon the manner in with each and every one of us fulfills his obligation to our country.[358]

Before the day ended, the government revoked the thirty-month limitation on military service periods and recalled 175,000 reservists. Now men would serve for the duration of the war plus six months.

***

Amid the headlines of Japan's thrust across the Pacific, newspapers published air raid rules for the nation; sirens would wail for seven minutes before an air attack — hopefully. People were instructed to shelter at home with the lights off, out of the path of flying glass. Motorists were instructed to pull to the curb, turn off their lights, and lie down. If incendiary bombs fell, people were to cover them with dry sand. In case of a gas attack, they were told to go to the room in their house with the least number of windows and doors and paste paper over the windows, and stuff the cracks under doors and windows with rags. *"AVOID HYSTERIA, FOLLOW OFFICIAL ORDERS AND PROCEED AS USUAL,"* one headline advised.[359]

San Francisco's first blackout and air raid drill, perhaps the first on the mainland, resulted in three people killed and three injured. Ann Stewart fell to her death when she leaned out her seventh-story window to see what was going on when the air raid alarm wailed. Drivers unable to see one another because of the fog, darkness, and blacked-out headlights collided near Alameda Naval Air Station at 2:30 AM. Both died, and their passengers were critically hurt. Two other head-on collisions injured three others. In San Francisco General Hospital with her husband at her side, Marie Sayre held the dubious distinction of becoming the first war victim on the mainland. Her husband, Donald, had failed to hear a sentry's command to stop as he approached the First Street entrance to the Bay Bridge. A bullet got his attention. Private Albert Rowand of the Home Guard's Company L had shot Donald's wife.[360]

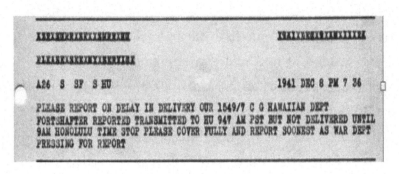

Servicegram (George Street Archive)

George focused his attention on a servicegram sent from the San Francisco office. The War Department was still investigating the delivery of Radiogram 1549. It became clear that someone was going to get blamed for the delay. By now, George realized that Radiogram 1549 was a crucial piece of intelligence and that Stevens had made a serious mistake by not time-stamping the radiogram when it was delivered.

He pulled Radiogram 1549 from the file cabinet and spent about an hour piecing together the story. He reviewed previous servicegrams and Sue Sharp's response sent on the afternoon of 7 December. George replied to San Francisco's latest query with a summary:

My own conclusion, after the interviews with Corporal Stevens of Fort Shafter, and our messenger, and an examination of

other delivery receipts of messages delivered on the route both before and after the Fort Shafter delivery was that the RCA messenger was at the Fort Shafter message center at approximately 9:40 AM.

George stated: "Stevens admitted to me on December 9th that he failed to time-stamp the RCA receipt as usual, but that he believed our messenger was there at Shafter between 9 and 9:30 AM."[361]

About Fuchikami's harrowing motorbike ride on the seventh, George wrote in the margins of a typed timeline he crafted: "... anti-aircraft shells falling and exploding in the downtown area and between town and area of Fort Shafter ... seven miles of delay, bedlam, and danger." He instructed Tadao Fuchikami to write a detailed account of his route. Barbara would later say, "They also tried to blame the delivery boy, who was Japanese. He did his normal route, but there were lots of blockades and barriers that slowed him down."[362] Street's handwritten sidebar on page 381 of Farago's book, *The Broken Seal,* reads: "Re the delivery and time of the delivery is grossly erroneous and based on a planted fabrication, probably by Army Signal Corps in the Washington records."

*Fuchikami's typed account of his
delivery route with George Street's handwritten annotation.
(George Street Archive)*

Chapter 20

Shell Shocked

With Honolulu now in total lockdown due to martial law, George and George Jr. took time out of their day to acquire safe-conduct passes so that they could drive after curfew. George received the seventy-third one issued. His ID card was makeshift — typed on a piece of paper glued to cardboard, covered with a thin piece of plastic, and secured with cellophane tape. It never left his wallet.

Safe-conduct pass (George Street Archive)

With his pass in hand, George Jr. arranged with the University of Hawaii's dean of engineering — his freshman-year mentor — to borrow survey equipment which the RCA crew needed to map the transmitter's relocation. He and Philbrick picked up a transit and measuring tapes and then headed to a strategy session with the Navy communications officer at Pearl Harbor. On the way to the meeting, George Jr. described the devastation in the harbor: "I observed seven battleships sunk or beached along with other smaller vessels ... Fires still burned on several ships and ashore ... This truly was a major catastrophe."[363] And Barbara was still not home.

***

FDR's office glistened with brass on the morning of 10 December. Forrestal, Stark, King, Marshall, Watson, and Beardall joined Secretaries Hull and Stimson, and Undersecretary of State Sumner Welles to discuss the business of war. Secretary of the Navy Knox was noticeably absent. Roosevelt had sent him to Oahu to find out what had gone wrong.

Knox had spent a restless night huddled in a blanket in the belly of a PBY seaplane. There were no game tables, bars, or comfy seats on this transpacific flight. Instead, he shared the space with blood and serum for the wounded on the long flight. As they eased into Honolulu's waters, smoke hung in the air like fog. It dimmed the mountains that hugged the city proper. Admiral Kimmel met Knox when he debarked and offered him a room in his home. Knox declined. He did not want to bias his investigation and booked a room at the Royal Hawaiian Hotel instead.

Grim-faced, Kimmel and Knox headed to Pearl Harbor. Through the car window, Knox witnessed the devastation — oil-slicked bodies still being retrieved from the harbor, burned-out hangars, strafed cars, scorched hunks of ships, and planes blown to bits.[364] According to Layton, "Even Knox, the veteran Rough Rider who had charged with Teddy Roosevelt up San Juan Hill during the Spanish-American War, was shocked to his boots by the shambles of Battleship Row."[365] Next, he visited hospital wards and comforted men he said were so badly burned they were barely recognizable as humans. Knox later confided to his aide that "the sight of those men made me as angry as I have ever been in my life."[366]

During the second day of his investigation, Secretary Knox cabled the inspector of naval aviation in San Diego:

The enemy has struck a savage, treacherous blow ... We must have ships and more ships, guns and more guns, planes and more planes, men and more men — faster and faster. There is no time to lose.[367]

Knox deduced that his Hawaiian command suffered from post-attack shock. He conferred with General Short and concluded that Oahu's fifth columnists, people in cahoots with the enemy, had contributed to the confusion of the U.S. military response. Knox returned to D.C., submitted his findings to Roosevelt, and advocated for a full investigative inquiry.[368] In an effort to restore public confidence and Navy morale, Knox recommended a reassignment of Admiral Kimmel. He also suggested the complete evacuation of all ethnic Japanese from Oahu, about thirty-five percent of the population.[369]

Secretary of War Henry Stimson dispatched an Army team to Oahu to hold an investigation similar to the one conducted by Secretary of the Navy Knox. He wanted to make sure the Navy's report was unbiased and so sent Major General Herbert A. Dargue and Colonel Charles W. Bundy and their staff to Honolulu. En route, their transport bomber crashed in the Sierra Nevada Mountains near Bishop, California. No one survived.[370] Secretary Stimson then decided to accept Secretary Knox's findings rather than risk more lives.

Once the U.S. declared war against Japan, Congress authorized the president to take over transportation systems, industrial plants, radio stations, power facilities, and ships, and to place rigid controls on communications. Censors and new regulations became part of RCA. Later that day, FDR signed an executive order to implement those controls, ordering "other agencies of the government to step in and take control of private radio broadcasting facilities."[371] The order also gave the War Department and the Navy Department the power to "use, control or close ... the radio facilities of the Nation."[372]

Meanwhile, Japan had cut the east/west telegraph cable stretching between Midway and Hong Kong. Commercial Pacific Cable Co. confirmed the cut. Now messages between the Far East and the West would have to be sent by wireless, which meant that "coded messages would be more accessible to enemy cryptographers," according to a New York City newspaper.[373]

In Honolulu, *the Honolulu Star-Bulletin* published General Order Number 14, signed by Military Governor Lieutenant General Thomas H. Green on 10 December.[374] It placed the press and radio services in Hawaii under strict military censorship. Wire services were limited to "the Associated Press, United Press, International News Service, [and] Transradio Press." Only radio stations KGU, KGMB, KTOH, and KHBC were allowed to continue on the air in Hawaii.

At HYPO, Woodward finally cracked the code of the Kita/Kuehn signal light dispatch, which would have been an easy task for Magic.[375] It had taken him four days to realize he had lined up the message-text backward. According to Layton, "if HYPO had possessed all the latest key recoveries, the decryption process would have involved about six hours of work."[376]

While Knox conducted his investigation, Hitler and Mussolini delivered a ranting speech to their respective countrymen in Germany and Italy and declared war on the United States. In response, Roosevelt addressed Congress in one of his most famous and inspirational speeches:

> **The long-known and the long-expected has thus taken place. The forces endeavoring to enslave the entire world now are moving toward this hemisphere. Never before has there been a greater challenge to life, liberty, and civilization ... I, therefore, request the Congress to recognize a state of war between the United States and Germany, and between the United States and Italy.[377]**

Ready for the fight and stoked with pride, troops as far away as Iceland declared, "We'll pin their ears back."[378]

!

Chapter 21

Paradise Burned

Four days after the attack

Barbara finally made her way home four days after the attack and arrived to an empty house. Her brother and father were at work and would not return for hours. She was alone. And at some point, she made a lifelong decision. She would never tell her brother or her close friends, and later her children, where she had been or what she had been doing during her absence. But, on 7 December, for the rest of her life, she remembered the attack. "It's Pearl Harbor Day," she would say as she passed the mashed potatoes to her four hungry children. They asked her to tell them about where she was and what she had seen. It was a different story each year — she was home or with her girlfriend — and then she'd change the subject. No amount of pestering could pierce her veil of silence.

Her girlfriend, interviewed decades later, said Barbara was not with her. Her boyfriend's son said his father talked about Barbara, but on 7 December, he was not with her. As an ROTC cadet-lieutenant, he became part of the Territorial Guard, deployed to man intersections and vital facilities.

On one Pearl Harbor Day, her husband answered the oft-repeated question, blurting out, "Picking up dead bodies out of the water." If looks could kill, Barbara's glare would have dropped him on the spot. "He's just making up stories," she barked. But her children never forgot their father's apology, as its tone had confirmed the blurted truth.[379]

When she returned home, according to George Jr., Barbara secured the house. "We painted the windows black. Headlights had to be painted black, with a horizontal blue stripe. Barbara blacked out windows that did not have heavy drapes, and taped the glass so it wouldn't shatter if impacted."[380]

Barbara listened to the radio a lot. Billy was gone, swept into the military. Her school was closed, and the beaches she loved were laced with barbed wire. Her girlfriend took shelter at the YMCA with her mom until they could get off the island. She had lost track of her other friends. Her youthful dreams had disappeared into the smoke that hung over Oahu. She rarely crossed paths with her dad, who battled to keep a lifeline open to the mainland. She was now mostly alone on a ship to nowhere, and in rough seas to boot.

It took less than a week after the attack for the Treasury Department to reap the consequences of seizing Japanese assets and restricting transactions. The department had to relax its edicts because the Pacific Coast was running out of vegetables and other foodstuffs. Mobs took out their anger in the back alleys of Seattle. Chow Get Min, a local teacher, was attacked and partially beheaded, with his hands tied behind his back. The *Oakland Tribune* reported, "He might have been killed by a person who mistook him for a secret agent working on the war situation, and there is no possibility that it was a Tong [Chinese gang] slaying."[381]

As the days progressed, George continued to receive servicegrams that asked for clarification about Radiogram 1549. Why did RCA deliver Marshall's message by motorcycle instead of "printer wire?"

He replied to the Army Chief Signal Officer: **"Installation of printer wire completed December 6, but testing before deployment still pending on December 7."** By now, George had

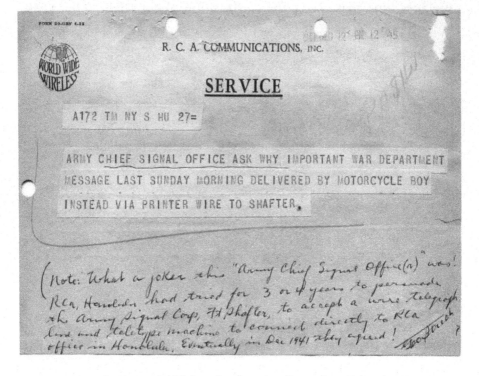

Servicegram with Street's annotation (George Street Achieve)

had enough, as revealed by what he wrote on the bottom of his reply. "Note: What a joke the 'Army Chief Signal Office(r)' was! RCA, Honolulu had tried for 3 or 4 years to persuade the Army Signal Corps, Ft. Shafter, to accept a wire telegraph line and teletype machine to connect directly to the RCA office in Honolulu. Eventually, in Dec. 1941, they agreed!"

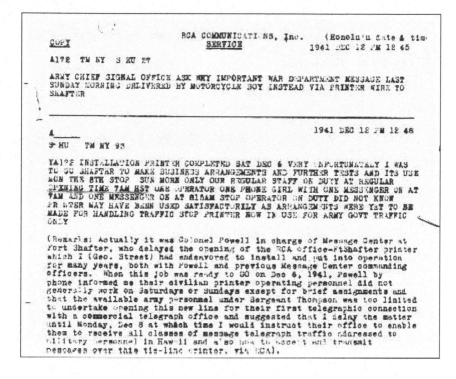

Servicegram regarding Colonel Powell (George Street Archive)

On 12 December, he wired a follow-up and let the cat out of the bag:

… it was Colonel Powell … who delayed the opening of the RCA office-Ft. Shafter printer … when this job was ready to GO on Dec 6, 1941. Powell, by phone, informed me their civilian printer operating personnel did not generally work on Saturdays or Sundays … Army personnel under Sergeant Thompson was too limited to

**undertake opening this new line ... and suggested that I
delay the matter until Monday, Dec 8 ....**

Then, at the end of a long day, George's intercom buzzed. The
FBI was on the line. When he picked up, the caller asked, "Street,
do you know who this is?

"I do," Street responded, recognizing the voice of a local FBI
agent.

"... don't say how you found out, but I thought you should
know that your man J.U. [Joe Unger] will not get to work tonight
on the 11 PM shift. The FBI has locked him up."

"What for? George asked.

"He is a Nazi sympathizer," the agent assumed, because of
Unger's German heritage.

"How can I reach Bob?" George snapped.

The caller gave him Bob Shivers' unlisted phone number. An
hour later, George had him on the phone. He told Shivers, "... that
man you have under arrest is my number one most reliable
employee, and it is almost impossible not to shut RCA down
without him. Furthermore, if he is an enemy sympathizer, you will
have to go a very long way to prove it. You have swallowed the
bait, hook, line and sinker of the radio operators' unions affiliated
with the C.I.O. [Congress of Industrial Organizations] who don't
like J.U. only because he happens not to like unions and will not
join them."[382]

Shivers told George before he hung up, "All right, Street, but
remember it's your head too, maybe. I'll release him immediately
to your custody."

Unger was back on the job — for a while. Forty-eight hours after the FBI released him into George's custody, he was picked up by the Army and locked up incommunicado on Sand Island, a former Immigration and Naturalization Service quarantine facility. Barbed wire capped the chain link fencing surrounding the compound and laced the twelve-foot-high gates. Canvas tents supplemented overcrowded clapboard housing. Shade was at a premium, but the views were great. Diamond Head, Waikiki Beach, Honolulu Harbor, and the vast Pacific Ocean surrounded the island. Aloha Tower pierced the skyline, a reminder of better times for those welcomed to Hawaii.

Joe Unger (George Street Archive, Relay Magazine)

The military housed Unger in quarters next to the mess hall with other Germans, including Bernard Otto Kuehn and some Italians. He could smell the food cooking next door, the scents being familiar because the cook was German. Kuehn's wife, Freidel, and daughter Ruth bunked in a cabin close to the women's barracks, alone, segregated from the other women and Bernard, probably to prevent the fabrication of untrue stories.

This time George had little recourse to effect Unger's release. George Jr. fumed and suggested that Unger's nonunion status was probably one of the reasons he was considered "suspicious by some hot-shot union member, who inferred he was a spy because he wasn't one of them."[383] George fought the military on Unger's behalf each step of the way and figuratively banged his cane on the desks of those who barred his way. He wrote letters, attended hearings, and butted heads with weary commanders who were just trying to do their jobs. Now critically shorthanded, George received a letter from Unger weeks after his arrest. Unger explained that he was only allowed one letter a month. George remarked, "In this letter, I could see he was writing guardedly." Now aware of Unger's location, George used the power of the pen to fight for Unger's release. He appealed to Colonel Bicknell several times. "Bicknell just stalled me off, once saying to me, 'This is war, things are different now,' as if I wouldn't know."[384]

For six weeks, George asked Bicknell and his staff about the date of Unger's hearing. They replied, "We don't know," or "Not yet."

"After getting the well-known brush off these four or five times, I could only assume that Colonel Bicknell was displaying his 'mighty authority' under the new Military Government of Hawaii. So I gave up on 'Bick'..."[385] George went over Bicknell's head and wrote to the commanding general of the Hawaiian Department and suggested that "an early hearing on the case would be in the interest of maintaining RCA's good and reliable communications facilities." He wrote a follow-up letter and even considered writing to President Roosevelt.[386] He received no response.

After weeks of petitioning, George was finally given a chance to testify on Unger's behalf. He was summoned to the quarantine station. MPs escorted Unger to the hearing, yet George sneaked an "unauthorized few minutes in the hallway" with Unger.

"I went into the hearing room; about ten officers from the rank of colonel on down were sitting at the table ... First, I was required to take an oath for swearing the truth. Then informed that anything I said may be held against me. Now, in this room full of strangers, I lit right out and said, 'Gentlemen, if I cannot prove the truth of this matter, you can lock me up too!'"

George explained that the FBI had released Unger into his custody. Then he attacked Bicknell. "... he hardly listened to me and did nothing," he told the tribunal. George hit hard with "this was still the United States of America as far as I knew, and I thought that G-2 was playing into the hands of the C.I.O. Union." A civilian, unknown to George, nodded his head in agreement! According to George, it took days for the Army to complete its "red tape and paperwork." Unger was cleared and allowed to return to work at RCA three months after his arrest. "There was absolutely no substance at all to the charges," George raged. "But this was not the end of troubles for J. U. After he was freed from the FBI and G-2, he was picked up ... by the Navy!" [387]

George sharpened his pencil again. By this time, he was on a confidential [Navy] committee to help weed out undesirable radio operators. George reminded the commandant of his defense of Unger and received a swift reply from the Marine Corps. In a couple of days, the district's legal officer "was in my office asking how to go about clearing Unger," George recounted. "He followed my outline, and in about two or three days, Unger was released. The Navy took about ten days overall. The Army, about one hundred days or more!"[388]

While he battled for Unger's release, George ran operations at RCA without Unger's help. He and the other Islanders braced for the feared invasion and continued the grim cleanup. Bodies of sailors, disintegrated and burned beyond recognition, were towed behind boats because they could not be lifted out of the water without falling apart. Rescuers could not match hundreds of body parts and chunks of viscera with the person that once was. Others became a gull's meal.

Life under martial law was bleak. Bars remained closed. Retail stores, movie houses, and restaurants were shuttered or told to close early, so that people could be off the streets by sundown. Honolulu was under constant patrol. The military suspended weather reports to keep the information from the enemy. People could only fill their automobile gasoline tanks half full. Machine gun nests bracketed bridge crossings. Residents filled sinks, containers, and bathtubs with water and colored their windows and their world black.[389]

Security regulations hit the news at a rapid-fire pace. Fishermen kept an eye out for enemy ships. The military surrounded harbors with anti-submarine netting. A nationwide broadcast asked all radio operators, including ham radio operators, to clear the airwaves.[390] RCA was allowed to transmit radiograms, since the censors were in place. They monitored all phone calls to the mainland when the local phone company patched the calls through RCA. All callers had to speak in English. Hester Adams and the other switchboard operators did not hesitate to disconnect calls if rules were broken. The Chinese population wore special ID buttons to distinguish them from the Japanese, and Japanese women no longer walked the streets in their kimonos. George Jr. remembered that "After the attack, the people of Hawaii responded admirably ... The populace dug in, changed their lives around, worked extra jobs and hours, and did the necessary things to maintain a viable wartime economy."[391]

The Businessmen's Military Training Corps (BMTC) grew to seventeen companies, totaling fifteen hundred men, two-thirds of whom were First World War veterans. Their primary function was security. They excluded ethnic Japanese from their organization, fearing they would collaborate with the enemy. George objected to segregation. He preferred to consider each man's honor and loyalty, based on his actions and not on his heritage.

In response to BMTC's white bias, Chinese Americans, Filipinos, Native Hawaiians, Puerto Ricans, Koreans, and sympathetic whites formed the Hawaii Defense Volunteers to help defend their island home.

Shivers and the Army had laid the groundwork in an attempt to prevent wholesale racism on the islands. The advisory group of Americans of Japanese Ancestry, the Oahu Citizens Committee for Home Defense, and the Committee for Inter-Racial Unity in Hawaii had shown up at Shivers' office on the morning of the attack. Now, the Committee for Inter-Racial Unity formed a morale section with several racial subcommittees to work among their communities, according to Shivers.[392] Their job was to act as liaisons with the FBI and the military governor's office. "They passed on orders, explained, and eased tension on all the islands. An Emergency Service Committee sprang from the Morale Section and helped people to demonstrate their loyalty in concrete ways," he explained.[393] Anti-Japanese bias soon regressed in Hawaii.

Shivers combated fear, prejudice, and paranoia, because it was only going to get tougher. Germans, Italians, Japanese, Bulgarians, and Croatians were ordered to "surrender firearms, weapons, ammunition, bombs, explosives, shortwave receiving and transmitting sets, signal devices, codes and ciphers, cameras, binoculars and similar devices, papers with invisible writing, and maps and blueprints of military or naval importance."[394] They had until noon the next day to turn in their items to the police department, and they had to carry their alien registration cards at all times. When there was no evidence of insurgency, they were allowed to move about freely.

Lava rock, dust, sand, and tension became the daily ration of the hardworking men and women who prepared for the invasion. There was little sleep to be had and no relaxation. The world that was once a tropical delight became an island fortress of concrete, wire, noise, and darkness, overcrowded with homesick men who worked their fingers to the bone.

George Jr.'s boat beached and forgotten on Hunakai Beach, was no more. He described how "it had been pulled up on the beach and was a shambles, as it had been commandeered along with other small boats to lay out the barbed wire. Barbed wire and redwood planking do not mix well. I disassembled the hull, outriggers, mast, rigging, and sails, and dragged the pieces home."[395]

Hawaii was no longer anyone's paradise. It wasn't even pleasant.

Barbara Street at barbed wire beach (George Street Archive)

Chapter 22

The New Reality

Oahu, Territory of Hawaii

After the attack seared its place in time, each day turned into shell-shocked flashes of change. Oahu, well ahead of the mainland in terms of preparedness, and time tested, now dealt with shortages. The city treasurer issued gas ration cards, ten gallons per month per car. Military regulators urged Hawaiians to buy chicken and pork to save beef for the boys on the front. Restaurants were allowed to stay open around the clock so they could feed the night shifts

Streets' bomb shelter (George Street Archive)

who prepared for the invasion that never came. Rents were frozen.[396]

Households in the territory constructed bomb shelters to protect against flying shell fragments. Plans were available from the U.S. district engineer. A six-foot-deep trench with a sand-covered roof was recommended for each home.

George Jr. and Barbara expanded their slit trench into the required shelter. George Jr. shoveled and dug each day after he finished work and his block warden rounds. He described it as "six feet by eight feet and six feet below ground level (to within a half a foot of the sea-water table) covered with two-inch-thick planks and tar paper … with a mounded roof."[397] They shored up the walls with wood. George Jr. then piled three feet of sand on the roof and constructed a hatch and a ramp for his dad. He also ran an extension cord from the house for a lamp and small radio. Four bunks, two collapsible cots, a card table, kerosene stove, lanterns, books, and games rounded out the shelter. Satisfied, George Jr. said, "We were ready. The Japs were expected back."[398]

Meanwhile, Hawaii continued to bury its dead. Bodies in coffins built at the local lumberyard lay in a well-dressed row. With each burial, six Marines raised their rifles and fired three volleys into the sunset. Locals stripped their gardens of flowers — poinsettias, asters, and hibiscus — so that each grave could be adorned. The sound of taps shrouded the silence.

Protestant Chaplain William A. Maguire and a Catholic priest blessed the boys who had lost their lives at Pearl. The chaplain remarked, "Since Monday, December 8th, men have been laid to rest — laid to rest, so that others could live and be free!"[399]

He recounted the heroism he had witnessed on the day of the attack. "At the Marine barracks where the wounded lay on tables, if a worse wounded man was brought in on a stretcher, a man with a leg missing or an arm missing would say: 'For God's sake, I'm all right. Put him on the table and take me out of here'... Men about me without clothes and badly burned, wrapped in blankets, begged me: 'I want to get back to my ship, I want to get back to my gun!'... if every American saw how quietly, yes quietly, these dead suffered, how gallantly they died, how courageously they thought of the man next to him, they'd glory in the dead and resolve that it would never happen again. They'd know too, that our front-line will never give up ...."[400]

It did not take long for the cemetery at Nuuanu to reach capacity. Soon, trenches on Red Hill, which overlooked the harbor, held more dead. Officers were embalmed, dressed in their formal white uniforms, and transported back to the mainland for burial at the national cemetery. Japanese airmen lost in the attack were laid to rest with the same dignity as the Americans.[401]

Bert Gottdiener left the Baltimore office of RCA to sign up for the military. He penned a letter to the Honolulu office on 15 December which was delayed by censor Lieutenant Colonel H. B. Turner. His letter appeared in the March 1942 RCA *Relay* magazine: "Undoubtedly the uppermost thought in your mind, along with the other one hundred thirty million Americans, is the war ... Manager George Street ... opened a branch in Waikiki to take care of the load ... lines formed like an army chow line ... To save time and facilitate office operations, radiogram blanks were passed out on the street ... so that when they finally entered the enchanted portals of the King Street office, the message was all set to go — typical of old RCAC [RCA-Communication] efficiency, eh?"[402]

By now, all messages had to be in "plain language." As men took leave to serve their country, RCA personnel across the country worked longer shifts to fill the gap and keep traffic moving. Armed guards protected equipment, and RCA laboratories continued to advance technology for the military.

At the 17 December Rotary Club meeting, hosted in the Alexander Young Hotel roof garden, George urged fellow members to "maintain its attendance and membership in the war emergency ... because the weekly meetings ... make possible the exchange of ideas among members and facilitate the formation of committees and other groups to meet community service problems...."[403] Ten days after the attack, Hawaiians were not panicking; they were planning.

Oahu grocers closed and took inventory. The results were grim. Oahu had just a thirty-seven-day supply of smoked meats and staples, seventy-five days' worth of flour and cereals, eighteen days of onions and potatoes, and only a thirteen-day supply of rice. Normally, Oahu received weekly supplies from the mainland. Now Islanders could only hope that ships would get past the Japanese submarines that stalked the Pacific. Even before the war, the massive influx of military and civilian contract personnel created an enormous demand for imported foodstuffs because Oahu produced only fifteen percent of the food it consumed.

On 20 December 1941, the first shipment of supplies left San Francisco for Honolulu. It contained a year's worth of sardines and 180 tons of cheddar cheese — initially intended for England. The shipment made it. However, when it arrived, there were no trucks available to haul it to warehouses because planners had conscripted them for ambulance service. The Army stepped up with men and vehicles. When the food warehouses overflowed, plumbing shops, schools, church auditoriums, and even automobile showrooms became storage facilities. And the rodents had a field day. Rain poured through leaky roofs. Worms carpeted the floors of inadequate facilities and crawled up the bags en masse onto the ceiling rafters.[404] Who would want to eat worms with their rice? Pigs feasted on the food not fit for human consumption, and within months the Army requisitioned twenty-five thousand rat traps from the mainland to crush the invasion.[405]

Food shortages became critical, and lines at the grocery store grew longer. The military shipped dependents back to the mainland so there would be fewer mouths to feed. Troops had to eat field rations.[406]

The Federal Surplus Commodities Corporation, which was in charge of food supplies under martial law, mistakenly ordered nine hundred tons of onions instead of three hundred tons. When they arrived, there was no place to store them. So, local newspapers ran "my favorite onion recipes" and lauded onion breath. Maui celebrated "Onion Week."

Households were encouraged to stash food to help alleviate storage capacity shortages. Barbara crammed cabinets and their bomb shelter with Spam, tuna, canned pineapple, peaches, vegetables, and tinned potatoes. George Jr. remembered that they "had plenty, primarily because it was difficult for their dad to shop, so he stocked up when he made his infrequent shopping trips. Meat became scarce, and Spam became our protein of choice." [407] Unfortunately, prolonged tropical rainstorms flooded the Streets' bomb shelter. Labels on their canned goods melted away, and mold took hold. Barbara remembered that, during an hours-long drill, she guessed at the contents of the cans, and once they ended up eating "tuna a-la-peaches." [408]

Plantation owners converted their pineapple and sugar cane fields to vegetable gardens, which destroyed their export market and resulted in a nationwide sugar shortage. Thousands of acres were under cultivation by March. However, there were no men to harvest the crops, and pineapple machinery did not work well on vegetables.

Copper, lead, chrome, and zinc for civilian use became things of the past. There was no new kitchenware until after the war ended. Building materials and basic supplies vanished in the riptide of war. The government requisitioned privately owned material supplies. Shoes, paper, silk, butter, and milk turned into remembered luxuries. "Use it up, wear it out, make it do, or do without" became a rallying call from the home front.

The days that followed the attack were unlike any George Jr. and Barbara had ever seen. Their world was hemmed in by barbed wire, curfews, censorship, roadblocks, and darkness. People faced fines of one hundred dollars — almost a month's salary — or one hundred days in prison for breaking the blackout rules. If wardens or police caught people lighting cigarettes in their backyard, the provost often ordered them to donate a pint of blood as their fine.

Authorities asked civilians to help whenever they could. The call for workers went beyond RCA due to the shortages created by men flocking to recruiting centers, and authorities detaining people with suspicious backgrounds or the wrong heritage. Middle and high school students made up the largest available reservoir of manpower on Oahu and stepped up to fill the void.

Taking a moment over breakfast — bacon maybe — coffee for sure, George read in his morning paper that there was a need for clothing for the Army personnel who had lost everything during the raid. "Able-bodied, patriotic men, and lusty youths" were asked to apply to the U.S. Army engineers with promises of good wages. The Army needed help with cleanup and new construction. George Jr. wrote, "There was a shortage of workers for commercial and military support services, and to that end, young men were essentially exempt from the draft." Instead of going to boot camp, they stepped into the shoes of cooks, maintenance men, and clerical workers to support the ever growing number of soldiers, sailors, and Marines. George Jr. felt a "current of excitement, a realization that we were at the forefront of potential danger...."[409]

Barbara did not return to Roosevelt High. Barbed wire laced the steps of her school when it reopened in February. Like so many other high school students, she gave up school and went to work. "After the attack, the school took on the formidable appearance of a building in the combat zone," read a caption in her yearbook.[410] Gas masks accessorized the student body. Students and volunteers dug trenches across the campus grounds. Air raid drills punctuated the school day. Barbara had enough credits to graduate and had earned a spot in the National Honor Society. A little over fifty percent of American high school seniors received diplomas in 1942, and Barbara was one of them.

That's when she began to work eighty hours a week for her father at RCA. In part because, as she recalled, "RCA instituted sending money orders by radiogram as a service to help facilitate the flow of funds in Hawaii."[411] In addition to working the counter at RCA, she drove a blacked-out jeep to construction sites and cantonment units to collect the money wired home by men and women on paydays.

Peggy Beers was usually Barbara's copilot when she drove to the cantonments for payday pickups. Wind whipped their hair, and bugs splattered the windshield as they sped from one pickup point to another. When it rained, water puddled at their feet and clouded the windows. Peggy hung out the side of the jeep as a spotter so they wouldn't drive off the road and plunge into the sea. Moonless, rainy nights kept the girls especially alert. Out of the darkness a red flashlight beam would penetrate the night, and Barbara would stop for an ID check. Red light traced her body. The sentries took a close look to make sure the girls matched their IDs. They were a welcome sight for men stuck in the middle of nowhere. The memory of flashing eyes, bright smiles, and the curve of a breast filled their long hours of sentry duty.

The girls did not worry about robbers, even though they stuffed the money in garbage cans when their money bags overflowed. According to Barbara, "Everyone was pulling together to protect their island; everyone was in the same boat. Why would they want to hurt each other? ... Somebody had to collect the money and instructions and take it back to the RCA office at night...." [412]

Instead of lounging at the beach when she had a few precious off-hours, Barbara and her friends helped out at canteens and passed out coffee and doughnuts to weary, homesick sailors. The demands of this new mass of masculinity on the long-established norms of the local population created a complicated business that aggravated the local boys and unleashed riptides of conflict. Clashes over girlfriends were inevitable, since women were few. The civilian population struggled to hold this vast sea of decompressing troops behind the breakwaters of moral decency. Parents taught their children about differences in military ranks to help them survive the tsunami of men that engulfed their island. George was such a father. He declared military men off-limits to his daughter, Billy included — pilots, especially so. He did not mince words when he explained his reasoning to Barbara. "What is a sky pilot going to do after the war, become a taxi driver?"[413]

After giving up their beds to the wounded, the prostitutes in Honolulu were in crisis. Where could they rent a room? They'd have to move into nice neighborhoods because there was no place else to go. Police Chief Gabrielson, however, was intent on enforcing the law restricting them to the red-light district. Madam O'Hara became the girls' general. She rallied the MPs and shore patrol. Servicemen were grateful and protective of the girls, who had serviced them in pleasure, and again when they were in pain. They were not forgotten. The MPs and shore patrol battled the local cops who were sent to oust them from nice neighborhoods.[414] It did not take long before Gabrielson retreated and turned over control of the brothels to the military. The Navy provided VD checks, and Honolulu had one of the lowest VD rates in any military town. In order to keep the men happy, the Army ordered the prostitutes not to raise their rates.

***

The hunt for a scapegoat continued. On 23 December, more servicegrams arrived at the King Street office — this time from RCA-New York. They pressed for details about the delivery of Radiogram 1549. George double-checked his facts and reaffirmed that there was no second delivery that morning. He confirmed that one messenger came in at 7 AM, made copies, and helped the phone operator stuff them into envelopes. Fuchikami arrived at 8:15 AM, arranged his route, and departed at 8:40. He spelled out, once again, the reason for delayed delivery times that Sunday — a war had broken out, after all! And he explained why the phone operator did not relay the message by phone: "… letters C G in the address [were] meaningless to her … she thought to phone the message but being in code decided against doing so as many times Shafter only reluctantly accepted messages from us over the phone in the past … 'too busy send them by boy' [was their typical response] …." Then he summarized his conversation with Stevens and said the message was delivered between "9:00 and 9:30 AM." 415

George also interviewed Corporal Stevens, who had failed to time stamp the coded message. Now, Stevens insisted that the message was delivered in a second run at 11:30 AM. Stevens had failed to time-stamp all five or six messages delivered by RCA. George held firm. He had proof that there was no second delivery. George concluded, in the understatement of the year, "We believe our boy, who took it out there with the others, did better than average in getting through at all this particular time because of certain conditions and dangers existing en route."[416] Then he slipped Radiogram 1549 with its mysterious coded message, signed "Marshall," into his desk drawer for handy access, in case questions should come up again.

The following servicegram copy, found among George Street's papers, was addressed to RCA's general manager (GM). It details the circumstances of the delivery. George underlined in red the words which he was destined to defend.

COPY   RCA COMMUNICATIONS, Inc.   (Honlulu date & time
                                      SERVICE

A____   1941 DEC 23 ____

3 HU GM NY (COPY 3 SF)

YA83 HU REGULAR HOURS PRIOR TO DECEMBER 7TH AND INCLUDING MORNING OF
DECEMBER 7TH WEEK DAYS CLOSED BETWEEN 1AM/6AM SATURDAYS HOLIDAYS CLOSED
MIDNIGHT SUNDAYS HOLIDAYS OPEN 7AM STOP SINCE DECEMBER 7th* OPEN
CONTINUOUSLY STOP WILL BE ABLE TO RECONFIRM DELIVERY DEC 7TH MESSAGE WITH
ACCEPTING CLERK IN ABOUT TWO HOURS

    (* Note correction in following message).

_____

A____   1941 DEC 23 ____

3 HU GM NY 34 RUSH

CORRECTION RE BEGINNING 24 HOUR SERVICE STARTED FROM SIX AM DECEMBER
EIGHTH AS WE COULD NOT PROCURE NECESSARY BLACKOUT MATERIAL TO PREPARE
OFFICE ON SUNDAY 7TH AND OFFICIALS FORCED US TO CLOSE SUNDAY NIGHT

_____

A____   1941 DEC 23 ____

3 HU GM NY

SORRY REPORT DELAYED SHAFTER ACCEPTING CLERK SEVERAL HOURS LATE KEEPING
APPOINTMENT STOP NORMALLY HAVE 2 DAY TIME SUNDAY MESSENGERS FIRST ONE ON
DUTY 7AM MAKES WATER COPIES OR ASSISTS PHONE OPERATOR IN PUTTING INCOMING
MESSAGES AFTER 7AM IN DELIVERY ENVELOPES SECOND MESSENGER ON DUTY 815AM AND
BOTH OF THEM START ROUTING MESSAGES REASON FOR WHAT MAY SEEM LATE START TO
YOU BECAUSE NORMALLY MANY COMPLAINTS IF SUNDAY DELIVERIES MADE EARLIER THAN
830 OR 900AM STOP THIS OF COURSE DOES NOT EXCUSE OUR STAFF FOR NOT
RECOGNIZING GOVERNMENT TRAFFIC STOP MESSAGE RECEIVED 733AM AND PROMPTLY PUT
INTO DELIVERY ENVELOPE BUT MY QUESTIONING PHONE OPERATOR WHO PUT IT UP FOR
DELIVERY STATED THAT LETTERS C G IN ADDRESS MEANINGLESS TO HER THEN ALTHO
SHE THOUGHT TELPHONE THE MESSAGE BUT BEING IN CODE DECIDED AGAINST DOING SO
AS MANY TIMES SHAFTER ONLY RELUCTANTLY ACCEPTED MESSAGES FROM US OVER THE
PHONE IN THE PAST EXPLAINING "TOO BUSY SEND THEM BY BOY" BEFORE BOY WAS
READY TO GO OUT GREAT EXCITEMENT HAD ALREADY STARTED SOME IN IMMEDIATE
VICINITY OUR OFFICE BUT BOY DID LEAVE OFFICE ABOUT 840AM WITH SEVERAL OTHER
MESSAGES FOR DELIVERY IN SAME AREA STATING THAT EXCITEMENT WAS ALL ALONG
THE WAY AND GOT CAUGHT HEAVY TRAFFIC JAM WAS TURNED BACK BY POLICE BUT BY
CIRCUITOUS ROUTE GOT TO SHAFTER HE BELIEVES BEFORE 1000AM STOP NORMALLY
TAKES MOTORCYCLE BOY ABOUT 20 MINUTES ON A STRAIGHT RUN TO SHAFTER STOP ON
DECEMBER 7TH UPON THE INITIAL DELIVERY INQUIRY OUR AFTERNOON PHONE OPERATOR
A RELIABLE AND EXPERIENCED PERSON STATED ACCEPTING CLERK CORPORAL STEVENS
ACKNOWLEDGED RECEIPT OF THE MESSAGE ABOUT 900AM STOP WE HOLD DELIVERY
RECEIPT INITIALED LETTER "S" WHICH STEVENS ACKNOWLEDGES AS HIS BUT HE FAILD
TO PUT USUAL SHAFTER TIME STAMP ON OUR RECEIPT AND ABOUT FIVE OTHER
MESSAGES WHICH WE ALLEGE DELIVERED IN THE FIRST DELIVERY THAT MORNING STOP
TODAY STEVENS STATED OUR MESSENGER MADE A SECOND TRIP BEFORE NOON AND
BELIEVES HE DID NOT RECEIVE THE MESSAGE IN THE FIRST GROUP BUT IN THE
SECOND GROUP DELIVERED ABOUT 1130AM STOP VERY CAREFUL INVESTIGATION

                          (continued)

_____

-4- Continued

WITH A WRITTEN REPORT FROM OUR OWN MESSENGER STATES HE DID NOT MAKE A
SECOND DELIVERY TO SHAFTER IN THE FORENOON BUT DID MAKE A SECOND
TRIP SOME TIME AFTER LUNCH STOP FROM ORIGINAL INVESTIGATION DECEMBER 7TH
TO 9TH I BELIEVE THE MESSAGE WAS AT SHAFTER BETWEEN 900 AND 930AM AND WE
BELIEVE OUR BOY WHO TOOK IT OUT THERE WITH THE OTHERS DID BETTER THAN
AVERAGE IN GETTING THROUGH AT ALL THIS PARTICULAR TIME BECAUSE OF CERTAIN
CONDITIONS AND DANGERS EXISTING ENROUTE

Servicegram series (George Street Archive)

It was becoming increasingly clear that even a few minutes'
warning would have resulted in fewer lives lost, even though the
fleet needed about four hours to launch.[417] In the modern Navy,

ships proceed from "cold iron" to "readiness for sea" in under thirty minutes. Ships circa 1941 required four or more hours; battleships needed six to eight hours to get underway.[418] According to Rear Admiral Robert A. Theobald, author of *The Final Secret of Pearl Harbor,* if an alert had been sent even three hours in advance of the attack, a surprise attack might have been averted.[419] If Radiogram 1549 had been sent as a RUSH or been addressed to the "Commanding General" instead of "C G," thus alerting RCA to its importance, perhaps men would have been at their battle stations to prevent the Rising Sun from blindsiding them in the gray light of dawn.

Against the backdrop of war and the aftermath of finger-pointing, in order to retain some semblance of normalcy, America went Christmas shopping. The romance novel, *Saratoga Trunk,* was immensely popular with wives and girlfriends.[420] Babe Ruth signed a movie deal. And gossip columns took up where those diversions left off.

Chapter 23

"Nothing Can Change the Facts"

Mainland, U.S.A.

Seven interminable days had passed since the attack. The headlines FDR read were grim. *"JAPS TAKE GUAM ISLAND ... MANILA BLASTED IN WORST RAID ... RUSS[IANS] CHASE RETREATING NAZIS ON ENTIRE FRONT."*[421]

Congress passed legislation that gave Roosevelt more power over Americans than King George III had before the revolution. FDR could reorganize the government, accept non-competitive bids for the military war machine, and censor just about anybody. He and his advisors worked to establish censorship of the press under the mistaken fear that the details of the attack would demoralize America's heartland. Reports of beheadings, enemy ships, aircraft sightings off the coasts, and trigger-happy guards shooting mainland citizens added to the panic and confusion. The president endorsed the War Department's request to lower the draft age to nineteen; so men aged nineteen to forty-four were now subject to compulsory military service. Soon forty million men were registered. The Army wanted eight million men. The United States Army Air Forces (USAAF) needed a million. The Senate quickly passed a bill to build no less than 150,000 tons of new warships.

In addition, communication overseas was locked down. The Navy banned all cable transmissions between Hawaii and the Philippines and all news reports to Japan, Germany, Italy, and Finland. All private pilots were grounded until they could pass a background check, a welcome precaution in the early days of the war, when aircraft sightings resulted in military sorties and unnecessary conflicts.[422] Americans were told to report anyone whose loyalties were in doubt. And the Statue of Liberty went dark.

Senator Charles Tobey of New Hampshire donned his boxing gloves and called for an investigation into Pearl Harbor. Other members of Congress joined in, angry about the "unspeakable disaster ... and criminal negligence."[423] Finger pointing, speculation, and innuendo were rampant, and not just at RCA. The press speculated that Japan was too stagnant to be able to pull off such a calamity, suggesting that Hitler and the Germans were the masterminds behind the attack.[424]

Shocked by the mounting tally of losses with each daily report from Hawaii's military command, Roosevelt withheld the bleak news from the public as long as he could. On the 15th of December, Secretary Knox finally addressed a stunned America and told the brutal truth. He listed the ships sunk and damaged, reported the losses known to date, and mistakenly underestimated the number of wounded.[425] He did not mention civilian casualties. It would be months, if not years before final numbers were known. He described acts of heroism and disclosed the use of Japan's two-man submarines. And Knox revealed that espionage had played a significant role in coordinating the attack.

President Roosevelt ordered the immediate removal of Rear Admiral Husband Kimmel, Lieutenant General Walter Short, and Major General Frederick L. Martin, commanders of the Navy, Army, and Army Air Forces in Hawaii. Their seconds in command would run the show until official replacements arrived. A possible court-martial depended upon the findings of a hastily called board of inquiry. The *Honolulu Star-Bulletin* reported: "Secretary of the Navy Knox said bluntly after a personal investigation of the Pearl Harbor incident, that he was convinced that the American services were 'not on alert' when the Japanese attacked...."[426]

On 18 December, FDR addressed the renewed clamor for answers and appointed a five-man commission headed by Associate Justice Owen J. Roberts of the Supreme Court. According to the news, it was "to determine why the United States armed forces were not on alert when Japanese planes attacked Pearl Harbor."[427] The other four members of the commission were senior officers of the Army, the USAAF, and the Navy. They were to proceed to Pearl Harbor for an on-the-spot investigation.

The Roberts Commission took testimony from 127 witnesses, including Kimmel and Short, who were denied representation and were not privy to other testimony.[428] For the first three days, the commission interviewed witnesses in Washington about their understanding of what happened in Hawaii. Washington's actions were not part of the investigation. Justice Roberts, aware of the existence of Magic incepts, would not allow them into the record, fearing Japan would discover that the U.S. had cracked their Purple code.[429] With respect to Radiogram 1549, General Marshall stated he did not know that Army radio circuits were down, on the morning of 7 December.[430]

Meanwhile, on the West Coast, five hundred Italian garbage men — determined to demonstrate their loyalty to the United States — gave up their Sunday day of rest and hauled sand to each block in San Francisco. If an incendiary bomb were dropped, the sand could extinguish the fire.[431]

On the previous day, air raid signals had wailed in California, from San Jose to Napa. Unidentified planes triggered an alert and blackout. In the ensuing darkness, traffic accidents injured scores of people. Vandals smashed out lights and helped themselves. Safecrackers in San Francisco got away with an unknown amount of cash. Two streetcars ran wild for five miles and injured two people. A car almost crashed into an Army truck filled with explosives on the Eastshore overpass. Fifty windows were broken in Berkeley, supposedly by air-raid wardens. Police raided the command in charge of the blackout because their lights were on, and a bonfire blazed on Government Island (now Treasure Island).[432] It was a hell of a blackout.

Across the bay in Oakland, eight hundred men formed a warden plan and a police reserve similar to Oahu's. A women's ambulance and motor corps was organized in Alameda; they asked station wagon owners to register their cars with them. A gun club offered free lessons. "We are now in a shooting war, and if our citizens are to give a good account of themselves, they should know how to handle guns," Captain John W. Strohm of Alameda advised.[433] Local scout leaders announced, "Services for National

Defense Under Way for All Troops in Oakland Area." They organized the boys for emergency service patrols.[434]

Concerns about a Japanese attack on the West Coast were well founded. Five days before Christmas, Japanese submarines *I-17* and *I-23* cruised in for the kill off the California coast. Two unarmed U.S. tankers, SS *Emidio* and SS *Agwiworld,* were theirs for the taking.

SS *Agwiworld* was twenty miles off Cypress Point, near Carmel, heading to San Francisco from Los Angeles, when a submarine broke the surface. "If I had a slingshot, I could have hit the damn thing," one seaman said.[435] "The Japanese fired eight shots at us. One cut the halyard, and the others whistled over us. We were spewing so much smoke when we got underway at full steam that the sub must have thought we were afire."[436] But there was little damage. Life vests on, the crew steamed to Santa Cruz harbor for refuge.

SS *Emidio,* two hundred miles north of San Francisco, off Cape Mendocino, wasn't as lucky. Japanese submarine *I-17* blasted her. *Emidio* sent out an SOS by wireless and raised a white flag, after *I-17* hit her with 14 cm deck guns. As men began to abandon ship, *I-17* continued to fire, killing three. A torpedo killed two others. Lookouts spotted the ship nine miles north of the cape, at Table Bluff, riding low in the water. "Planes immediately took off in pursuit of the enemy submarines," the *Honolulu Advisor* reported.[437] A PBY Catalina flying boat dropped depth charges, but *I-17* escaped to fight another day. A Coast Guard cutter rescued the survivors. The remains of *Emidio* drifted down the coast and broke apart on the rocks off Crescent City.

Because of the two attacks, the president declared the Pacific Coast to be a defense zone. Folks in the San Francisco Bay area woke up to the *Oakland Tribune's* headline, *"BAY DISTRICT IS NOW RATED FRONT LINE."*[438] That meant that the coast was a "combat zone and, therefore, the place only for fighting forces," according to Lieutenant General John DeWitt, commander of the Fourth Army.[439] The Ninth Corps area headquarters that handled communication, supply, and transportation logistics for the Western states and the territory of Alaska, withdrew to Salt Lake City.[440]

The Navy took control of all ship movements and cautioned vessels to stick to the main shipping channels. The Coast Guard issued a firmer warning: "a vessel entering or navigating the waters of a defensive area including San Francisco Bay does so at their own risk."[441]

Japanese submarines in Hawaiian waters continued to wreak havoc. Within days of the Pearl Harbor attack, a Japanese submarine sank SS *Lahaina,* an unarmed merchant ship. Survivors drifted for days before spotting palm trees bent in the breeze. Overjoyed at the sight of land, Concezio Del Tino and Alfred Lunquist jumped out of the lifeboat two hundred yards from Kahului beach, on the island of Maui.[442] It was raw and bristled with basalt. No one ever spotted the two men again. The remaining thirty survivors, including one dead seaman, rode the swell until their twenty-four-foot boat scraped sand, at six in the morning. After establishing that they weren't an enemy landing party, locals gave the survivors food and coffee. As *The Honolulu Advertiser* reported, Colonel C.B. Lyman of Maui's medical disaster committee "was on the job minutes after the beaching of the lifeboat and rushed the crew members to Puunene Hospital."[443]

The crew's captain, H.O. Matthiesen, told reporters, "We met heavy weather during the ten days at sea and swamped many times ... Hillard Moore, a Negro mess man, disappeared over the side 19 December after muttering that he was going to catch a bus and go home."[444]

Matthiesen and his fellow survivors commended Hawaiian Henry J. Fern, who "performed heroically at the oar and sail." They said "he and a Japanese American proved particularly valuable in aiding the surfing of mountainous waves."

***

Meanwhile, one thousand men shipped to Honolulu to help rebuild island defenses, Congress having allocated $512 million for defense housing. George held little hope that any of those men would be available to work at RCA, and new regulations continued to increase his workload.

Regulations for transpacific calls were revised:

- **No communication with anyone in a country under enemy control.**

- **Operators needed the caller's full name and occupation, and the addresses of the telephones in use for both parties on the call, as well as the nature of the call.**

- **If a personal call turned into a business call, it would be disconnected.**

- **Only English could be spoken.**

- **No information about ship movements, camps, war material, mines or minefields, aids to navigation, conditions of social, political or economic unrest, or weather conditions could be discussed.**

The military assured Oahu's residents that the water, milk, and food supplies were well protected. Liquor stores remained closed. Sandbags lined city streets. Sentries with fixed bayonets stood behind concrete barricades and tile box barriers.[445] Stores were allowed to be open from 10 AM to 4 PM. "Come on out and shop," newspapers prompted. "Only three days left until Christmas!"

The Roberts Commission arrived in Hawaii on 22 December. They focused their interviews on military and civil service personnel at Fort Shafter. They did not question George, since he was neither military nor a civil servant. RCA's general manager contacted him on 22 December to advise him that the War Department was complaining about how long it had taken RCA-Honolulu to deliver the message. The annotation, written by George, again expressed his opinion about the late delivery.

While the commission was in town, Corporal Stevens arrived late, on 23 December, for an appointment he and a sergeant had made with George. Stevens wanted George to change his story. "The two of them tried to get me to say that an RCA messenger made a second delivery to Fort Shafter, during the forenoon of December 7." Stevens was afraid that he might be court-martialed. George refused to lie, and told them, "The original story was in accordance with RCA's own records." Nothing could change the facts. They were as solid as the cane he held in his hand.

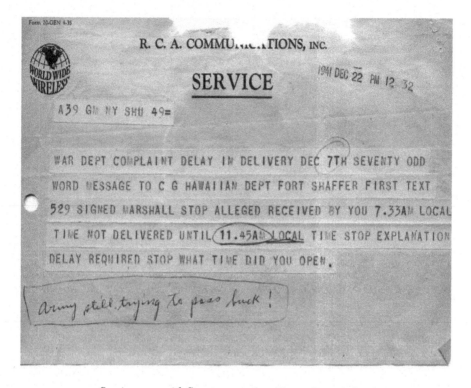

Servicegram with Street annotation (George Street Archive)

Chapter 24

The Cost of War

On 18 December, RCA's vice president, W.A. Winterbottom, telegraphed that he was "satisfied with [the Honolulu office's] performance under such dangerous conditions."

RCA's internal publication, *Relay,* dated January 1942, replicated the exchange:[446]

> **George Street, Superintendent**
> **RCA Honolulu**
>
> **It has always been a tradition that RCA personnel rise to any emergency, but the manner in which you and your staff in Hawaii have met the present situation is more than commendable, it is magnificent. With Hawaii part of the United States, it was vitally necessary that everything be done to maintain uninterrupted communication between Hawaii and the mainland and under your able direction supported by a loyal and efficient staff; this has been done. Please accept for yourself and extend to all of your people my sincere congratulations for a job well done.**
>
> **W.A. Winterbottom**

George replied: **"Your kind and thoughtful message very much appreciated by all. Many thanks and the season's greetings from all the Hawaiians."**[447]

Winterbottom's praise was the best Christmas present George ever received.

***

It was raining at 7 AM on Christmas morning, when the PBY Catalina splashed down in Pearl Harbor's East Loch. Spray obscured the windscreen as the plane rocked to a halt. Rear Admiral Chester W. Nimitz stared through a water-splashed window at the upended hulls of USS *Oklahoma* (BB-37) and USS *Utah* (BB-31), enveloped in a rainbow-colored sea, pock-marked with debris. "This is a terrible sight, seeing all these ships down," Nimitz remarked.[448] The acrid smell of oil and burnt surfaces assaulted the men when they disembarked.

Admiral Bellinger and his staff eased up to the hatch of the PBY in a whaleboat so slick with oil that they all stood for the short ride to shore. Admiral Kimmel and Admiral Pye, acting commander in chief, waited for him on the submarine wharf. There was no fanfare when Nimitz formally took command from Kimmel on the deck of submarine USS *Grayling* (SS-209), described by a seaman in the mess as the "only available deck left afloat."[449] From that moment on, Nimitz's flagship was always a submarine.

Honolulu's holiday season was about as bad as it could get. Christmas lights that usually welcomed arrivals no longer glowed. Dust, grime, and ash dulled empty streets. Police arrested twenty-three people for being out without authorization and broke into stores to switch off lights because the city was still under blackout orders. They reportedly arrested three men for burying ten thousand rounds of .22 caliber ammunition and two hundred twelve-gauge shotgun shells in the yard of the Honolulu Junk Company on South King Street. Newspapers featured ads for bomb shelters. Radios and batteries were available for purchase, but only to American citizens with permits.

The mail censor asked the public to omit rumors, references to military and naval movements, defense activities, and horror stories in their letters to friends and family on the mainland. He issued orders about how the populace was to handle mail:

- **Place the return address of the sender on the envelope.**

- **Mail without delay. Do not allow mail to accumulate.**

- **Write the language [the letter is written in] on the outside of the envelope.**

Translators for twenty-seven different languages read and censored each letter. They redacted phrases and words that did not pass muster or returned the letter to the sender if it contained too much information. Letters and cards George Jr. and Barbara received from the mainland now bore censor stamps and were resealed with tape.

The government requisitioned the luxurious passenger liner SS *Lurline* and retrofitted her to hold as many people as possible. She was nicknamed "Mickey Mouse" after being converted to a transport ship. Boudoirs and cargo holds became bunkrooms. Canvas cots chained to pipes hung four high. There was barely enough room between bunks to roll on one's side. Metal posts supported beams hung with cots in the Grand Ballroom.[450] A second ballroom became a playground.

Before year's end, seventeen unarmed merchant freighters, tankers, and passenger ships were sunk in the Pacific.

On the day Nimitz arrived, 3,504 mandatory evacuees crowded the counter of Matson Lines. The next day SS *Lurline, Matsonia,* and *Monterey* headed to San Francisco in convoy, crammed with the first load of evacuees from Honolulu. Among the passengers were fifty-seven wounded, tended by a doctor and two nurses. Not wanting to delay, the captains did not get a complete headcount until they were underway. Nine Japanese submarines stalked the waters between Seattle and Baja, but they did not attack.

SS *Prusa,* a cargo ship headed from Honolulu to Baltimore, was not as lucky. A torpedo from Japanese submarine *I-172* sent her to the bottom on the nineteenth of December. Survivors scrambled for lifeboats and watched their ship sink in nine minutes. The men drifted for three days before picking up a favorable wind that took them toward Oahu. At 8 AM on Christmas Day, a Navy plane spotted the hollow-eyed men and dropped tomatoes, fruit juice, and water. Two days later, the fourteen lucky men sailed into Honolulu Harbor aboard the Coast Guard cutter, *Tiger.*[451] Ambulances and private cars drove them to Queen's hospital.[452] They did not know that eleven of their crew, including their captain, had survived in a second lifeboat. They sailed 2,700 miles before a Fijian government vessel spotted them and transported them to the Gilbert Islands, a cluster of atolls barely above sea level.[453] But they did not care. It was land — white beaches shaded by palm trees — and the U.S. military was there.

During the holidays, destroyer USS *Allen* (DD-66) picked up the crew of SS *Manini*, another unarmed merchant ship. A plane had spotted the survivors on 21 December and dropped provisions and a note telling them they were 153 miles from Honolulu. The next day another airplane dropped more rations and a message telling them a ship was on the way. "On Christmas night, a navy aircraft dropped another note. It asked if we 'needed any help.' We signaled back, 'We sure do!'"[454]

Days later, more *Manini* men were found. Sixty hours of rough seas had prevented them from setting sail. A seaman remembered that their biggest hardship "was the sight of airplanes in the distance while they had no means of signaling their distress. We took turns at the oars for an hour, then rested two hours. We had instruments for latitude only, not longitude."[455]

The crewmen credited their survival to training. Before the ship settled under the waves, each grabbed what he could. One scooped up cigarettes, another the Bible his mother had given him; one only had time to snatch his trousers and shoes. As they rowed, they spent their time figuring out exactly how they would retrofit and supply their lifeboats for the next cruise.

SS *Manini* lost one man, "M. Tompkins, a buddy only 25 years old. He had lowered the after-end of the lifeboat on the port side, and as it slid down the boat-fall, the boat surged forward, leaving him stranded on the deck." When they shouted, "Jump for it," he said he could not swim. "Maybe he jumped after all but got sucked down ... Everybody was scared but not panicky, scared of being sucked down as the ship started settling fast." The seaman concluded that "Somebody has to go to sea. You can't live forever. And if your name is on one of those iron cigars, you'll sink no matter where you are." [456]

Off the California coast, chief cook Thomas Watkins had a hunch. Today reminded him of a torpedo attack he'd lived through in the Great War; so he put on his best suit. "I didn't want to lose my good suit," he explained.[457]

He tied his apron over his suit to prepare a roast for the thirty-five-man crew of SS *Absaroka*. While he gazed at San Pedro's retreating shore from the galley window, Japanese submarine *I-17* raised her periscope.

Watkins recalled, "She was coming head-on ... and she shot a torpedo. I've seen torpedoes coming at me before. They've wasted that one, I said, and sure enough, it went wide. But then came another. I could see it was going to get us. There was a sort of slow jar with nothing but a rumble."[458]

The galley turned upside down. "I remember saying to myself, 'Thomas, be careful and don't get that Sunday suit wet.'" At 10:40 AM, people on the shore saw the waterspout. "I went to my lifeboat station, and we got the boat over the side without trouble. Nobody was excited."[459] *Absaroka* did not sink.

After a short time, ten crew members and the captain re-boarded and called for a tow back to San Pedro. The remaining twenty-four crew members returned to shore aboard a Coast Guard cutter, while four tugs struggled to haul SS *Absaroka* back to the harbor with a "hole in its side large enough to drive an automobile through."[460] They lost one crew member to the blast. Navy planes "dropped depth bombs in an effort to knock out the submarine," according to the report in the *Star Press*.[461]

Before year's end, seventeen unarmed merchant freighters, tankers, and passenger ships were sunk in the Pacific by the Japanese. By war's end, over 1500 were sent to Davy Jones's Locker, the most of any service.[462] Only survivor stories made the news.

Elsewhere, RCA operators at Point Reyes, California, were on alert. They had picked up a signal, and then listened for five days before they heard it again. One of the operators called the San Francisco FBI office. "Sounds like a mobile marine unit at 6908 kilocycles, and it could be close," he reported.[463]

The San Francisco FBI office got on the phone with the FCC monitoring station in Portland, Oregon, the Pan American Airways system at Treasure Island, in San Francisco Bay, and the FCC monitoring station near Los Angeles. They all tuned in to the mysterious signal at 6908 kilocycles. Using direction finders, the three stations triangulated the location of a Japanese submarine. Pan Am sent the bearings to the Navy. Ten minutes later, a PBY bore down on the heading.

The sub spotted the PBY. "Dive! Dive!" the bridge ordered. Depth charges rained down on the submarine, fore and aft of its position. Two minutes later, Army bombers joined the PBY and drilled holes in the ocean with their depth charges.[464] Then, because of the masterfully coordinated effort between RCA, the FBI, the Navy, and the Army, an oil slick spread over the water off the Mendocino coast. Now there was one less Japanese predator hunting in the Pacific.

***

While George and Barbara worked at RCA, George Jr. spent the rest of December surveying areas in pineapple fields along the base of the Koolau Mountain Range, north of Pearl City looking for a site to relocate RCA's transmitter. The six-foot-high sugar cane fields made access difficult.[465] George Jr., Philbrick, and crew worked six to eight hours in the field and then returned to the office to write up their findings. George Jr. did the drafting and said, "We ended our day at 1 – 2 AM, bushed."[466] Before hitting the sack, he checked on his block of thirty homes for blackout status.

On the last day of the year, George Jr. hit the streets of his ward to make sure residents were responding to the notification just published in the *The Honolulu Advertiser*. It read, "IMPORTANT NOTICE TO ALL RESIDENTS OF OAHU." They had to register for fingerprinting. The form they needed to complete requested information about their number of beds, the capacity of their automobiles and trucks, the makes and models of their radios, their suitability for caring for evacuees, and a description of each person's skills, including Boy Scouts and Red Cross training.[467]

As the people of Hawaii came to grips with the new normal in Honolulu, headlines across the nation spoke of world affairs: Manila was about to fall, the Dutch East Indies was bombed, the British battled in Malaya, and Hitler renewed his victory promise. Commandos crashed Rommel's birthday party to no avail, and worse yet, MacArthur's troops were retreating.[468] FDR demanded that the U.S. use half the national income for the war effort.

Still, babies were born, people wed, and the bad guys got arrested. Benny Goodman played at the Terrace Room in the Hotel New York, and Kitty Carlisle, with Dick Gasparre and his Orchestra, entertained the folks at the Persian Room on New Year's Eve. After the surprise attack on Pearl Harbor, few headlines featured the words "Happy New Year."

Chapter 25

A New Year

One day shy of a month since the attack on Pearl Harbor, FDR once more braced himself before Congress. He extended his right arm and curled his fingers under the lip of the podium to help take the weight off his polio-weakened legs. Speaking in a slow, deliberate cadence he said, "In fulfilling my duty to report upon the State of the Union, I am proud to say to you that the spirit of the American people was never higher than it is today ... We have not been stunned. We have not been terrified and confused ... the grim resolution which here prevails bodes ill for those who conspired and collaborated to murder world peace." FDR continued with "The militarists of Berlin and Tokyo started this war. But the massed, angered forces of common humanity will finish it."

He then laid out production goals for the year:

"First, to increase our production rate of airplanes so rapidly that in this year 1942, we shall produce sixty thousand planes.

Second, to increase our production of tanks so rapidly that, in this year 1942, we shall produce forty-five thousand.

Third ... twenty thousand anti-aircraft guns.

Fourth ... merchant ships ... six million deadweight tons ...."

Then Roosevelt goaded his enemies. "These figures and similar figures of a multitude of other implements of war will give the Japanese and the Nazis a little idea of just what they accomplished in the attack at Pearl Harbor." He concluded with "There never has been, and there never can be, successful compromise between good and evil. Only, only total victory can reward the champions of tolerance, and decency, and freedom, and faith."

The standing ovation was thunderous. And Rosie the Riveter was born.

Middle-class women turned in their aprons and donned coveralls and dungarees. They wrapped their hair in kerchiefs and caps and put their evening gloves in the drawer. It was up to them to fill the void, while their men went off to war. Women jumped at the chance for financial gain and the opportunity to express their patriotism, as they extended their roles of caregivers beyond the walls of their homes.[469] They worked because they cared for their families, their country, and themselves. They worked to keep them safe.

They learned to drive tractors and heavy equipment, weld, work on factory lines, and use machines of all types, and they learned how to fix them when they broke down. Gone were the days of the "fragile woman" whose female proclivities were regulated with opiates. Gone were the apron strings that bound them to their mothers' world, and gone were the Victorian rules laid down by their fathers.

Women relied on women, even though men still ran the show. Magazine articles, propaganda posters, movies, and books sharpened their image. However, prejudice, class status, and male-dominated businesses shaped their reality. They received less pay, often with no other benefits, faced sexual harassment, and were on their own when it came to childcare. Mothers were expected to work a "second shift" after work, in order to keep the home fires burning.

Women who had worked before the war due to their poverty led the way and taught the new workforce the ropes, often without recognition. African American women worked in segregated units, drank at separate water fountains, used separate bathrooms, ate at separate tables, and lived in segregated neighborhoods. But they worked just as hard for their country. In the early years of the war, enemy agents tried to trick the "Negro people into disloyalty ... to weaken national unity by acts and speeches against this minority group, according to the *Pittsburgh Courier*."[470] The NAACP and the National Negro Congress battled for equity. Other minorities suffered a similar fate, but few were disloyal to the American cause.

Rosie the Riveter became the symbol of the home front. Virtuous, strong, and capable, women shouldered the burden in America's struggle to remain free.[471] Naysayers worried that women workers would become "accustomed to the world of men, including their power, independence, and monetary gain," according to the authors of *Reflecting Freedom*.[472] Others worried that they would lose their feminine wiles.

There was no going back. Women were the largest source of labor available to drive the industrial war machine. "Wendy the Welders" used assembly line techniques and needed little training to assemble the massive ships. By mid-April, at the Richmond, California shipyard, men and women had built a ten-thousand-ton liberty ship in just forty-four days.[473]

Hollywood also lent a hand. Set designer John Stewart Detlie camouflaged the roof of Boeing Plant #2 in Seattle — all 26 acres of it. Acres of canvas formed lawns, roads, and treetops on the roof of the factory. Plywood houses, cars, and people who never moved replicated a typical middle-class neighborhood designed to fool the enemy, if they dared to fly over.[474]

The recruitment of women from top-notch eastern schools began shortly after the Pearl Harbor attack. Only four percent of women had a four-year college degree in 1942, primarily because financial rewards were limited for women with degrees in America. Now Washington needed them for code-breaking. They wanted linguists, mathematicians, librarians, women with knowledge of Latin and Greek, and those who could "make sense of a large amount of data"— the very skills that often labeled them as boring in polite society.[475] And they also had to know how to keep their mouths shut.

Deans sent recommendations to the military — usually for women in the top ten percent of their classes, with good moral character and gumption. The War Department sent the women a summons and asked them to report to Washington for testing— for what, they did not know. It was all very secret. By the end of the war, eighty percent of the Navy's codebreakers were women. Their official job description was "secretary." The transition of the accepted role of American women in society was now in full bloom.

Life in Hawaii continued to change just as dramatically. In early January 1942, George Jr. was pulled back to Hawaiian Electric to help repair a circuit at Pearl City that had shorted out. His workload at RCA had been reduced to only eight to ten hours a day, so he was comfortable returning to Hawaiian Electric. His dad and sister held down the fort, now more of a crash pad than a sanctuary. Because of the threat of attack, Hawaiian Electric decided to build a power plant underground to supplement the Pearl City station. George Jr. spent six months drafting new electrical circuits. Ultimately, the government spent $300,000 dollars to reinforce its primary power plants. George Jr. wrote, "I continued my nightly rounds as Block Warden on returning home from work (about 1-2 AM) and weekly stood a watch at the Block headquarters."[476]

By the end of January, the Roberts commission had presented its findings to the president. The committee had interviewed Powell about the delivery of Marshall's final warning message. Powell falsely stated that the RCA messenger left Radiogram 1549 on the desk, without a receipt, and that it was found at 11:55 AM.[477] The committee summarized twenty-one different conclusions, deciding:

The warning message of December 7 intended to reach both commanders in the field at about 7:00 AM, Hawaiian time, December 7, 1941, was but an added precaution in view of the warnings and orders previously issued. If the message had reached its destination at the time intended, it would still have been too late to be of substantial use.[478]

The Commission omitted all references to Magic to maintain secrecy.[479] They charged Admiral Kimmel and General Stark with dereliction of duty, failure to confer and heed warnings and orders received on 27 November, and failure to adapt and use existing plans to meet the emergency. Admiral Theobald, commander of the Pacific Fleet destroyers, questioned the commission's findings because of inept stenographic recordings and lack of legal representation.[480]

On 25 January 1942, as the Roberts Commission was concluding its work, shells rained down on the city of Kahului, on Maui. The Japanese had shelled Maui twice before in December and the islands of Kauai and Hawaii once, with minor damage. Today's attack lasted just minutes. A Japanese submarine from the Second Submarine Squadron surfaced, fired, and dove. No one was hurt, and the property damage was minimal.

That same day Japanese submarine *I-22* bombarded the Navy base on Johnston Atoll, west of the Hawaiian Island chain, again inflicting negligible damage. Lloyds of London discontinued bomb insurance for the United States and Canada. Two days after the shelling of Maui, the military ordered visitors, the wounded, and all dependents of Navy and civil defense workers to evacuate to the mainland. Next on the evacuation list were dependents of employees of government projects. Last up were dependents of permanent residents, which included George Jr. and Barbara.

In February, schools reopened, and all Nisei — children of Japanese immigrants born in the United States — were discharged from the Hawaii Territorial Guard, even those previously promoted from ROTC. The discharged Nisei petitioned the governor and the military with oaths of loyalty. They eventually formed the Varsity Victory Volunteers, a one hundred sixty-man labor unit supervised by the Army Corps of Engineers. The Nisei proved their loyalty daily. Eleven months later, they became part of the 442nd Regimental Combat Team and served for the rest of the war.[481]

On 19 February 1942, Roosevelt signed Executive Order 9066, which gave the U.S. armed forces the ability to declare sections of the United States as military areas. One third of the mainland, including West Coast cities, ports, industrial and agricultural areas, was designated as such. The military could exclude any or all persons of foreign-enemy ancestry from their homes, farms, and businesses. American citizenship offered no protection. To make matters worse, the cost of the war had mushroomed from $729 to $1400 per second by 1942, doubling the cost of living in just six months.[482]

On Oahu, military areas expanded, and "The Island of Oahu was converted into a fortress," George Jr. explained. "By the end of February 1942, most of the barrier reefs extending offshore, such as the one fronting the beach near our home, had been studded with streetcar rails, angled

RCA office with blacked-out windows, June 1942
(George Street Archive)

outward and spaced three to four feet apart. Directly behind the rails was a barrier of barbed wire. More barbed wire angled from the reef edge to the beach, where additional barbed wire was installed along the dune line." George Jr. described that "on the beach, at each intersection was constructed a concrete bunker, housing up to three machine guns. These were spaced about five hundred yards apart. A three-inch field piece was located at selected points."[483]

The bunker near the Streets' home was manned by a squad that the neighborhood adopted as its own. They were "our boys ... the residences made sure they had more than enough food and reading material," George Jr. relayed. Residents invited them to dinner during their off-hours, and George Jr. enjoyed sitting with them for a chat. "We almost looked forward to the Japs invading across the reefs. I didn't carry a gun, but I had a well-sharpened hunting knife."[484]

The influx of men needed to shore up Hawaii's defenses led to men outnumbering women by the hundreds in Honolulu. Some guessed a thousand to one. Long lines became the norm at the USO facilities. Bishop, King, and Hotel Streets crawled with men on liberty. If a serviceman was lucky enough to belly up to a bar, he drank his fill fast. Men had to be even quicker in brothel "bullpens." Using an assembly line set up, each woman serviced ten to twelve men an hour for twenty days a month.[485]

George worked even longer hours to ensure that the words and wages of war made it to their destinations. Armed guards manned the entrance of RCA and checked IDs. A light trap was constructed between the counter and the street so that customers could have access during a blackout. RCA also relocated five key technical personnel to Honolulu to assist in moving wartime traffic across the Pacific.[486]

Then George received equipment so that radiophotos, today's faxes, could be sent between Honolulu and the mainland. Walter L. Roe, installed the equipment. On 29 December he boarded an American Airlines Skysleeper for his flight to San Francisco, where he installed a terminal before boarding a steamer for Honolulu. The ship carried eight times its peacetime capacity. Roe joked, "I was lucky to get a private stateroom … with five other fellows."[487]

He arrived in February and connected RCA-Honolulu's radiophoto equipment. Now drawings, documents, and photos in black and white supplemented Honolulu traffic.[488] Meanwhile, RCA re-established the circuits to the Dutch East Indies and the capital of Sumatra.

By April, radiophotos went live. George "faxed" birthday wishes to RCA past-president Edward J. Nally. The first photograph sent from Honolulu to San Francisco was of Admiral Nimitz, decorating officers in their dress whites under the massive guns of a battleship. From San Francisco, the photograph was picked up and recorded in New York.[489]

Barbara Street, left, inspects the new radiophoto (fax) machine (George Street Archive)

RCA also implemented ship-to-shore phone calls. They patched vessels calling KQM — RCA's Koko Head station — on their battery-powered transmitters to the local telephone exchange.[490]

George wrote a piece for RCA's internal magazine, *Relay*, in appreciation of the equipment provided by RCA's engineers. He explained, "Our radio operators, clerks, and messengers, with loyal devotion to the job to be done, not once, but many times, have met our opportunity by serving many additional thousands of patrons … Never forget Pearl Harbor."[491]

Chapter 26

No Goodbyes

In April, four months after the attack, Honolulu went to Alert Level Two. Level One triggered blackouts and curfews, and required safe-conduct passes. Level Two stepped up preparations for an invasion. Level Three indicated that an incursion was imminent. This time there was no confusion about the order. [492]

The military probably raised the alert level in anticipation of the Doolittle raid, America's surprise attack on Tokyo, scheduled for 18 April 1942. Oahu stepped up preparations according to the order. The military converted a portion of the Hawaiian-ancestry boarding school into a temporary hospital. Saws whined, and hammers pounded, deadening the cries of mynah birds. If the worst happened, and Japan counterattacked, the children at the school had their names taped on their shoulders for identification purposes. They also shared their dormitories with dependents of servicemen, who fled the bases. [493] Churches and living rooms became their school rooms.

Leaving the RCA building at 1 AM on a dark night in April, George Jr. and his dad were startled by a sudden flash in the mountains behind Honolulu. [494] Searchlights streaked the sky; blips swept across radar screens, but the air raid sirens did not wail. Was it friend or foe? Then, lights bracketed a bomber. George Jr. later wrote that the Army did not "want the city illuminated by people opening doors as they raced to shelters."[495] Spotlighted and aglow like a shooting star, the pilot jettisoned his bomb load harmlessly in the backcountry and flew into the night. An explosion set the night sky afire. A Japanese bomber had attempted a sneak attack. Some months later, a San Francisco radio picked up a Japanese announcement saying that their "bomber attack in April had annihilated Honolulu."[496]

Then another explosion rocked Honolulu. This time air raid sirens did wail, and people took to the hills in fear, but it was a false alarm. Instead of an air raid, the owner of a wooden lunch shack had accidentally set his establishment on fire. Flames scorched the sky like a torch in a cave.[497]

***

As a wartime precaution, the government overprinted Hawaiian paper money with the word "Hawaii." [498] The U.S. planned to declare the overprint notes worthless if the Japanese captured the Territory, thus depriving the invaders of cash. From January 1942 to June, the government

Overprint note

confiscated and replaced two hundred million dollars with Hawaii's overprint money. The military opted to burn the recalled notes at a local crematorium rather than to risk sending them to the mainland by steamer.

The maximum amount of currency an individual (civilian or military) could legally possess was two hundred dollars. Businesses were allowed five hundred dollars. No one was above the law. The provost judge, Lieutenant Colonel John R. Hermann, sentenced Saburo Kuniyoshi, a Japanese alien, to eighteen months of hard labor in an Oahu prison and fined him $1500.00 for possessing $4,138.38. He ordered Kuniyoshi to buy war bonds with the balance of the confiscated funds. Mrs. Tsuyo Arakaki was fined $150 and told to buy $350 worth of war bonds because she hid $700 inside a chair at the boarding house she ran. Others received similar sentences, along with Lieutenant Colonel Hermann's reprimand. "It seems you do not try to obey the law. Were you an American alien in Japan instead of a Japanese alien in America, the punishment would be much stricter."[499] George Jr. remembered a prostitute, convicted of having more than two hundred dollars, defending herself by stating "that her sister had whored half of it!"[500]

By April, Pele, the goddess of volcanoes and fire, had had enough of war and war preparations. Rats, workers, contractors, and the U.S. military had invaded her islands. So she blew her top, and Mauna Loa erupted on the island of Hawaii. Pele threw up a mile-long curtain of molten lava that crinkled, hissed, and sputtered toward the town of Hilo. The Army Air Forces took to the sky and dropped bombs on the cooling edge of the southern flow, splitting it into three streams. Then they blasted missiles at the smoldering river to complete the job. The Army diverted Pele's wrath and saved Hilo. They kept the news of Pele's ire under wraps for fear that Japanese planes would home in on the blazing light of her fury.[501]

Then, air raid sirens blared, and Honolulu went to Alert Level Three. The Japanese were on the move! Aircraft scrambled and reconnaissance planes circled.

George Jr. later wrote, "We knew something serious was about to happen ... Block wardens began setting up an evacuation plan for the area east of Diamond Head ... the Army anticipated a possible invasion along the east and southeast shores of O'ahu."[502] They set up their first line of defense at Koko Head and their second line in the east foothills below Diamond Head. The Streets' house was smack-dab in the middle of the expected Japanese landing zone at Hunakai Beach.

By mid-May, block wardens and the military had moved women and children who lived in the area between Diamond Head and Koko Head downtown. Barbara had to leave. The Army recommended that she pack a four-day supply of food, two blankets, a raincoat, warm clothing, gas masks, toiletries, and a flashlight.[503] Schools morphed into evacuation centers. Residents who relocated to private homes checked in with their block wardens. George and George Jr. elected to remain at their house. They were never there anyway because they were always at work.

Barbara likely stayed with a friend, rather than with Nina Street, who lived in an apartment downtown. Barbara and Nina had never gotten along, and never would. After divorcing George, Nina worked as a cashier at a cantonment unit set up for civilian contractors. She also volunteered to deliver food to the leper colony at Kalaupapa on Molokai Island. The colony sheltered at the base of one of the highest sea cliffs in the world. Her employer provided a motorboat, the only way to reach the isolated community. She and George stayed in touch only for financial reasons. As long as Barbara and George Jr. remained on the island, she would have nothing to do with him or them. Her stubbornness and selfishness were rooted in bedrock and the kids had to go if George ever wanted her back. George didn't have time for her nonsense. Neither did the kids.

George Jr. and his fellow block wardens stood duty around the clock. George Jr. lamented, "We had blessed little sleep." He and his friend, Curt Shoemaker, were fire watchers during the alerts. When the sirens blasted, they pounded upstairs to a cupola on top of Hawaiian Electric. It was the second-highest point in the city, topped only by the Aloha Tower. There, they scanned the city and sky for enemy airplanes or other signs of an attack. On one occasion George Jr. remembered, "… we observed a flight of B-17s on their takeoff climb over the city heading over the ocean. After a half-hour or so, the all-clear would sound, and all would go back to work. I wondered how Curt and I would have responded to a firebomb dropping in our lap, let alone a strafing attack."[504]

As part of the response to Alert Level Three, the military ordered all remaining military dependents evacuated to the mainland. The old *Aquitania,* a four-stack Cunard liner, commissioned before the Great War, was pulled out of the boneyard and converted to a transport. According to George Jr. it was longer than any pier in Honolulu and had to be tied onto several docks. Its black hull and gray superstructure loomed over the city like an oversized cutout in a diorama. Several Monopoly games kept the older children busy as she zigzagged her way across the Pacific, retreating to the mainland.

Meanwhile, HYPO worked around the clock to crack the JN-25 code that Tokyo used to communicate with its fleet. It was a manual code, not one punched out on a Red or Purple machine. If they cracked it, Washington would have a direct line into the Japanese command center.

The code consisted of 45,000 five-letter groups.[505] HYPO and Washington had figured out about twenty percent of them, but constantly changing additives made it tough for the code breakers. Commander Rochefort and his crew at HYPO used direction finders and traffic analysis to fill in some missing pieces. They had successfully nailed down the "when and where" of the Battle of the Coral Sea, boosting Nimitz's confidence in the Hawaiian team. Then, on the 25th of May, they cabled headquarters on Kodiak Island, Alaska, that the Japanese planned an amphibious operation to secure an advance base in Alaska's Aleutian Island chain. Japan's armada departed that same day. The crypto guys in Washington were not happy with Rochefort's methods, nor with Rochefort for that matter, but they could not deny his results.

Then another puzzle piece dropped into place. HYPO picked up references to the Aleutians again, and "campaign" and "aircraft in the second K campaign." This suggested that Japan was planning a multi-phased attack similar to the one on 7 December 1941.[506] Rochefort also wheedled out that an invasion force was headed to "AF." HYPO knew "H" was code for Hawaii, and "AK" referred to the French Frigate Shoals. Where was AF? Rochefort figured it stood for Midway. Washington disagreed. They did not believe that "AF" was the Japanese code for Midway, because it was the U.S. code for Midway. It was too much of a coincidence.

Rochefort put the "AF" designator to the test at the suggestion of his assistant, Lieutenant Commander Jasper Holmes. He sent a fake message about a water shortage at "AF" knowing the Japanese would intercept it. With Nimitz's blessing, he used a submarine cable to send a plain-language message, as well as a coded message in a crypt he knew the Japanese had broken. Japan's listening post on Kwajalein picked it up and sent it on to their headquarters. Then, the U.S. intercepted a message from Tokyo that ordered the invading Japanese fleet to include a two-week supply of water with their provisions. With this proof, there was no doubt that "AF" meant Midway in the J-25 code. Rochefort tactfully let another station tell Washington the news.

Next, Rochefort had to deduce *when* the attack on Midway would take place. Japan's two-week water supply order narrowed it down; it would be before 15 June. That left Nimitz a week to get his task force to Midway. Using IBM punch cards, the remarkable recall ability of the analysts, and sheer gut feelings, Lieutenant Joseph Finnegan homed in on the dates used in Japanese cables. He and Rochefort backtracked through old intercepts and found "at 1900 6 June arrive at AF." Japan's fleet would be within air-strike distance of Midway on the third or fourth of June![507] Rochefort now had the dates, and Nimitz pulled the trigger.

Six months after the Pearl Harbor attack, on 3 June 1942 (U.S. date), the tide turned in favor of the U.S., at the Battle of Midway. It was Barbara's eighteenth birthday. That same day, Japan attacked Dutch Harbor in the Aleutians. Japan had split its forces again and executed another coordinated attack, intent on securing footholds closer to American shores.

While these battles raged, George Jr. received a phone call at Hawaiian Electric.

The caller asked him if he still wanted passage to the mainland. George Jr. said, "I had to stop a minute to reflect on why they asked me. I had completely forgotten my application for transport in December. I had applied to the Military Transportation Command so I could attend the University of California, Berkeley." [508] George Jr. wanted to join the ranks of the five percent of high school graduates that went to college, and become an officer in the Navy as his dad had been. A degree from Cal on an ROTC scholarship would cinch his plan.

George Jr. said, "Yes."

"Get your gear, and report for embarkation at 10:00 AM."

That was it. George Jr. had packed two nested baskets, strapped together months earlier and had two hours before having to report. He later explained, "It was hectic … signing out from my two jobs, getting clearance from the Territory of Hawaii Tax Bureau, and borrowing my father's car to pick up my gear and return to the city. Goodbyes were brief and to the point." He could not locate Barbara to say farewell.

"I walked to the ship, several blocks away, paid for my ticket, twenty-one dollars, and boarded." His ship was *President Johnson*, built in 1903 and converted to a troop transport to carry several thousand men in pipe berths. According to George Jr., "Less than a hundred individuals came aboard. We departed on the evening of 3

June 1942 in company with the old *Maui* and several destroyers."[509] It was months before he would learn that the battles of Midway and Dutch Harbor had occurred on the same day he left to launch the rest of his life.

It took ten tense days to make the crossing. George Jr. did not know why they had an escort, and he did not know their destination until the Golden Gate Bridge emerged through the fog. George Jr. remembered decades later that, when he debarked, San Francisco was overflowing with soldiers, sailors, and **girls**. He shared a room with another guy in a small hotel and then took a ferry to the East Bay the next day. His first stop was the draft board, as his Honolulu 1-Y deferred status no longer applied. At the university, he signed up for the V-7 Navy College Training Program, an accelerated course for officer candidates. He was one of twenty-two young men who made the cut. Boot camp was tough, but he survived and even excelled. Then he spent seven months in intense training as a midshipman. During that time, he became ill and then recuperated at Oak Knoll Naval Hospital, in Oakland. Wrecked and wounded men from the frontlines joined him. When he improved, George Jr. taught math to recovering men to help pass the time.

After returning to the university, on the night before his commissioning ceremony, his commander informed him that he had washed out because of his time in the hospital. George Jr. was shocked that he was being separated from the Navy. He was number two in his class. Seven decades later, his disappointment still echoed in his words. George Jr. completed his degree and registered for the draft. If the Navy would not have him, maybe the Army would.

Barbara was not around to say goodbye to her brother, because she had attended the Roosevelt High Class of '42 graduation and all-night dance party with George Jr.'s buddy, Curt Shoemaker. Graduation was a somber affair on the evening of 2 June. There were no caps and gowns, and the curfew prevented them from returning home. Barbara remembered it "as a quiet celebration but a fun one."[510]

She received her 1942 yearbook at graduation. Unlike her 1941 yearbook, inscribed with numerous good wishes, this one had few. She was lucky to get one at all. The yearbook staff was determined to get the book published, showing a degree of dedication that epitomized the spirit and resourcefulness of the students:

> **There was no paper in Honolulu on which to print an annual. School yearbooks don't rate priority in the frontline battleground. But someone else's misfortune proved to be to our advantage when a shipload of paper, destined for the Philippines and Batavia, was turned back after the blitz and landed in Honolulu. No Ink! Plenty on order but no shipping priority! It was ordered by cable and delivered from the mainland by parcel post. Covers? You can't possibly have hardcovers! There's nothing left! Here, our printers again came to the rescue. They dug up some scrap board and brought some bolts of cloth which was originally meant to be for girls' dresses.**

Oh, but glue to fasten the covers on with? That's been frozen by the military governor! ... Makeshift, ingenuity, and good luck have all been ours in the production of this wartime annual.[511]

George Jr. had been Barbara's anchor in the storm that now engulfed her life. She felt more vulnerable and alone than ever before, and Barbara shed tears when she found out he'd left. Without Nina around, her dad expected her to keep the house and insisted she not evacuate to the mainland. She'd have to wait three years to leave home, because the age of majority was twenty-one. Her father was strict about how she spent her time, exacting about her behavior, and draconian about whom she dated. His reputation, good standing, and Victorian view trumped her wishes for fun and freedom. Barbara avoided the house and him, and like Nina, she could not be tamed.

***

Three weeks after the Battle of Midway, off Fort Stevens near the Columbia River bar in Oregon, Japanese submarine *I-25* surfaced. It had followed the salmon fishing fleet into the harbor to avoid the mines laid across the river entrance. Hatches opened, water dripped, and men scrambled to their battle stations. Commander Meiji Tagami ordered a turn, so that their stern faced the shore. Chief Gunner Sensuke Tao manned his position. "I shot the gun with my right hand," Tao recalled. "I did not use any gunsight at all — just shot."[512]

Fort Stevens was at the receiving end of those shells. Captain Jack R. Wood remembered, "When the first shot echoed across the harbor, I jumped off the cot and ran up to the command post ... everybody just started running ... most weren't dressed." Sergeant Laurence Rude of "B" Battery added, "It was a real madhouse ... the men were going in and out like a herd of elephants," as they hustled to their battle stations.[513] Then radar position reports were called in. A submarine was just out of range of the batteries on the beachhead. When the men got to their guns, Ken Evans said, "I wanna shoot. I wanna shoot. He's right out in front of me!" But Evans had to wait for the order to "Fire." At another battery awaiting the same order, Henry K. Scott asked, "Sergeant, if I made sure all phones were open, then lit a piece of paper and yelled *Fire!,* would I be court-martialed if my guns went into action?"

"Yes, sir!" exclaimed the sergeant.[514]

I-25 fired seventeen shells at Fort Stevens before slipping back under the water, unscathed. The only thing the submarine gunner hit was the backstop of a baseball field. Scott did not burn a piece of paper and yell an alarm. The Americans had held their fire, in order not to reveal their artillery positions as targets. At war's end, Oregon was unique among the 48 states, having had a fort attacked, a forest firebombed, and six people killed by Japanese military action.

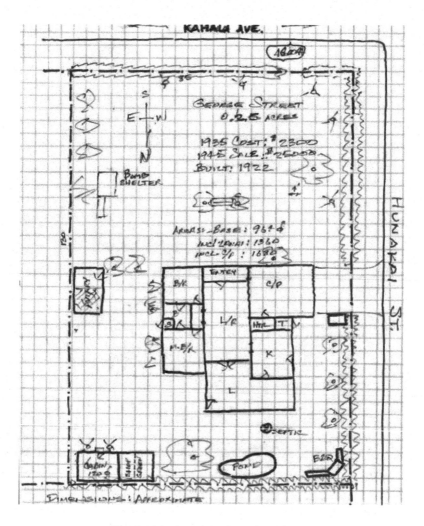

Sketch of the Street residence by George Jr.

George Street and George Jr., c. 1941 (George Street Archive)

Barbara Jean (Street) Olsen 1941
Senior Class picture (George Street Archive)

Chapter 27

Paradise Lost

By now, the Hawaii George loved was gone. Nina was gone, but fondness lingered. George Jr. was gone. And Barbara may as well have been gone. She was rarely at home.

As a young man, George relished the romance of the tropical island paradise. He got his first taste of Hawaii when he was a radio operator on steam-schooners bound for the Orient. His ships stopped in Honolulu for coal and a bit of R&R, and George fell in love with the islands. At the age of twenty-three, RCA assigned him to the position of radio-circuit supervisor at Koko Head, and he lived the words in James Michener's book, *Hawaii*. Hawaiian love songs cast their spell as he gazed into the deep, brown eyes of hula girls in ti leaf skirts, who undulated in impossible ways. Brown-skinned and beautiful, they raised a young man's blood in ways that Victorians never dared mention.

White and black sand beaches, pristine and breathtaking against turquoise blue water, were not laced with barbed wire and ringed with railroad ties back then. The valleys of Oahu's two volcanic mountain ranges were verdant and wild, not cramped with houses and tents and veined with asphalt. The magic of Hanauma Bay's coral reef, vibrant with solitude and color, now sprouted spikes to ward off landing parties. Hawaii's royalty crouched under the shield of a military provost. Battleships and concrete bunkers rose above the morning haze and overshadowed the Oriental temples, colonial churches, and sacred sites that once commingled in misted clouds of peace. Plantations that once covered the landscape with pineapple and sugar cane now cultivated air bases, cantonments, camps, and anti-aircraft emplacements. The military paved impassable roads. No longer did automobiles get stuck in the mud for two or three days until it hardened. The adventure of sleeping rough under a mosquito net next to a stranded car was gone — replaced by curfews, sentries, and wardens.

The Japanese did not invade. Instead, the U.S. military and civilian workers took over the island. Welders, mechanics, miners, construction crews, clerical workers, and truck drivers swarmed Oahu from every state in the Union, as the Army promised good pay and a great life on a tropical island.

Only some found paradise. After the attack, civilian crews that worked for the Army swelled from about nine thousand to seventeen thousand in less than a year. Schools became dormitories. Unwanted furniture littered parks. Hotels turned into offices. Proprietors received compensation only if the military had the time to process the paperwork. Relocated family men did not last long. Several left when they discovered that "three hots and a cot" meant they rotated shifts as well as a bed shared by two other men for six days a week. It was men used to construction-camp life who survived and thrived.

Honky tonk towns flourished under palm trees. Tattoo shops inked three hundred to four hundred civilian workers, sailors, and soldiers a day. Shooting galleries and pinball machines competed with hula girls who posed for pictures. A joint Army and Navy disciplinary board declared gyp joints out-of-bounds to protect the gullible. Many of them were headed for the grizzly battlefields of the South Pacific.

Libraries, art galleries, movie houses, service bands, symphonies, and the Bishop Museum adjusted schedules and performed to the tune of the military's needs. Twenty-five thousand men played records in a designated room at the library.[515] Churches rented fleets of bicycles and comfortable beds, helping to build a bridge between the troops and the people they were being trained to shoot.

The USO Victory Club held lunchtime dances so lonesome sailors could swing dance with girls like Barbara during their lunch break. The YMCA, converted to a USO Army and Navy club, offered over six hundred programs each month. Men could rent beds, take ballroom dance classes, watch silent movies, and go on guided sightseeing tours.

Wealthy ranch and plantation families opened their homes to exhausted pilots and submariners for five days of good food, genteel entertainment, and restful sleep, without charge. In lush tropical surroundings, these bone-weary men played bridge and tennis, golfed, swam in private pools, and went horseback riding. Two hundred hostesses nurtured a continuous stream of house guests, wrote letters to them when they shipped overseas, and helped them keep in touch with their loved ones back home. The lucky ones returned to experience this little corner of paradise, again and again. Lifelong bonds of gratitude ensued.[516]

The Royal Hawaiian Hotel on Waikiki expelled its guests, in order to welcome military men. Cots clogged the suites. The famous Coconut Grove bar became a soda fountain. The hotel hosted over 200,000 men during the war, and the Navy footed most of the bill. Officers paid a dollar a day; enlisted men paid nothing.

Other hotels were just as welcoming, and still, streets overflowed. At times some six hundred men stood in line to rent lockers and swimsuits. Up to eight hundred men waited in line to enter an establishment built for three hundred. At a dance on Kauai, there were just sixty-four girls for six hundred men.[517]

Twelve became the legal age for workers. Girls typed and filed. Boys hustled material and loaded ships. Science teachers became lab technicians, and economics teachers kept records. Professors supervised, and used their "teacher's voice" to snap people into line. Dental clinics sprang up in community halls, gyms, and even Japanese temples. Sewing, surgical dressing, and knitting corps entrenched themselves in living rooms to make plaster of Paris bandages, face masks, hospital garments, ditty bags, canvas bags, and cold-weather garments for the men headed to Alaska and the Aleutians.

Navy wives became Gray Ladies and assisted in hospital wards and recreation centers. They wrote letters for the wounded, organized parties for the lonely, and supplied books and magazines for recuperating men. The Red Cross Motor Corps drove men to picnics and outings, continued to deliver supplies, and rendered aid as needed. The Hawaiian Sugar Planters' Association, in cooperation with the Navy, produced penicillin for the troops.[518]

Fort Ruger now included an amphibious training camp near Koko Head. Fort DeRussy on Waikiki became a rest and recreation site. Kapiolani Park housed office and refrigeration supplies, and a vacant lot on Queen Street, in the center of Honolulu, became a storage site for explosives.

George set up branch offices at the Waikiki Foto Shop, the local YMCA, the Kemoo Center at Schofield Barracks, and the RCA station at Kahuku. His advertisements for new employees were unceasing: "Phone operator must be typist. Ph. Geo Street, RCA 6116 for appointment."[519] Among the ads for maids, cooks, and clerks that filled the classified ads, RCA sought messenger girls over the age of sixteen. Letters to the editor complimented the remarkable patience and courtesy shown to harried customers when they filed their radiograms. One message delayed by the censor resulted in a "hopping mad" customer, and prompted the following compliment: "… the clerk at RCA handled me like an ambassador … she could have tamed Hitler." [520] George trained his staff well.

In six months, three provost courts handled nineteen thousand civilian cases. Hauled in on the day of their arrest, the accused would stand in a semicircle with the prosecutor. The provost controlled oral arguments and witnesses, if any. Attorneys were discouraged from speaking for the clients, to the point where the judge would frequently say in open court that he did not want them to participate. The provost asked questions and cross-examined witnesses, time permitting. Then he rendered a verdict on the spot. For drunkenness he required a hundred dollar fine. Juveniles were sent to detention homes for being out after curfew, showing a light, quitting a job without permission, and even for failing to register carrier pigeons.[521] Needless to say, there was criticism about the military justice system. It bore the face of fascism and didn't end until 24 October 1944, nearly three years after the attack.

Within a year of the attack, newspapers featured half and full-page ads for the sale of war bonds. The *Honolulu Star-Bulletin* advertised, "Buy a little anniversary present for Mr. Hirohito … someday, we'll bomb that quivering coward so deep into his bomb shelter even rats can't find him[522] Another read, "Are you Mad? Rededicate yourself to revenge — Buy War Bonds." Each purchase included a free "Remember Pearl Harbor" pin.[523]

Within days of her twenty-first birthday in 1943, Barbara left Honolulu. Once she hit the age of majority, her father could no longer refuse her evacuation, and he released her trust fund. She reconnected with her mother, Kathryn (Heunisch) Street, and George Jr. in San Francisco, which she described as a city "whose heart beats in time to the waves washing against its shore." Like so many other evacuees, she traveled on the once luxurious SS *Lurline*. Barbara remembered that the staterooms, converted to hold double their previous capacity, with cots bolted to the bulkheads, offered passengers just one blanket per cot and no sheets or pillows. Nina and George remarried as soon as Barbara left, and Nina remained by George's side until she died.

Barbara had no difficulty in finding work when she arrived in California. The unemployment rate was less than two percent. After a brief stint in a fish cannery, she landed a job at Armory Ordinance, located in a twenty-eight-story, wedding-cake-style skyscraper at 100 McAllister Street. The Army had purchased the building when war broke out to house their Ordnance Department, a passport office, and the local draft induction center. It was one of the tallest buildings in San Francisco, with fantastic views of downtown. A stained glass window over the entry doors filled the lobby with light. Barbara worked on an NCR bookkeeping machine — a calculator and typewriter — happy to give up her cannery job. She helped account for the weapons systems and ordnance needed across the globe.

Initially, Barbara lived in a boarding house at 2300 Van Ness. Then she and her new friends, Betty Jane Smith and (Bernice) Gloria Selke, rented Apartment 25 in the four-story corner building at 1600 California Street in Polk Gulch, at the base of Nob Hill. Bay windows and fire escapes dressed the front of her second-story apartment. There was access to the roof for sunbathing and private gatherings. The building still stood when she drove by it on her 50th wedding anniversary, in 1995. The three girls joked that they were in an apartment full of "BS" because of their initials — Betty Smith, Bernice Selke, and Barbara Street. And they had a ball.

"Yosemite Valley for a long weekend? You bet!" Barbara had never been in snow. Her new friends, Gladys Williams and Irene Graves, were going to take the bus from Oakland to Yosemite to visit a relative who was recuperating at the Ahwahnee Hotel, and they invited Barbara to join them. One day up, one day back, and two days of fun in the snow.

When the Ahwahnee was first converted to a U.S. Naval hospital in 1943, it was used for the rehabilitation of shell-shocked warriors. Doctors soon discovered that the isolation and claustrophobic towering mountains in Yosemite Valley made the men worse. "If the patients weren't nuts when they got to Yosemite, the boredom there soon sent them over the edge," reported a staff member.[524]

Then, Captain Reynolds Hayden took command. Within months, the neuro-psychiatric center was phased out and turned into a general physical rehab unit. He had headed the Naval hospital at Pearl Harbor during the attack, and he knew just what the men needed — socialization. Quickly, he established transportation to the Badger Pass ski run, created a toboggan run, and built a bowling alley, crafts department, pool hall, and wood and machine shops. He arranged for bus transportation to and from Merced, Fresno, and Oakland, so that families and friends could visit. Curry Company, the hotel's operator, supplied tents, cabins, and stores for the guests.

The Ahwahnee News, typewritten, mimeographed, and chock full of humor and news, included the schedule for skiing, skating, tobogganing, game night, happy hour, movies, and bingo. Lessons were free. Barbara and women her age were more than welcome. When she arrived, Barbara hopped into the back of the military transport, jam-packed with sailors, and headed to Badger Pass. Ready for the slopes, she tucked her wool pants into her ankle boots and proceeded to fall more than she skied. But Dale, Red Walt, and Tommy didn't seem to mind.[525]

Chapter 28

Aftermath: Investigations and Recriminations

1944

In 1944, the Rotary Club appointed George as chairman of the International Service Committee. He arranged for Army Captain Charles S. Dayton to speak at their luncheon about Japanese culture and their mindset. The war wasn't over, and as much as he disliked the internment of U.S. citizens, in Japanese detainment centers, Dayton was wary, like so many others.

He told his audience, "The current cartoon idea of making the Japanese out as a nit-wit is dangerous." He summed up his description of Japanese culture by pointing out that it was founded on a fierce Samurai tradition.[526] It's important to know your enemy, but it is more important not to be narrow-minded and blinded by misinformation and hatred.

Then in May, Hawaiians saw black smoke roiling from Pearl Harbor again. Windows rattled. An explosion made ears ring, and the air smelled like cordite. It was Sunday, and the detonations were as big as the ones on 7 December. "I thought it was another invasion...." recalled Navy corpsman, Tony Julian.[527] Six landing craft, three tank landing craft, seventeen attack landing vehicles, eight 155-millimeter guns, and twenty buildings were blown to smithereens. Eleven tugs of varying sizes and two other landing craft were damaged. Men died, and the Japanese had not fired a shot.

The blast was an accident. A tank landing ship (LST-353), moored in the West Loch while it loaded ammunition, had blown up, and the fire that swept through Pearl Harbor was an inferno. There was nothing mentioned in the newspapers until four days later. The military issued a brief statement tucked into the front page news of the *Honolulu Star-Bulletin.* "Pacific fleet headquarters announced today that an explosion and fire which occurred on Sunday cost some loss of life, a number of injuries and resulted in the destruction of several small vessels." Within days, the military towed the debris offshore, along with the remains of a Japanese midget submarine not involved in the incident. Reports of the number of men dead varied from 163 to 392. Scores more were wounded. The government classified the West Loch disaster as Top Secret, and the story remained under wraps until 1962. The explosion is now known as the "Second Pearl Harbor."

With the nation focused on the war effort and the Japanese, there were no additional inquiries into the Pearl Harbor attack until 1944. What was done was done, and the business of war took priority.

The military brass in Washington offered up Kimmel and Short as scapegoats, not RCA, George, or Fuchikami, as the Street family had feared. Their ouster did not silence the public's demand for the truth.[528] Short and Kimmel "retired" in 1942, and both took positions in the public sector. Short worked at Ford Motor

Company in Dallas, and Frederic R. Harris Company, a New York City shipbuilding firm, hired Kimmel.

Kimmel wanted to clear his name. He requested a court-martial in open court, even at the risk of losing his military retirement income. Judge Advocate General Cramer and Secretary of War Stimson agreed to waive the statute of limitations, so that Kimmel could have his showdown after the war. Bending to pressure from the press late in the war, Knox assigned Admiral Hart to collect testimony from officers to prepare for the court-martial.[529]

The Hart Inquiry

On 22 February 1944, Admiral Thomas Hart, USN (Ret.) began to gather evidence, before wartime hazards took their toll. He was not required to make any specific recommendation.[530] His collection of statements did not include Magic, even though he was fully aware of its existence.[531] He interviewed forty witnesses, but not George. Hart's inquiry ended on 15 June 1944. Concerned with Hart's finding, Congress called for a formal Navy court of inquiry and an Army board hearing in July.

Army Pearl Harbor Investigation

Authorized by Congress, the U.S. Army Pearl Harbor Board convened on 20 July 1944 to investigate the facts pertaining to the Pearl Harbor attack. Congress wanted the board to issue recommendations. The Army heard from one hundred fifty-one witnesses but prohibited the mention of Magic or any intelligence gleaned prior to the attack. This ruling forced Army personnel to perjure themselves.[532] When asked to testify, Admiral Kimmel made the first move to introduce Magic and its secrets into the record. A Navy man, Kimmel was not bound by the Army's prohibition regarding Magic. He requested Magic records for the Naval court of inquiry, which ran concurrently with the Army's hearing.

On 28 August, the board agreed to admit Magic and consular documents into the record, over the objection of Admiral Stark. The question of Washington's involvement came to light. Previous ambiguous testimony was clarified.

The board then traveled to Hawaii and San Francisco to take additional statements. Once again, George was not called to testify. During this time, Kimmel's son, a submarine commander, was killed, and Knox died of a heart attack. When a new picture emerged from the documents submitted by Kimmel, Congress called for more investigations and the release of all the material previously held by the Roberts Commission.

After thirty-three days, the board held that General Short should have placed his command at a higher state of alert and kept himself informed about the Navy's aerial reconnaissance effectiveness since he was in charge of Oahu's defense. It determined that Short had failed to implement the Joint Coastal Frontier Defense Plan. In other words, he bungled his duties. And for the first time, Washington was censured when the board determined that General Marshall also failed in his duty by not keeping Short fully informed. Marshall was further criticized for not keeping himself abreast of Hawaii's state of readiness and failing to forward the fourteen-part telegram to Short.[533] The board also admonished Marshall for his failure to contact Short after he realized Short had implemented a sabotage alert level instead of a general attack alert level, upon receiving the 27 November warning message.[534]

Regarding the late delivery of Radiogram 1549, General Marshall explained that he was not aware that commercial circuits were used to transmit the final warning message to Honolulu. Colonel French confirmed that he had not told Marshall the Army circuits were down. Marshall also stated that he did not telephone Short because of the lack of security on telephone lines and that he did not want the Japanese to find out that they had broken the Purple code[535] In the end, the Army board deemed Radiogram 1549 to be inconsequential.

General Gerow, chief of the War Plans Division, was also found to have failed in his duties because he did not keep the Hawaiian Command informed about Magic. The board found that he should have been more concise in the war warning message of 27 November and that he should have acted upon the joint Army and Navy plan. By implicating Washington, the board contradicted the findings of the Roberts Commission. The investigative team omitted all references to Magic when they released the report to the public.

Naval Court of Inquiry

The Naval court of inquiry convened on 24 July 1944 by the same act of Congress. The court fully exonerated Admiral Kimmel and held Admiral Stark in Washington responsible for not keeping Kimmel informed. Theirs was the first inquiry that considered testimony relating to intelligence. Once again, the investigators did not ask George Street to testify. Admiral Stark was criticized for not conveying the information garnered from radio intelligence and not sending a war warning message to his Hawaiian command on the morning of 7 December. Again, because of the need to maintain wartime secrecy, the Navy struck all testimony relating to Magic before releasing its public report.

Clarke Investigation

In September of 1944, General Marshall ordered a War Department investigation into the handling of top-secret communications, since the Army and Navy courts of inquiry had opened Pandora's box. Congress and the State Department were suspicious about the time various messages had been received and acted upon. They questioned the overall organization of data and the claims that accused General Marshall of ordering the destruction of the Winds code messages. It was an informal investigation conducted at a round table by Colonel Carter W. Clarke, chief of Army Military Intelligence. Clarke called twelve witnesses. He found no evidence to support the claim that G-2 ever received the Winds Code or that it destroyed any documents.[536]

Colonel French addressed the tie line that George tried to activate on 6 December. He had not mentioned it in his testimony to the Roberts Commission, which misspelled his name as "France."[537] Clarke did not follow up. Again, George was not called to testify. If Powell had authorized the activation of the tie line, Radiogram 1549 would have appeared at Fort Shafter within minutes. However, it is unlikely that it could have been decoded before 7:55 AM, the official time of the start of the attack. It's possible, however, that Colonel Powell could have become a sacrificial lamb when it was discovered that he put off the activation of the tie-line until 8 December simply because his civilian contractors did not work on Saturdays.

Clarke's final report said, "It appears that the teletype arrangement between RCA in Honolulu and Fort Shafter was not operating at the particular hour the message was received, with the result that it was dispatched by a messenger on a bicycle who was diverted from completing delivery by the first bombing."[538] Not only did the committee's report misstate the delivery time, but it also indicated that Fuchikami rode a bicycle, instead of a motorcycle, and delivered it *after* the first bombing instead of *during* the first bombing. Stevens' failure to time stamp Radiogram 1549 continued to promote misinformation. The committee protected its own and gave Stevens and the Signal Corps a pass.

Clausen Investigation

Two months later, Secretary of War Stimson asked Army Major Henry C. Clausen to conduct a follow-up to supplement the Army board's prior findings. Armed with a memorandum of authorization from Stimson and the backing of G-2, Clausen opened the floodgates. His investigation unearthed a trove of intelligence material, including information about Kuehn, the Moris, and the Japanese consulate. Clausen later testified before a congressional committee and published his findings in *Pearl Harbor: Final Judgement,* a 1992 book, coauthored with Bruce Lee.

Clausen's investigation uncovered two key messages received by Captain Mayfield from George Street that were decoded after 9 December. One radiogram was from Yoshikawa to Tokyo, sent on 6 December 1941, specifying that "now" would be a good time for a surprise attack. It included updated information about anti-torpedo nets and barrage balloons in and about Pearl Harbor. The second key message handed over by George was the 3 December telegram that described the Kuehn signal-light system. Again, George was not called to testify.

Hewitt Inquiry

The Navy also conducted a follow-up investigation — the Hewitt Inquiry — from May to July 1945. Radio intelligence and Magic were discussed in detail. There was no required secrecy, as the war had ended. This time, witnesses testified under oath, and Hewitt cross-examined them. For the first time, George Street was asked to provide testimony as well as telegrams and correspondence. A joint congressional hearing referenced these documents later that year. Shown is the Hewett Inquiry request for documentation, sent to George Street. Annotation at the side of this telegram reads: **"I testified under oath re msg copies at CINCPAC office Pearl Harbor. Geo Street"**

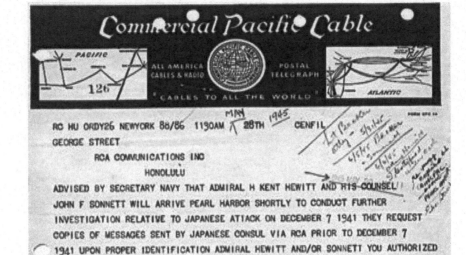

*Two radiograms regarding Hewitt Inquiry with Street's
annotations (George Street Archive)*

```
COPY
                          COMMERCIAL PACIFIC CABLE
                                                      Honolulu time & date
RC HU ORDY 26  NEWYORK 88/86  1130AM  28TH           1945 MAY 28 AM 11 10


GEORGE STREET
    RCA COMMUNICATIONS INC
       HONOLULU

ADVISED BY SECRETARY NAVY THAT ADMIRAL H KENT HEWITT AND HIS COUNSEL
JOHN F SONNETT WILL ARRIVE PEARL HARBOR SHORTLY TO CONDUCT FURTHER
INVESTIGATION RELATIVE TO JAPANESE ATTACK ON DECEMBER 7 1941 THEY REQUEST
COPIES OF MESSAGES SENT BY JAPANESE CONSUL VIA RCA PRIOR TO DECEMBER 7
1941 UPON PROPER IDENTIFICATION ADMIRAL HEWITT AND/OR SONNETT YOU
AUTHORIZED AND DIRECTED TO COOPERATE WITH THEM TO THE FULLEST EXTENT AND
TO FURNISH THEM SUCH INFORMATION AS YOU HAVE IN YOUR POSSESSION

                                DAVID SARNOFF


                                                      1945 MAY 28 ____
A____

STREET HU  SARNOFF NY 6

YOURS RE HEWITT AND SONNETT ACKNOWLEDGED


Note:  Several days after receipt of above instructions from Mr. Sarnoff.
I was called to Pearl Harbor and in the presence of Admiral Hewitt
and Mr. Sonnett a transcript was made of questions put to me and my
responses by a secretary.  I have no copy, nor was I provided with one
of the testimony taken.  This interview or inquisition became a part of,
I believe, the "Navy's Investigation" of the PearlHarbor disaster.  I
was at this part of their investigation for an hour or perhaps and hour
and a half.
              George Street    1/9/63
```

During the Hewitt Inquiry, Layton, the former combat intelligence officer for Admiral Kimmel, now a captain, testified that he understood that Mr. Sarnoff had obtained immunity for his manager in Hawaii regarding the handover of messages to the Navy. Captain Mayfield stated that RCA's handover messages were delivered in the late forenoon because "… This arrangement was at the desire of the manager of RCA and was for his own security, inasmuch as he was violating instructions and desired to have these messages copied and delivered to me or my representative only in such manner as would best safeguard and protect him as well as me."[539]

JOINT CONGRESSIONAL COMMITTEE INVESTIGATION

In the aftermath of the victory over Japan, Congress, aware that prior investigations were riddled with bias and secrecy, demanded a full investigation into all the events and circumstances relating to the Pearl Harbor attack. Members of the committee gathered all relevant information relating to Magic and other classified documentation to supplement what was considered to be a suspicious record. They included testimony from the prior investigations and questioned all participants still living. The resulting forty volumes of testimony and exhibits include items supplied by George during the Hewitt Inquiry. The investigation clarified conflicting and incomplete testimony. And heads rolled.

Two months before the congressional hearing, the Navy produced a report, declassified on 1 December 2011:

Despite the fact that all messages in Japanese diplomatic channels were not available by 7 December and that the daily reports mailed from Hawaii and Corregidor were at least two weeks en route to Washington, by late November 1941, U.S. Navy officials in Washington, Pearl Harbor, and Manila well knew that war with Japan was imminent....

The report concluded:

In summary, the U.S. Navy's radio intelligence program from 1924–1941 is a story of trial and error. Through

**much of the period, particularly the closing months of
1941, the tactical and strategic benefits from
cryptanalysis and traffic analysis were not clearly
understood or appreciated. Despite early successes
against Japanese naval communications, U.S. Navy
decision makers either ignored or forgot the utility of
such information. Plagued by shortages in personnel and
equipment, problems of communication, and interservice
rivalries, the small program nevertheless developed a
core intercept and analysis program at Pearl Harbor and
Corregidor, which would prove invaluable, but not until
after Pearl Harbor.**[540]

Short and Kimmel were held responsible for the devastation at
Pearl Harbor. The committee's findings censured President
Roosevelt in its minority report. The majority report found
Secretaries Stimson and Knox, Generals Marshall, Gerow and
Short, and Admirals Stark and Kimmel culpable. Marshall was
chastised because he failed to send Radiogram 1549 as a RUSH or
URGENT message. [541] The committee concluded:

**They [the Hawaiian Command] failed to defend the
fortress they commanded — their citadel was taken by
surprise. Aside from any responsibilities that may appear
to rest in Washington, the ultimate and direct
responsibility for failure to engage the Japanese on the
morning of December 7 with every weapon at their
disposal rests essentially and properly with the Army and**

Navy commands in Hawaii, whose duty it was to meet the enemy against which they had been warned.[542]

During the investigation, an incomplete and inaccurate story of Radiogram 1549's origination and delivery emerged. The handling of Radiogram 1549 was detailed for the public, but the time of delivery to Ft. Shafter remained misstated as 11:45 AM Hawaii time.

The congressional committee concluded that "it was the failure of communications (between French and Marshall) and not the selection of an improper channel that occasioned the delay [of the delivery of Radiogram 1549]."[543] The Joint Committee on the Investigation of the Pearl Harbor Attack also posited that the Communications Act of 1934 — that which Sarnoff and George had ignored when George handed over communiques to the Navy — had benefited the Japanese and hindered U.S. counter espionage agencies. They recommended that such an act should never impede national security again.[544]

***

Piecing together testimony from the various hearings relating to Pearl Harbor and timelines proposed by authors Admiral Layton, Gordon Prange, Henry Clausen, and Bruce Lee, it seems likely that Corporal Stevens turned in Radiogram 1549 for *decoding* at 11:45 AM Hawaii time, after keeping it in his pocket for almost two hours. With no time stamp to clarify the delivery time of Radiogram 1549 to Fort Shafter, and because George was not called to testify until the Hewitt Inquiry, no one questioned the discrepancy. The fact that Stevens wanted George to change his testimony to say there was a second forenoon delivery lends credence to this speculation. The message was decoded at about 2:48 PM Hawaii time and hand-delivered to General Short around 3:45 PM. The unnecessary debate over who was going to give it to Short for fear of his wrath accounted for almost an hour's delay.[545]

More than one author has assumed that the telegram was delivered in the afternoon by Western Union, not RCA. The confusion continued for years, as evidenced by a newspaper clipping in George Street's archives, datelined 29 January 1946, Washington, D.C. The headline read, *ROBERTS REVEALS HOW SHORT MESSAGE* [Radiogram 1549] *HERE WAS DELAYED*. The article stated that the messenger boy hid in the bushes and that an RCA "official," George, of course, denied the story. The news reporter quoted him as saying, "We don't have boys who go to sleep in bushes."

On the sidebar of the clipping, George wrote, "A gross canard made up by the people in the Army Signal Corps." Underscored in red, he wrote, "Lies, Untrue! Not so." His anger had not abated when he wrote to Ladislas Farago over twenty years later, "If any messenger was seen 'crawling into the bushes' it undoubtedly would be for the purpose of relieving himself to a call of nature! ... The rank canard was circulated for years, and for my part, I could believe it may have been concocted, planted, and promoted by members of the Army Signal Corps."[546]

***

There still is much debate about why Marshall did not act sooner to send a warning message or why he did not have it phoned to the command in Hawaii on the secure transpacific radio line or designate it "URGENT." According to testimony before the Hewitt Inquiry, the Navy did not have a scrambled telephone line to Pearl Harbor, and the Army's scrambler was "not secure against an expert."[547] Colonel French stated in the *Congressional Record* that the reason he did not pick up the phone and call Pearl Harbor with General Marshall's warning was that the signal center never used the phone for classified messages. General Marshall confirmed this. Other testimony clarified that a single message sent to numerous commands was usually teletyped so all would receive it simultaneously. Phone calls to each would not have been as fast.[548]

George Street was not as understanding. He blamed Washington. "What an old fashioned idea General Marshall had — not to use the phone but to actually forward a telegram to an office that he did not know, nor did his signal officer know would not be open for business until 12:30 Washington time!!!" He continued, "I feel sure that the untruths that persist regarding the delivery in Honolulu of General Marshall's 'warning' telegram — such as it was — to Fort Shafter are the results of the Signal Corps' early and longtime efforts to have a scapegoat, or some kind of a 'whipping boy,' or a distraction from truth … Marshall's message was simply filed much too late in Washington, due to the irresponsible and reprehensible funny business going on there, to be effective in Hawaii. [They should have] allowed time for reasonable transmission (actual transmission time Washington to Honolulu was forty-five minutes) and then another forty minutes, or more, for decoding it at Fort Shafter."[549]

***

By the end of the year, George was on his way to a new assignment in New York. George's last official act as manager of RCA-Honolulu was presenting Alexander McLain with a twenty year pin. His promotion to RCA's traffic bureau seems odd. Had he asked to return stateside? He'd devoted ten years of his life to RCA-Honolulu and had made friends in high places. It made no sense. The weather in New York had not suited him in 1934, when he was recovering from polio. Why would he want to go back to that climate? Was Sarnoff being kind and allowing him to work out his last years at an easier post? David Sarnoff took a personal interest in his employees and often reassigned them to less demanding jobs to keep them on the payroll.[550] Nonetheless, RCA reassigned him without ceremony. There wasn't even a call from Sarnoff.

There are other possible reasons for the transfer. George's greatest advocate, mentor, and business friend, W.A. Winterbottom, had died and been replaced by Thompson II. Mitchell. George had supplanted Mitchell when he took over RCA-Honolulu in 1935. George said of Mitchell, "He supervised some pothole digging at Point Reyes of Bolinas for an antenna, then was sent to Los Angeles to supervise the rebuilding at the Marine Coast Station and stayed on there as a 'District Manager.' I was then District Manager in Pacific Northwest-Seattle. RCA had asked me two or three times to go take over the Honolulu job."

George turned it down for personal reasons (he was in the middle of divorcing his first wife) and was told, "then we are forced to send Mitchell from L.A. who does not have qualification or experience enough!!"

Was Mitchell flexing his muscles and reassigning favorites? Had George's lack of cooperation with Mayfield left a bad impression with Sarnoff? Or was it because he destroyed evidence sought by investigators when he followed FCC regulations and got rid of radiograms that exceeded their normal shelf life? Newspapers announced his move, and good wishes poured into the office. *Relay* featured a lengthy and glowing account of his tenure.

***

Although Radiogram 1549 did not arrive in time to warn the military command of an impending attack at Pearl Harbor, it did accomplish much. The resulting investigations into the surprise attack exposed flaws in military and diplomatic intelligence-communication systems. The congressional committee concluded: "In many respects, the picture presented by radio intelligence was among the most significant information relating to when, and to a degree, where the Japanese would possibly attack."

The investigations surrounding Radiogram 1549 and other missed messages embarrassed America's military leaders and helped establish a coordinated intelligence system. President Truman signed the National Security Act of 1947, which created the National Security Agency. Before the agency's formation, intelligence units worked independently in the Departments of Commerce and Agriculture, the Board of Economic Warfare, the

FBI, the Secret Service, the Customs Service, the F.C.C., cable and communications companies like RCA, and in each branch of the military. Shipmasters, business representatives abroad, and a private intelligence group headed by Vincent Astor also gathered intelligence data.[551] All the intelligence pouring in from these agencies and entities, and other countries as well, had no single coordination center and were presented piecemeal to different people.

Bureaucratic confusion, incorrect analysis, and denial doomed Pearl Harbor's final warning message to failure. The mistakes and delays encountered in sending and delivering Radiogram 1549 underscored the disastrous results reaped from convoluted military protocols, interservice rivalry, and personal power struggles. It also exposed the insanity of allowing diplomatic pressure to override prudent, cautious, and coordinated military strategy.

The surprise attack kindled a fire that ignited the hearts of America's Greatest Generation and unleashed a response that will forever illuminate the annals of history. It united the nation, fortified America's fighting spirit, and elevated the love of country. Men, women, and children moved with a single purpose — to protect their families, neighbors, and America's freedom.

***

In 1968, George Street expressed his passionate opinion about why America was caught flat-footed at Pearl Harbor:

> **Of all the stuff, off and on, that I have read, in the past twenty-seven years, I have concluded certainly that Roosevelt wanted the U.S.A. in the European war, and**

wanted the Japanese to strike the first blow at us to help his wanted war get started. And he probably mentioned this to Henry Stimson, the secretary of war, and also to Admiral Stark and General Marshall, his top military people in Washington; and in my mind they were so imbued that they too made the decision that some kind of sacrifice must come about, which in this case turned into a holocaust with about twenty-five hundred Navy and Army boys dead and thirty-six hundred more wounded. Let alone the loss and damage to a great part of the Pacific fleet of naval vessels and many aircraft.

George continued:

So Mr. Roosevelt got his war started! And neither Stark nor Marshall seemed to care enough to give their outfits better information and keep them posted. Some leaders! I think the word 'traitors' suits them all very well. Why should any one soldier or sailor die just to satisfy the egoism of a president? Was it all really necessary? Well, more books will continue to be written about it, and no one will ever, it seems, solve, "man's inhumanity to man."[552]

Epilogue

George Street was promoted to the position of assistant manager of the traffic bureau for RCA and transferred to New York in 1946 — a position he held until his retirement in 1962. George provided information for Walter Lord's *Day of Infamy,* James Michener's *Hawaii,* Ladislas Farago's *The Broken Seal: "Operation Magic" and the Secret Road to Pearl Harbor,* and RCA's archives. He was depicted in the movie *Tora! Tora! Tora!* His character in the movie elicited the following from George:

"That RCA telegraph office scene and that tall guy with the mustache (me, I suppose. Actually I was home in bed, just about ready to get up) was a real doozy. After the book was published, and I had read it, I was in direct communication with the author. He made the same mistake that a lot of authors make. He could have, and should have contacted me before he finished his book, and it would not have had the phony [time] which is a gross canard apparently made up by the Signal Corps as a cover-up for just another failure."

To commemorate Pearl Harbor's tenth anniversary, George Street was contacted by the *New York Times* and asked for details about the delivery of Radiogram 1549. In 1952, Street and Fuchikami were guest speakers for the WNBT "Pearl Harbor Day" TV special.

Upon retirement, George Street and wife, Nina, moved to the sunny climes of Sarasota, Florida. They had divorced and remarried twice while in Honolulu. Their relationship stabilized after Barbara Jean and George Jr. left home. George received his fifty-year Mason pin and fifty-year Masonic Scottish Rite blue prayer cap in 1968. When Nina died unexpectedly in 1977, George Sr., confined to a wheelchair, contracted with his neighbor to provide meals and housekeeping. Eventually, they joined households. George died in Sarasota, Florida in 1993 at the age of 95, while under the gentle care of Anna and Sonja Madera and Sonja's son, Dana.

George Street Jr. completed a Bachelor of Science degree in mechanical engineering at the University of California, Berkeley after he was "surveyed out" of the Navy.

He retired early as an engineer with the General Electric Company in 1985 to care for his ill wife, Martha. After her death, he indulged his love of sailing and made long haul crossings from the mainland to Hawaii — twice. He also joined his sons, David and Paul, on fishing expeditions in Alaska. He remarried in his 70's. He and Carol sailed, and traveled, and had the time of their lives. His children, David, Paul and Joanne, and two stepdaughters, Patricia March and Anne Norm, continue to enrich his life. He remains hale and hearty, living close to the sea, in Port Townsend, Washington.

George Street, Jr. 2021
(Photo by Patricia March)

Barbara Jean (Street) Olsen joined the crowd on Market Street to celebrate VJ Day when the *San Francisco Chronicle* printed the half page headline, *"PEACE"* in August of 1945.

In October of 1945, she married a "sky pilot," U.S. Naval aviator, Arthur Valarie Olsen, at Old St. Mary's Church in San Francisco. Lieutenant (Junior Grade) Olsen's first duty station was

Barbara (Street) Olsen and her husband, Lt. Arthur Valarie Olsen, Maui 1945 (author)

on Maui. Of the twenty-five military wives who arrived with Barbara to join their husbands on Maui, twenty-three, including Barbara, left the island pregnant. Art Olsen was a career carrier pilot who also served in Korea and Vietnam. When he retired, he taught naval aviators on simulators at NAS Corpus Christi. Art and Barbara's union produced four children—James, Valarie, Kathryn, and William. Tony Bennett's song, "I Left My Heart in San Francisco," always brought a sparkle to Art and Barbara's eyes.

Barbara's mother, Kathryn (Kay), joined the household after she retired from the civil service. Kay provided child care, enjoyed squadron parties, and treasured the active military life she shared with the family. At her 100th birthday party, Kay was still dancing, margarita in hand.

Barbara treasured the excitement of being a military wife, and later enjoyed birding, until her unexpected death in July of 2012, in Corpus Christi, Texas. Her beloved husband, Artie, died three months later. Barbara always grew Hawaiian flowers in their yard.

Joe Unger was remembered by George Jr. as a nice guy who built a bed set out of orange crates when he was first married in Hawaii. George Jr. liked and trusted him enough to loan him a hundred dollars in 1941.

In 1946, Unger sent a letter to George Street about changes the Honolulu office experienced after George transferred to New York. He wrote about how he dodged the police because he had not installed "1946 deluxe" windshield wipers on his car.

In a letter to Barbara, George wrote:

"Joe Unger was in to tell me this morning he is sprouting a family and now has a baby boy. He bought a country house and lives in New Jersey and is surrounded by woods, a trout stream and fifty acres of land he is buying...."[553]

Tadao Fuchikami was not detained during the massive sweep of arrests that shook the islands and forever changed people's lives. A *Honolulu Star-Bulletin* correspondent interviewed him when he was 79 years old. Fuchikami stated that he did not know he was delivering an important message until the FBI questioned him. It would be ten years before he learned the exact wording, according to an interview conducted by the *Honolulu Star-Bulletin* in 1996. When interviewed by Thurston Clarke, author of *Pearl Harbor Ghosts*, he confided, "I wished I could have had the message sooner. Then I would have warned people, and I might have been a national hero. For a while, I thought that the Day of Infamy might have been my fault."[554]

According to a memorandum from George, Fuchikami later became a sheet metal worker at Hickam Field. He was also a technical advisor for the 1970 film, *Tora! Tora! Tora!*. Fuchikami retired as a civilian employee, enjoyed golf in his retirement, and made coat hanger and golf ball sculptures. He passed away at the age of 89 years, on 7 February 2006. The U.S. Public Records, 1970-2009 Index, listed him as the owner of a residence on Ahuula St., Honolulu, the same address he had entered on the handwritten statement that described his heroic delivery of Radiogram 1549.

The Final Toll of Pearl Harbor:

- One hundred eighty-eight aircraft were destroyed, three-quarters of those based at Pearl Harbor; one hundred fifty-nine were damaged.

- Eight battleships, three light cruisers, three destroyers, one minelayer, and five other naval vessels were sunk or severely damaged.

- Two thousand three hundred thirty-five American servicemen and sixty-eight civilians were killed. Half of the servicemen killed were aboard USS *Arizona*. Friendly fire killed most of the civilians.

- One thousand one hundred seventy-eight military and civilians were wounded.

- The Japanese lost twenty-nine planes, five mini-subs, and sixty-four servicemen.

- The Congress' joint committee recommended twenty-five improvement points for the Army and Navy after its investigation.

- Walter Short retired in 1942 as a major general. He maintained that he did not receive adequate intel from Washington and received the court-martial hearing he requested to vindicate his record.

- Presidents Reagan, Nixon, and Clinton turned down the requests made by Admiral Kimmel's family to restore his four-star rank. A 1995 Pentagon investigation concluded that other officers were culpable, but they did not exonerate Kimmel. In May of 1999, the United States Senate passed a nonbinding resolution exonerating Kimmel and Short. They requested that the president restore both men posthumously to their full rank. Neither President Clinton nor Bush did so. In 2000, the Senate again issued an exoneration of Kimmel.

Additional details about the Moris, Robert Shivers, Tadao Fuchikami, and Japanese spy Yoshikawa can be found at the author's blog, *The Footfalls of History,* www.valarieanderson.com.

Appendix A: Timeline

Below, shown in Hawaii time and the corresponding Eastern Standard Time, is the sequence of events that placed George Street's RCA Communications-Honolulu office in the critical path of Pearl Harbor's final warning message. It was developed by this author, James R. Olsen, and Patricia March from the National Geographic Timeline, the *Congressional Record,* George Street's archives, and Ladislas Farago's book, *The Broken Seal,* except as noted.

7 December 1941

1:00 AM (6:30 AM EST) Commander Kramer returns to Magic and discusses with Captain McCollum the last section of the intercepted 14-part message. They deliver it to Admiral Stark. Kramer gives the 14th part to the president. FDR remarks that "it look[s] as though the Japanese are going to sever negotiations." (Layton, et al., 300).

~3:30 AM (9:00 AM EST) Colonel Bratton, U.S. Army, reads the last section of the 14-part intercept.

3:42 AM (9:12 AM EST) Less than two miles off the entrance to Pearl Harbor, U.S. Navy minesweeper, *Condor,* detects a periscope and sends a signal-light message to U.S. Navy destroyer, *Ward:* "Sighted submerged submarine on westerly course, speed nine knots."

4:00 AM (9:30 AM EST) General Marshall receives message to call Colonel Bratton. (Layton, et al., 302)

5:00 AM (10:30 AM EST) Marshall returns Bratton's call. Marshall says he will meet him in the office rather than have Bratton come to him. (Layton, et al., 303)

5:05 AM (10:35 AM EST) Stark makes decision not to call Kimmel because it is 5:05 AM in Hawaii. He tries unsuccessfully to reach FDR.

~5:50 AM (11:20 AM EST) Marshall arrives at the office and reads all fourteen parts of the intercepted message. He refuses to let Bratton interrupt him with the news about the 1:00 deadline stated in the last section of the 14-part message. (Prange, et al., 493) (Layton, et al., 305)

~6:05 – 6:10 AM (11:35 PM EST) Japanese carriers turn into the wind. First wave of 183 planes takes off and uses Honolulu radio music station as a direction finder.

~6:10 AM (11:40 AM EST) Marshall decides to send a warning message to Pacific outposts. He handwrites it and calls Stark. Stark says there is no need to include Hawaiian Naval command as a recipient, as the 27 November war message should have done the job. (Prange, et al., 494)

~6:12 – 6:15 AM (11:42 – 11:45 AM EST) Stark calls back and tells Marshall to go ahead and send the message with "Inform the Navy" added to the warning. Stark offers to send it on

Navy channels, but Marshall says he thinks he can get it through quickly. (Prange, et al, 494)

~**6:18** AM (11:48 AM EST) Marshall hands the message to Colonel Bratton who, in less than a minute, delivers it to Colonel French at the Signal Corps' office down the hall.

~ **6:25** AM (11:55 AM EST) French can't read Marshall's handwriting. Bratton dictates the message to a typist. (Prange, et al., 494)

6:28 AM (11:58 AM EST) French receipts message for coding and transmission. He tells Bratton that the outposts will have it in about thirty to forty minutes, 20 to 30 minutes before the 1:00 deadline. (Clausen, on page 137, incorrectly calculated a six-hour time difference, not a five-and-a-half hour difference. (Layton, et al., 306)

6:30 AM (12:00 PM EST) The Caribbean Defense Command receives the final warning message one hour and 25 minutes before the attack. (Prange, et al., 495)

6:36 AM (12:06 PM EST) Philippines receives final warning message one hour and nineteen minutes before the attack. (Prange, et al., 495)

6:41 AM (12:11 PM EST) San Francisco Presidio receives final warning message one hour and eleven minutes before the attack. (Prange, et al., 495)

6:42 AM (12:12 PM EST) French learns Army circuits to Honolulu are down. He selects Western Union/RCA path for transmission. (Prange, et al., 495)

6:45 AM (12:15 PM EST) USS *Ward* fires on a Japanese midget submarine.

6:48 AM (12:18 PM EST) Western Union (WU) D.C. office receipts and cables message to WU-San Francisco. WU-SF puts it in a pneumatic tube to RCA-SF.

6:53 AM (12:23 PM EST) USS *Ward* reports to Pearl Harbor Naval HQ, "We have dropped depth charges upon sub operating in defensive sea area."

7:00 AM (12:30 PM EST) RCA-Honolulu office opens fifty-five minutes before the attack.

7:02 AM (12:32 PM EST) U.S. Army privates J. L. Locker and G. Elliot at the Opana Mobile Radar Unit detect over fifty aircraft approaching the island from the northwest.

7:05 AM (12:35 PM EST) Japan launches the second wave — 167 aircraft.

7:15 AM (12:45 PM EST) USS *Ward* reports its action to Admiral Kimmel, who decides to wait for confirmation because of previous false sightings.

7:17 AM (12:47 PM EST) RCA-SF sends the final warning message to Honolulu. Total transmission time between D.C. and Honolulu is 45 minutes (Annotation on Radiogram 1549).

7:20 AM (12:50 PM EST) Lieutenant K. Tyler, U.S. Army at Fort Shafter receives Opana Mobile Radar Unit's sighting report. He tells the radarmen not to worry about it because a squadron of B-17s is expected from the mainland.

7:30 – 7:40 AM (1:00 –1:10 PM EST) Admiral Kimmel receives updates on submarine encounters.

7:33 AM (1:03 PM EST) RCA-Honolulu office receives Radiogram 1549 twenty-two minutes before official attack time.

7:34 AM (1:04 PM EST) Radiogram 1549's envelope is time stamped and it is pigeon-holed for normal delivery.

7:50 AM (1:20 PM EST) USS *Curtiss,* moored in berth X-ray 22 goes to general quarters after being strafed by Japanese planes.[555]

7:53 AM (1:23 PM EST) Commander Mitsuo Fuchida issues *"to ra to ra to ra"* message.[556]

7:55 AM (1:25 PM EST) NAS Kaneohe, Wheeler and Hickam Fields are attacked. The official time of the Pearl Harbor attack is set as 7:55 AM.

7:58 AM (1:28 PM EST) Cdr. Logan Ramsey instructs his radioman to send out in plain English, "Air Raid, Pearl Harbor. This is not a drill." (Prange, et al., 517)

8:00 AM (1:30 PM EST) Japan attacks Thailand. Five hours later Thailand requests a cease fire. Because Thailand is west of the International Date Line, the official date is 8 December.

8:00 AM (1:30 PM EST) B-17 Flying Fortresses from the mainland dodge Japanese and friendly fire on Oahu, as do the planes arriving from the carrier *Enterprise.*

8:03 AM (1:33 PM EST) George Street receives a call at home from William Steed at RCA-Honolulu. Steed informs him of the attack and requests instructions.

8:04 AM (1:34 PM EST) Radio KGMB disc jockey, Webley Edwards announces, "Attention, this is no exercise. The Japanese are attacking Pearl Harbor. All Army, Navy and Marine personnel are to report for duty." (Allen, 25) (Shirley, 139)

~ 8:05 AM (1:35 PM EST) Barbara Street gets on a bus to downtown Honolulu.

8:10 AM (1:30 PM EST) USS *Arizona* takes first hit and sinks in nine minutes. George Jr. startled awake.

8:10 AM (1:30 PM EST) General Short moves to Alert Level Three status. (Prange, et al., 525)

8:11 AM (1:31 PM EST) George Street dictates a message regarding the attack for RCA-Honolulu to send to RCA-New York and news agencies.

~ 8:15 AM (1:45 PM EST) George Jr. sees a dogfight above Hunakai Beach.

8:15 AM (1:45 PM EST) Messenger boy Tadao Fuchikami arrives at RCA Honolulu office.

~8:15–8:30 AM (1:45–2:00 PM EST) Street says RCA deliveries must go out.

8:17 AM (1:47 PM EST) USS *Helm* attacks two-man Japanese sub.

8:17 AM (1:47 PM EST) FDR learns of the Pearl Harbor attack, approximately twenty-seven minutes after the attack begins.

~ **8:20** AM (1:50 PM EST) Secretary Knox in D.C. receives a message from Admiral Kimmel, "Air raid on Pearl Harbor. This is not a drill." (Congress, Summary Report, 439)

8:30 AM (2:00 PM EST) FDR calls Secretary Knox for confirmation.

8:36 AM (2:09 PM EST) Seaplane tender USS *Curtiss* (AV-4) fires a 5-inch round at surfaced mini-submarine *I-22tou,* decapitating Lt. Naoji Iwasa.[557]

8:40 AM (2:10 PM EST) RCA messenger Fuchikami departs RCA with Radiogram 1549 and others.

~**8:45** AM (2:15 PM EST) First wave of Japanese aircraft returns to carriers, having inflicted ninety percent of damage to Pearl.

~**8:45** AM (2:15 PM EST) George Jr. returns home and turns on radio KGU.

8:50 AM (2:20 PM EST) USS *Nevada* heads to sea and is bombed by pilots of the second wave of Japanese planes, who hope to block the harbor with *Nevada.* Japanese encounter heavy anti-aircraft fire.

8:50 AM (2:20 PM EST) Japan's ambassadors, unaware of the attack, present the fourteen-part message to Secretary Hull, missing the 1:00 deadline set by Tokyo by an hour and twenty minutes.

~**8:50** AM (2:20 PM EST) George Jr. departs for his block warden meeting.

8:52 AM (2:22 PM EST). The White House delivers its first press release regarding the bombing.

8:54 AM (2:24 PM EST) Second wave of Japanese aircraft attacks Pearl Harbor.

~**9:15** AM (2:45 PM EST) Governor Poindexter of Honolulu is on the phone with FDR when a bomb drops in front of the Governor's mansion and kills one man.

9:30 AM (3:00 PM EST) USS *Shaw* explodes.

9:30 AM (3:00 PM EST) Japan attacks Singapore.

9:30 AM (3:00 PM EST) FDR meets with advisors and receives damage reports.

~ **9:40 – 10:15** AM (3:10 PM EST) RCA messenger Tadao Fuchikami delivers Radiogram 1549 to Fort Shafter. Corporal Stevens initials but does not time stamp it or the other messages delivered with Radiogram 1549.

~**9:45 – 10:00** AM (3:15 PM EST) The second wave of Japanese aircraft returns to carriers (Allen, 18)

10:10 AM (3:40 PM EST) Japan attacks British Malaya.

11:19 AM (4:49 PM EST) RCA-Honolulu receives the first servicegram requesting information about the delivery of Radiogram 1549. Office manager Sue Sharp investigates.

11:41 AM (5:11 PM EST) U.S. Army orders broadcasting stations off the air (Allen, 26)

11:45 AM (5:15 PM EST) Radiogram 1549's stated delivery time in the *Congressional Record* which is probably when Cpl. Stevens requested its decoding.

1:00 PM (6:30 PM EST) Japan calls off the third wave of attack planes.

1:00 PM (6:30 PM EST) Adm. Layton and others learn that Singapore, Hong Kong, Guam, Philippines have been attacked. (Layton, et al., 322)

2:17 PM (7:47 PM EST) RCA-SF sends a second request asking for information about the delivery of Radiogram 1549.

2:43 PM (8:13 PM EST) RCAs office manager, Sue Sharp, sends a servicegram indicating that Radiogram 1549 was signed by Stevens at 9:00 AM.

2:58 PM (8:18 PM EST) Radiogram 1549 is delivered to Short's adjutant general, Colonel Dunlop. (Prange, et al., 567).

~3:45 PM (9:15 PM EST) Radiogram 1549 decoded (Layton, et al., 320) [Layton indicated that it was decoded four hours after receipt, based on receipt time of 11:45 AM.]

4:00 PM (9:30 PM EST) General Short receives decoded message [~ 9.5 hrs. after it was receipted by French in the Signal Corps]. Shortly thereafter Adm. Kimmel receives his copy and throws it into the trash can. (Layton, et al., p 321)

~5:00 PM (10:30 PM EST) George Jr. returns home to find his father having a medical emergency.

~ **6:30** PM (12:00 AM EST) George Jr., departs to black out windows at RCA-Honolulu.

~ **7:00** PM (12:30 AM EST) RCA-Honolulu shut down by the Army.

~ **9:15** PM (2:45 AM EST) George Jr. witnesses friendly fire on planes from USS *Enterprise.*

8 December 1941

~**5:00** AM (10:30 AM EST) George Jr. and Mac are startled awake by the sound of heavy arms fire from Fort Ruger.

~ **6:00** AM (11:30 PM EST) George Jr. returns home on a blown tire.

~ **7:00** AM (12:30 PM EST) FDR's "Day of Infamy" speech is broadcast.

7:35 AM (1:05 PM EST) RCA-Honolulu receives a servicegram from RCA-San Francisco asking them to explain the delay of Radiogram 1549's delivery.

9 December 1941

George Street and George Jr. receive their safe conduct passes when RCA is allowed to resume operations.

11:24 AM (4:54 PM EST) Servicegram to RCA-Honolulu from RCA-SF references requests from Western Union, RCA-New York, and War Department regarding the delayed delivery of Radiogram 1549.

12:21 AM (5:51 PM EST) Delivery details of Radiogram 1549 sent to RCA-SF by George Street.

12 December 1941

12:45 PM (6:15 PM EST) A series of servicegrams from the Army chief of staff and RCA-New York's general manager asks for details regarding the delivery of Radiogram 1549, and why the tie-line was not in operation.

18 December 1941

RCA-Honolulu receives a servicegram from the general manager of RCA-NY commending the staff on a job well done.

22 December 1941

RCA-Honolulu receives a servicegram from RCA New York stating that the War Department is asking why Radiogram 1549, received at 7:33 AM, 7 December, was not delivered until 11:45 AM.

23 December 1941

George Street sends a series of servicegrams detailing why the Honolulu office opened at 7 AM Sundays, how Radiogram 1549 was not marked "Rush", and that "C G" was listed as recipient, and how it was not time stamped by the Signal Corps. Street states that the approximate delivery time of Radiogram 1549 was 9:00 AM. He also explains why Honolulu could not go to twenty-four hour service.

26 December 1941

George receives servicegram from RCA's general manager (W.A.
Winterbottom): "Re Shafter Message I feel satisfied with
performance under such dangerous conditions."

Appendix B: Mori Telephone Call
6 December 1941

The initial "J" stands for the person speaking from Japan, "H" for the person speaking from Hawaii, Dr. M. Mori. Transcribed from the Hewitt Inquiry Vol. 36, pages 523-535.

IC (J) Hello, is this Mori?

(H) Hello, this is Mori.

(J) I am sorry to have troubled you. Thank you very much.

(H) Not at all.

(J) I received your telegram and was able to grasp the essential points. I would like to have your impressions of the conditions you are observing at present. Are airplanes flying daily?

(H) Yes, lots of them fly around.

(J) Are they large planes?

(H) Yes, they are quite big.

(J) Are they flying from morning till night?

(H) Well, not to that extent, but last week they were quite active in the air.

(J) I hear there are many sailors there, is that right?

(H) There aren't so many now. There were more in the beginning part of this year and the ending part of last year.

(J) Is that so?

(H) I do not know why this is so, but appears that there are very few sailors here at present.

(J) Are any Japanese people there holding meetings to discuss US – Japanese negotiations being conducted presently?

(H) No, not particularly. The minds of the Japanese here appear calmer than expected. They are getting along harmoniously.

(J) Don't the American community look with suspicion on the Japanese?

(H) Well, we hardly notice any of them looking on us with suspicion. This fact is rather unexpected. We are not hated or despised. The soldiers here and we get along very well. All races are living in harmony. It appears that the people who come here change to feel like the rest of the people here. There are some who say odd things, but these are limited to newcomers from the mainland, and after staying here from three to six months, they too begin to think and feel like the rest of the people in the islands.

(J) That's fine.

(H) Yes, it's fine, but we feel a bit amazed.

(J) Has there been any increase in ..?.. of late? That is, as a result of the current tense situation.

(H) There is nothing which stands out, but the city is enjoying a war building boom.

(J) What do you mean by enjoying a war building boom?

(H) Well, a boom in many fields. Although there is no munitions industry here engaged in by the army, civilian workers are building houses for the army personnel. Most of the work here is directed towards building houses of various sorts. There are not enough carpenters, electricians and plumbers. Students at the High School and University have quit school and are working on these jobs, regardless of the fact that they are unskilled in this work.

(J) Are there many big factories there?

(H) No, there are no factories, but a lot of small buildings of various kinds are being constructed.

(J) Is that so?

(H) It is said that the population of Honolulu has doubled that of last year.

(J) How large is the population?

(H) The population increase is due to the present influx of Army and Navy personnel and workers from the mainland.

(J) What is the population?

(H) About 200,000 to 240,000. Formerly there were about 150,000 people.

(J) What about night time?

(H) There seems to be precautionary measures taken.

(J) What about searchlights?

(H) Well, not much to talk about.

(J) Do they put searchlights on when planes fly about at night?

(H) No.

(J) What about the Honolulu newspapers?

(H) The comments by the papers are pretty bad. They are opposite to the atmosphere pervading the city. I don't know whether the newspaper is supposed to lead the community or not, but they carry headlines pertaining to Japan daily. The main articles concern the US-Japanese conferences.

(J) What kind of impression did Mr. Kurusu make in Hawaii?

(H) A very good one. Mr. Kurusu understands the American mind and he was very adept at answering queries of the press.

(J) Are there any Japanese people there who are planning to evacuate Hawaii?

(H) There are almost none wishing to do that.

(J) What is the climate there now?

(H) These last few days have been very cold with occasional rainfall, a [phenomenon] very rare in Hawaii. Today, the wind is blowing very strongly a very unusual climate.

(J) Is that so?

(H) Here is something interesting. Litvinoff, the Russian ambassador to the United States, arrived here yesterday. I believe he enplaned for the mainland today. He made no statements on any problems.

(J) Did he make any statements concerning the US–Japan question?

(H) No. Not only did he not say anything regarding the US- Japan question, he also did not mention anything pertaining to the Russo-German war. It appears he was ordered by his government not to make any statement.

(J) Well, that means he was very different from Mr. Kurusu.

(H) Yes.

(J) What kind of impression did Litvinoff make?

(H) A very good one here. He impressed the people as being very quiet and a gentleman.

(J) Did he stop at the same hotel as Mr. Kurusu?

(H) Yes, at the Royal Hawaiian Hotel overnight. He has already enplaned for the mainland.

(J) Do you know anything about the United States fleet?

(H) No, I don't know anything about the fleet. Since we try to avoid talking about such matters, we do not know much about the fleet. At any rate, the fleet here seems small. I don't know whether all of the fleet has done this, but it seems that the fleet has left here.

(J) Is that so? What kind of flowers are in bloom in Hawaii at present?

(H) Presently, the flowers in bloom are fewest out of the whole year. However, the hibiscus and the poinsettia are in bloom now.

*(J) Does not seem to know about poinsettias. He admits he doesn't know.

(J) Do you feel any inconvenience there due to the suspension of importation of Japanese goods?

(H) Yes, we feel the inconvenience very much. There are no Japanese soy and many other foodstuffs which come from Japan. Although there are enough foodstuffs (Japanese) left in stock to last until February of next year, at any rate it is a big inconvenience.

(J) What do you lack most?

(H) I believe the soy is what everyone is worried about most. Since the freeze order is in force, the merchants who have been dealing in Japanese goods are having a hard time.

(J) Thanks very much.

(H) By the way, here is something interesting about Hawaii. Liquor sells very fast due to the boom here. The United States, which twenty years ago went under prohibition, is today flooded with liquor. British and French liquors are also being sold. The Japanese merchants, whose business came to a standstill due to the suspension of importation of Japanese goods, engage in liquor manufacture. The rice from the United States is used in brewing Japanese sake here and the sake is exported back to the mainland.

*(H) explains that the Japanese sake brewed in Honolulu is called "Takara-Masamuno"; that a person named Takagishi was the technical expert in charge of the brewing; that said Takagishi is a son-in-law of the Grand Chamberlain Hyakutake, being married to the latter's daughter; and that said Takagishi returned recently to Japan on the Taiyo Maru. He adds that Japanese here and the Americans also drink sake. He informs (J) that Japanese chrysanthemums are in full bloom here and that there are no herring-roe for this year's New Year celebration.

(J) How many first generation Japanese are there in Hawaii according to the last surveys made?

(J) About fifty thousand.

(H) How about the second generation Japanese?

(H) About 120,000 or 130,000.

(J) How many out of this number of second generation Japanese are in the United States Army?

(H) There aren't so many up to the present. About 1,500 have entered the army, and the majority of those who have been drafted into the army are Japanese.

(J) Any first generation Japanese in the Army?

(H) No. They do not draft any first generation Japanese.

(J) Is that right, that there are 1,500 in the army?

(H) Yes, that is true up to the present, but may increase since more will be inducted in January.

(J) Thank you very much.

(H) Not at all. I'm sorry I couldn't be of much use.

(J) Oh no, that was fine. Best regards to your wife.

(H) Wait a moment please?

(J) Thank you.

Acknowledgements

This is a work of nonfiction. As such, every effort has been made by the author to research original material relating to the events: letters and documents retained by George Street, firsthand accounts from his son, George Street, Jr., and his daughter, Barbara Jean (Street) Olsen, newspaper clippings, RCA circulars, transcripts of the eight investigative hearings, and books written by people who were present during the events.

In many cases, I sought at least two confirming references, due to the sensational nature of news reporting at the time, a view shared by FDR when he formally requested that reporters take care that their facts were correct. Themes of other scholarship relating to the Pearl Harbor disaster probe more deeply in some areas than I do in this work. I touched upon them only to shed light on the matrix of my grandfather's story.

Henry C. Clausen, investigator into the handling of intelligence after the Army, Navy, and Roberts hearings were completed, uncovered inconsistencies in the previous hearings. Clausen's book, coauthored with Bruce Lee, became my checkpoint for earlier works. Ladislas Farago, chief of research and planning, Special Warfare Branch of U.S. Naval Intelligence during WWII, compiled extensive research and firsthand interviews with many of the participants, including my grandfather. His book, *The Broken Seal*, originally published in 1967, provided valuable insight into the intelligence field.

I am also indebted to many authors for the wealth of published information about the Pearl Harbor disaster. Roberta Wohlstetter's analysis of the intelligence processes in the 1960s provided me with an in-depth reference.

In my quest for details, people who knew my mother and grandfather enriched the backstory. Peggy (Beers) Cantwell, who worked at RCA with my mother, and Sonja Madera, longtime caregiver and companion for my grandfather in his final years, were able to offer additional insight into his character. My mother's dear friends, Leah Pummel, and Sandi MacDiarmid and my sister, Kathy Klattenhoff, provided confirming insights into my mother's secretive ways. The richness of George Jr.'s narratives, the collective memories of Peggy and Sonja, and my grandfather's letters gave me the backstory that no amount of academic research could have revealed. My appreciation for them all cannot be adequately expressed.

Priceless help from family and friends motivated me throughout this project. Special thanks go to my brother, James R. Olsen, author and former Air Force captain. He spent countless hours assisting with researching, sharing his insights, and contributing valuable background content and writings. My "little brother," Bill Olsen, USN (Retired), guided me through the maze of military jargon and explained how ships get underway.

I would also like to thank several early readers who gave me valuable feedback, including Brenda Gates-Smith, Carla Merrill, and Burt and Carol Douglass. Joyce Kesterson, whose sister was born in a Japanese relocation camp, helped me locate someone who attempted a translation of the Mori radiogram. Unfortunately, time had changed the meaning of several romaji words; so the translation could not be guaranteed. Karen Gilden, a wonderful author in her own right, was the one who looked me in the eye and said, "Why don't you write this book?" She took the time to complete a tedious line and grammar edit of an early draft, as did Linda Weber, a retired paralegal. Special thanks go to my writer's group, *Sisters Write,* for their weekly critique and encouragement. Thanks, also, to Pat March, Colin Lamb, editor Beth Jusino, nonfiction author and editor Jim Barnett, and beta reader Thad Anderson for their honest appraisal of this work. My husband, William Anderson, never gave up on me and was brave enough to say something was irrelevant when it was. I can't thank him enough.

The "Texas Twins and Queens of Commas," Martha Collins and Nancy Glaspie, examined every word I typed, determined to make my draft as close to perfect as possible, and I am so very grateful. I'd also like to thank the Naval Institute for their review, which shaped this final draft. Steffanie Lynch performed a detailed line edit, examining readability and consistency with a fine tooth comb. Jim Lough scrubbed and polished my work, catching text and punctuation errors, questioning prose, formatting inconsistency, and more. I can't thank him enough for lending me his eagle eyes. Any remaining mistakes are mine and mine alone.

My deepest thanks go to the men and women who fought and died and survived Pearl Harbor's disaster. Without their bravery, courage, valor, and sheer strength of will, this story might never have been told. Included in that group is my uncle, George Street, Jr. His firsthand accounts, energizing enthusiasm, and never-ending encouragement inspired me beyond measure. George, you are my hero and will forever remain in my heart.

"Remember Pearl Harbor"

Works Cited

Agawa, Hiroyuki. *The Reluctant Admiral: Yamamoto and the Imperial Navy*. Tokyo: Kodansha International, 2000.

Allen, Gwenfread. *Hawaii's War Years, 1941-1945 (Pacific War Classics)*. Kailua, HI: Pacific Monograph, 1999. State of Hawaii approved version.

Bartlett, Bruce R. *Cover-up: The Politics of Pearl Harbor, 1941-1946*. New Rochelle, NY: Arlington House, 1978. Kindle Edition.

Budiansky, Stephen. *Battle of Wits: The Complete Story of Codebreaking in World War II*. New York: Free Press, 2000.

Burlingame, Burl. *Advance Force Pearl Harbor*. Annapolis, MD: Naval Institute Press, 1992.

Caphin, Helen Geracimos. *Shaping History: The Role of Newspapers in Hawaii*. Honolulu, HI: University of Hawai'i Press, 1996.

Chernin, Ted. "My Experiences in the Honolulu Chinatown Red-Light District." *The Hawaiian Journal of History, vol.34* (2000).

Clarke, Thurston. *Pearl Harbor Ghosts: The Legacy of December 7, 1941*. New York: The Ballantine Publishing Group, 2001. Paperback and Kindle editions.

Clausen, Henry C. and Bruce Lee. *Pearl Harbor: Final Judgement*. New York: Crown Publishing, 1992. First edition.

Coe, Lewis. *Wireless Radio: A History*. Jefferson, NC: McFarland &

Company, Inc., 1996.

Commission on Wartime Relocation and Internment of Civilians. *Personal Justice Denied,* Chapter 11 scanned. *National Archives: Japanese Americans.* December, 1982. https://www.archives.gov/research/japanese-americans/justice-denied/chapter-11.pdf. 4 April 2020.

Craig, David and Shelley Tanaka. *Attack on Pearl Harbor: The True Story of the Day America Entered World War II.* New York: Random House, 2003. Kindle edition.

Cressman, Robert J., Naval Historical Center. *The Official Chronology of the U.S. Navy in World War II, Indexed Edition.* United States: original publisher United States Naval Institute Press 1999, 2016. Uncommon Valor reprint edition.

Einstein, Albert. "Letter to FDR, August 2, 1939." n.d. *FDR Library/Atomic Bomb.* http://fdrlibrary.marist.edu/archives/pdfs/docsworldwar.pdf. 15 May 2020.

Evans, Dr. David C. (Trans./Editor) and Dr. Raymond Gish. *The Japanese Navy in World War II: In the Words of Former Japanese Naval Officers.* Annapolis, MD: Naval Institute Press, 1969. Originally published in *US Naval Institute Proceedings.*

Farago, Ladislas. *The Broken Seal: "Operation Magic" and the Secret Road to Pearl Harbor.* New York: Random House, 1967. Hardcover.

Federal Bureau of Investigations. *Bernard Otto Kuehn.* Case files.

Washington, D.C.: Department of Justice, 2011.

Freidel, Frank. *Franklin D. Roosevelt: A Rendezvous with Destiny.* Boston: Little, Brown and Company, 1990.

Ganske, Richard (2013, December 7) "To You, Our Fallen." *The Strategy Bridge.* https://thestrategybridge.org/the-bridge/2013/12/7/to-you-our-fallen, 7 June 2021.

Gillon, Steven M. *Pearl Harbor: FDR Leads the Nation into War.* New York: Basic Books, 2011.

Gose, Eileen Tannich and Kathy Wiederstein DeHerrera. *Reflecting Freedom: How Fashion Mirrored the Struggle for Women's Rights.* Charleston: Authors, 2017. Paperback.

Gray, R. Jean. Our Man of Peace in a Time of War–SAC Honolulu Robert Shivers during World War II. December 2016. https://fbistudies.com/wp-content/uploads/2016/12/FBI-Grapevine-DEC16-History.pdf. 19 May 2020.

Green, Major General Thomas H. Martial Law In Hawaii December 7, 1941– April 4, 1943. circa 1946. https://www.loc.gov/rr/frd/Military_Law/pdf/Martial-Law_Green.pdf

Hagen, Jerome (1999, December 4) "After a Deadly Day, U.S. Pilots Greeted by a Cloud of Friendly Fire." *Honolulu Star-Bulletin*/newspapers.com/image 273287470, 7 July 2021.

Hanyok, Robert J. and David P. Mowry. "United States Cryptologic History Series IV." 2011 World War II Vol. X National Security Agency. *West Wind Clear: Cryptology and the*

Winds Message Controversy – a Documentary History. https://www.nsa.gov/Portals/70/documents/about/cryptologic-heritage/historical-figures-publications/publications/wwii/west_wind_clear.pdf. 6 April 2020.

Hare, Roger. "They Will Always Be Remembered." 2000. USS *West Virginia.* Http://usswestvirginia.org/stories/story.php?id=23. 16 May 2020.

Honey, Maureen. *Creating Rosie the Riveter: Class, Gender, and Propaganda during World War II.* Amherst, MA: The University of Massachusetts Press, 1984.

Horodysky, T. *American Merchant Marine at War: U.S. Merchant Ships Sunk or Damaged in World War II.* 21 January 2004. http://www.usmm.org/shipsunkdamaged.html. 2 April 2020.

Hotta, Eri. *Japan 1941: Countdown to Infamy.* New York: Alfred A. Knopf, 2013.

Isonaga, Sue. "Sue Isonaga's Story" 2006. *The Hawai'i Nisei Story: Americans of Japanese Ancestry During WWII.* http://nisei.hawaii.edu/page/sue.html. 2 February 2017.

Johnson, Chalmers A. *An Instance of Treason: Ozaki Hotsumi and the Sorge Spy Ring.* Stanford, CA, 1990. Second edition.

Kerber, Linda K, Jane Sherron De Hart, Cornelia Hughes Dayton, and Judy Tzu-Chug Wu. *Women's America: Refocusing the Past.* New York: Oxford University Press, 2016.

Kern, Gary. How Uncle Joe Bugged FDR: Historical Document. 14 April 2007. https://www.cia.gov/library/center-for-the-study-of-intelligence/csi-publications/csi-studies/studies/vol47no1/article02.html. 15 May 2020.

Layton USN (Ret.), Rear Admiral Edwin T., Captain Roger Pineau, USNR (Ret.) and John Costello. *"And I Was There": Pearl Harbor and Midway – Breaking the Secrets*. Old Saybrook, CT: Konecky & Konecky, 1985.

Limon, Peter T. and Natalie Meehan. *A Pearl Harbor Survivor's Expose on Pride, Prejudice and Prostitutes*. Authors, 2015.

Lord, Walter. *Day of Infamy*. New York: Henry Holt and Company, 1985. Sixtieth Anniversary edition.

Lyons, Eugene. *David Sarnoff; A Biography*. New York: Harper & Row, 1966.

Marshall, George Catlett. *The Papers of George Catlett Marshall*. Baltimore, MD: Johns Hopkins University Press, 1986. Six volumes.

Martin, F.L. and P.N.L. Bellinger. *A Joint Estimate Covering Joint Army and Navy Air Action in the Event of Sudden Hostile Action Against Oahu or Fleet Units in the Hawaiian Area*. Exhibit 21. Washington, D.C. Library of Congress: U.S. Congress, Hart Inquiry, March 1941.

Masatake, Okumiya, with Martin Caiden. *Zero!* New York: Ballantine Books, 1956.

McWilliams, Bill. *Sunday in Hell: Pearl Harbor, Minute by Minute*. New York: E-Reads/E-Rights, Ltd. Publishers, 2011. Paperback.

Morgenthau, Henry. "Transcript of Telephone Call between FDR and

Treasury Secretary Henry Morgenthau, Jr." 7 December 1941. *Franklin D. Roosevelt Day by Day.* http://www.fdrlibrary.marist.edu/daybyday/resource/16386/. 19 May 2020.

Morison, Samuel Eliot. *The Rising Sun in the Pacific, 1931- April 1942: History of the United States Naval Operations in World War II.* Boston, MA: Little, Brown and Company, 1984. Volume three of fifteen volumes.

Mosley, Leonard. *Hirohito: Emperor of Japan.* London: Weidenfeld and Nicolson, 1966.

Mundy, Liza. *Code Girls: The Untold Story of the American Women Code Breakers of World War II.* New York: Hachette Books, 2017.

National Park Service. Yosemite's World War II Hospital. n.d. https://www.nps.gov/articles/yosemitehospitalwwii.htm. 27 July 2018.

Nelson, Craig. *Pearl Harbor: From Infamy to Greatness.* New York: Scribner, 2016.

Odo, Franklin. *No Sword to Bury: Japanese Americans in Hawai'i during World War II.* Philadelphia, PA: Temple University Press, 2004. Kindle edition.

Ogawa, Dennis M. and Evart C. Fox, Jr. "Japanese American Internment Unit for Modern History of Hawai'i." 2008. *Hawaii Internment: the Untold Story.* Japanese Cultural Center of Hawai'i.

http://hawaiiinternment.org/sites/default/files/Modern%20Hist ory%20of%20Hawaii_0.pdf. 3 March 2018.

O'Hara, Jean. *Honolulu Harlot.* RCT Publishing, 2016.

Ohira, Rod. "Natsunoya Tea House Banquet Room." n.d. *History.* http://www.natsunoyahawaii.com/about-us/history. 18 April 2017.

Olsen, Barbara Jean [Street]. *"Collected Works."* unpublished, 1941-2012.

Olson, Wyatt for *Stars and Stripes.* "'2nd Pearl Harbor,' kept top secret until 1962, commemorated." 21 May 2016. https://www.stripes.com/news/2nd-pearl-harbor-kept-top-secret-until-1962-commemorated-1.410773. 20 May 2020.

Panko, R. "Pearl Harbor VF-6; The Deadly Night of December 7 1941." 14 January 2013. *Pearl Harbor Aviation Museum.* https://www.pearlharboraviationmuseum.org/blog/vf-6-the-deadly-night-of-december-7-1941/. 30 March 2018.

Parker, Frederick D. *"Pearl Harbor Revisited: United States Navy Communications Intelligence 1924-1941."* United States Cryptologic History, Series IV World War II Volume 6. Center For Cryptologic History: National Security Agency, 1994. 97.

Prange, Gordon W., Donald M. Goldstein, and Kathrine V. Dillon. *Miracle of Midway.* New York: Penguin Books, 1982. Kindle edition.

Prange, Gordon W., Donald M. Goldstein, and Katherine V. Dillon. *At Dawn We Slept: The Untold Story of Pearl Harbor.* New

York: McGraw-Hill, 1981.

Repplin, J. "1941 Pearl Harbor Willamette Football Team." 17 December 2015. *Willamette University Hatfield Library News.* http://library.willamette.edu/wordpress/blog/2015/12/17/1941-pearl-harbor-willamette-football-team/. 20 May 2020.

Rodriggs, Lawrence Reginald. *We Remember Pearl Harbor!* Newark, CA: Communications Concepts, 1991.

Rottman, Gordon L. *SNAFU: Situation Normal All F***ed Up: Sailor, Airman, and Soldier Slang of World War II.* Oxford: Osprey Publishing, 2014. Dictionary.

Rupp, Leila J. *Mobilizing Women for War: German and American Propaganda, 1939-1945.* Princeton, NJ: Princeton University Press, 1978.

Schreiber, Mark. "Japan Reconsiders and Reinterprets the Pearl Harbor Attack." 24 December 2016. *Japan Times.* https://www.japantimes.co.jp/news/2016/12/24/national/media-national/japan-reconsiders-reinterprets-pearl-harbor-attack/#.WqvqbmbMz0A. 16 March 2018.

Shinsato, Douglas T. and Tadanori Urabe. *For That One Day: The Memoirs of Mitsuo Fuchida, Commander of the Attack on Pearl Harbor.* Kamuela, HI: eXperience, Inc., 2011. Kindle edition.

Shirley, Craig. *December 1941: 31 Days That Changed America and Saved the World.* Nashville, TN: Nelson Books, 2013.

Shivers, Robert L. *Cooperation of the Various Racial Groups with*

Each Other and the Constituted Authorities Before and After December 7 1941. Presented in 1946. Honolulu, Hawaii: out of print, 1946.

Slone, Robert. "Vol. 53 No.12." *Paradise of the Pacific* December 1941. Magazine.

Socota, Vic. "06 Jun Station HYPO Tour!" 21 May 2016. *Naval Intelligence Professionals.* https://navintpro.org/news/2016/05/21/06-jun-station-hypo-tour!/. 26 September 2017.

Soga, Yasutaro. *Life Behind Barbed Wire: The World War II Internment Memoirs of a Hawaii Issei*. Honolulu: University of Hawaii Press, 2008.

Soria, Harry B., Jr. "'The Lost Tapes': My Father's Secret Pearl Harbor Mission." 7 December 2016. *The Daily Beast.* https://www.thedailybeast.com/the-lost-tapes-my-fathers-top-secret-pearl-harbor-mission?ref=scroll. 24 February 2018.

Staff. *Arlington County, VA Weather History*. 5 November 2019. https://www.wunderground.com/history/daily/KDCA/date/19 41-10-17. 20 May 2020.

Sterling, George E. "The History of the Radio Intelligence Division Before and During World War II, 1940-1945." FCC Commissioner. *A Collection of Articles and Manuscripts of George E. Sterling, Chief Radio Intelligence Division (1940-1946).* http://users.isp.com/danflan/sterling/ridhist.pdf. 02 February 2017.

Stinnett, Robert B. *Day of Deceit: The Truth about FDR and Pearl*

Harbor. New York: Free Press, 2000.

Street, George. "George Street Archives." unpublished, 1898-1995. Archived by the author.

Street, George Jr., Valarie J. Anderson, and Patricia March. *A Compendium of the Life and Times of George Street Sr.* Sisters, OR: unpublished, 2013. Softcover.

Stuppy, Mary. Letter to her mother, Popsie, and Marie, dated Sunday, December 7, 1941 with permission from her daughter, B. J. Pike, Los Angeles, CA, unpublished.

Summerland Amateur Radio Club. "Radiotelegraph and Radiotelephone Codes, Prowords and Abbreviations (Third Edition)." 2002. https://books.google.com/books?id=e0IKBgAAQBAJ&prints ec=frontcover&source=gbs_ge_summary_r&cad=0#v=onepa ge&q&f=false. 15 May 2020.

The National WWII Museum. "Remembering Pearl Harbor." *A Pearl Harbor Fact Sheet*. New Orleans, LA: the National WWII Museum, 7 December 2001. https://www.census.gov/history/pdf/pearl-harbor-fact-sheet-1.pdf. 15 May 2020.

Theobald, Robert A. *The Final Secret of Pearl Harbor: The Washington Contribution to the Japanese Attack*. New York: Devin-Adair, 1954.

Thomas, Rhys. *Hotel Street Harry*. United States: RCT Publishing, 2016.

Todd, George P. "Early Radio Communications in the Fourteenth Naval District, Pearl Harbor, Territory of Hawaii." 1985. *Navy Radio.* http://www.navy-radio.com/commsta/todd-hawaii-01.pdf. 2 February 2020.

Toll, Ian W. *Pacific Crucible: War at Sea in the Pacific 1941-1942.* New York: W.W. Norton, 2012.

Tomokiyo, S. *Development of the First Japanese Cipher Machine: RED.*27 March 2014. http://cryptiana.web.fc2.com/code/redciphermachine.htm. 20 May 2020.

U.S. Congress. "Hearings Before the Joint Committee on the Investigation of the Pearl Harbor Attack. *By 96th Congress, 1st Session.* Washington, D.C.: Library of Congress, 1946. Cited as PHH.

U.S. Congress, 77th Congress, Senate Commission. *Document No 159: Attack Upon Pearl Harbor by Japanese Armed Forces.* Washington, D.C.: U.S. Congress, 1942. http://www.ibiblio.org/pha/pha/roberts/roberts.html.7 July 2018.

U.S. Congress, 79th Congress, *Summary Report of the Joint Committee on the Investigation of the Pearl Harbor Attack.* New York: De Capo Press, 1972. cited as Congress, Summary Report.

Unger, Debi, Irwin Unger, and Stanley Hirshson. *George Marshall: A Biography.* New York, NY: HarperCollins Publishers, 2014.

Victor, George. *The Pearl Harbor Myth: Rethinking the Unthinkable.* Washington, D.C.: Potomac Books, 2007.

Volkman, Ernest. *Espionage: The Greatest Spy Operations of the 20th Century.* New York: John Wiley & Sons, Inc, 1995.

Webber, Bert. *Retaliation: Japanese Attacks and Allied Countermeasures on the Pacific Coast in World War II.* Albany, OR: Oregon State University Press, 1975.

Weintraub, Stanley. *Pearl Harbor Christmas: A World at War, December 1941.* Cambridge, MA: De Capo Press, 2011.

West, Rodney T. *Honolulu Prepares for Japan's Attack: The Oahu Civilian Disaster Preparedness Programs May 15, 1940 to December 8, 1941.* Honolulu, HI: Author, 2003.

Whitehead, Don. *The FBI Story: A Report to the People.* New York: Random House, Inc., 1956.

Widner, James F. "Bombing of Pearl Harbor." 5 July 2000. *Radio Days.* http://www.otr.com/r-a-i-new_pearl.shtml. 6 April 2020.

Willmot, H. P., Haruo Tohmatsu, and W. Spencer Johnson. *Pearl Harbor.* London: Cassell, 2011.

Wohlstetter, Roberta. *Pearl Harbor: Warning and Decision.* Stanford, CA: Stanford University Press, 1962.

Wortman, Marc. *1941: Fighting the Shadow War: A Divided America in a World at War.* New York: Atlantic Monthly Press, 2017.

Yardley, Herbert O. *The American Black Chamber.* New York: Ballantine Books, 1981 reprint. Paperback.

Yoshikawa, Takeo and Norman Sanford. "Top Secret Assignment. 1960 December." *US Naval Institute Proceedings Magazine.* https://www.usni.org/document/yoshikawa-takeo-and-norman-stanford-1960-86-12-694?magazine_article=7893. 16 March 2018.

Index

Notes

Prologue: Japanese Imperial Year 2591
[1]Yardley, *The American Black Chamber*, 187-207.
[2]Tomokiyo, *Development of the First Japanese Cipher Machine: RED*.
[3]Parker, *Pearl Harbor Revisited: United States Navy Communications Intelligence, 1924-1941*, 45, declassified 12-01-2011.
[4]Budiansky, *Battle of Wits: The Complete Story of Codebreaking in World War II*.
[5]Mundy, *Code Girls: The Untold Story of the American Women Code Breakers of World War II*, 99.
[6]Clausen and Lee, *Pearl Harbor: Final Judgement*, 46.
[7]Layton, et al., "And I Was There," Pearl Harbor and Midway Breaking the Secrets, *81*; Farago, *The Broken Seal: "Operation Magic" and the Secret Road to Pearl Harbor*, 101.
[8]Farago, *The Broken Seal: "Operation Magic" and the Secret Road to Pearl Harbor*, 108.
[9]Clausen and Lee, *Pearl Harbor: Final Judgement, 44-46*.

Chapter 1: Purple Haze
[10]*The Honolulu Star-Bulletin*, 25 March 1938.
[11]George Street Archives, Binder 2, Section 1938, page 10b.
[12]Todd, *Early Radio Communications in the Fourteenth Naval District, Pearl Harbor, Territory of Hawaii*.
[13]*Farago, The Broken Seal: "Operation Magic" and the Secret Road to Pearl Harbor*, 35.
[14]George Street Jr., Interview 20 July 2019.
[15]George Street Archives, Letter to George Jr., dated 2 February 1975.
[16]Ibid, Letter to Barbara [Street] Olsen, dated 31 December 1972.
[17]Ibid, Letter to George Jr., dated 7 March 1964.
[18]Ibid, Divorce Decree, dated 14 October 1941.
[19]Ibid, Letter from Shecklen, dated 12 April 1931.
[20]Interview George Street, Jr., 20 July 2019.

Chapter 2: The Need to Know
[21]Kern, *How Uncle Joe Bugged FDR: Historical Document*.
[22]Lyons, *David Sarnoff: A Biography*, 180.

[23]Freidel, *Franklin D. Roosevelt: A Rendezvous with Destiny*, 17.

[24]Lyons, *David Sarnoff: A Biography*, 86.

[25]Ibid, 176, 224.

[26]Freidel, *Franklin D. Roosevelt: A Rendezvous with Destiny*, 393.

[27]Layton, et al., *"And I Was There," Pearl Harbor and Midway-Breaking the Secrets*, 117; Clausen and Lee, *Harbor: Final Judgment*, 46;Wohlstetter, *Pearl Harbor: Warning and Decision*, 176 footnote.

[28]Layton et al., *"And I Was There," Pearl Harbor and Midway-Breaking the Secrets*, 27.

[29]Budiansk, *Battle of Wits: The Complete Story of Codebreaking in World War II.*

[30]Staff, *Arlington County, VA Weather History.*

[31]Stinnett, *Day of Deceit: The Truth about FDR and Pearl Harbor*, 105; PHH, Vol 20, 4468; "FDR: Day by Day." – Date of luncheon confirmed in White house Usher book.

Chapter 3: Sitting Duck

[32]Wohlstetter, *Pearl Harbor: Warning and Decision*, 28-29.

[33]Martin and Bellinger, *A Joint Estimate Covering Joint Army and Navy Air Action in the Event of Sudden Hostile Action Against Oahu or Fleet Units in the Hawaiian Area, March 31, 1941.*

[34]Sterling, *The History of the Radio Intelligence Division Before and During World War II, 1940-1945 – A Collection of articles and manuscripts of George E. Sterling, Chief, Radio Intelligence Division, (1940-1946), FCC Commissioner, (1948-1954)*, 7.

[35]Prange, et al., *At Dawn We Slept: The Untold Story of Pearl Harbor*, 78.

[36]George Street Archives, Binder 6, p. 77, Attachment (a) to Letter to Ladislas Farago, dated 14 February 1968.

[37]PHH, Vol. 36, 478.

[38]George Street Archives, Binder 5, page 86, Editorial remarks addressed to Ladislas Farago, dated 14 February 1968.

[39]Ibid, Appointment certificate, signed by Secretary of the Navy Curtis D. Wilbur, 21 November 1927.

[40]Ibid, Letter from the Navy Department, signed C.W. Nimitz Chief of Bureau by direction, dated 12 December 1941.

[41]Prange, et al., *At Dawn We Slept: The Untold Story of Pearl Harbor*, 79.

[42]George Street Archives, Binder 5, page 77; Attachment (a) of Letter to Ladislas Farago, dated 14 February 1968.

[43]Ibid, 76; Attachment (a) of Letter to Ladislas Farago, dated 14 February 1968.

[44]Ibid.

[45]Ibid.

[46]Ibid.

[47]Ibid.

[48]"HYPO" was the U.S. military's phonetic radio code for the letter "H." Later it changed to "How." Now it is "Hotel."

[49]Wohlstetter, *Pearl Harbor: Warning and Decision,* 33.

[50]Socota, Vic. "06 JUN Station HYPO Tour!"

[51]Layton, et al., *"And I Was There," Pearl Harbor and Midway-Breaking the Secrets,* 93; Farago, *The Broken Seal: "Operation Magic" and the Secret Road to Pearl Harbor,* 227; PHH, Vol. 39, 453.

Chapter 4: Mending Fences

[52]George Street Archives, Undated newspaper clipping.

[53]*Honolulu Star-Bulletin,* 15 November, 1941, photo caption.

[54]Ibid.

[55]Nelson, *Pearl Harbor: From Infamy to Greatness,* 15.

[56]Gray, *Our Man of Peace in a Time of War – SAC Honolulu Robert Shivers during World War II,* 2.

[57]Ibid, 5.

[58]Wohlstetter, *Pearl Harbor: Warning and Decision,* 30.

[59]Ibid; Prange, et al., *At Dawn We Slept: The Untold Story of Pearl Harbor,* 80.

[60]Wohlstetter, *Pearl Harbor: Warning and Decision,* 34.

[61]PHH, Part 8, 3455; Wohlstetter, *Pearl Harbor: Warning and Decision,* 25.

[62]Wohlstetter, *Pearl Harbor: Warning and Decision,* 280-285; O'Donnell, *Operatives, Spies, and Saboteurs.*

[63]Clausen and Lee, *Pearl Harbor: Final Judgement,* 47, with permission.

Chapter 5: Preparing for War

[64]Farago, *The Broken Seal: "Operation Magic" and the Secret Road to Pearl Harbor,* 227.

[65]Ibid, 227.

[66] Allen, *Hawaii's War Years,* 85.

[67] West, *Honolulu Prepares for Japan's Attack: The Oahu Civilian Disaster Preparedness Programs May 15, 1940 to December 8, 1941,* 22.

[68] *Honolulu Star-Bulletin,* 19 March, 1941.

[69] Allen, *Hawaii's War Years,* 88.

[70] Ibid, 166.

[71] {Pistols} *The Honolulu Advertiser,* 10 Jun 1941, 4; {Ration cards} Ibid., 8 July 1941; {86,000 homes} Ibid., 23 May 1941; {Defense plan} Ibid., 9 July 1941.

[72] West, *Honolulu Prepares for Japan's Attack: The Oahu Civilian Disaster Preparedness Programs May 15, 1940 to December 8, 1941,* 34.

[73] Allen, *Hawaii's War Years,* 91.

[74] Sloane, Robert. *Paradise of the Pacific,* Vol. 53, No, 12, December 1941. (Publication prepared prior to Dec. 7).

[75] Barbara [Street] Olsen, 2010 interview.

[76] 1941-42 *The Roundup* Roosevelt High School yearbook, annotated picture, 53.

[77] Barbara [Street] Olsen, 2010 interview.

[78] Allen, *Hawaii's War Years,* 95-96.

[79] Ibid, 100.

[80] Ibid, 97.

[81] Street Jr., Anderson, March *A Compendium of the Life and Times of George Street Sr.,* 163.

Chapter 6: Inside Outside

[82] Farago, *The Broken Seal: "Operation Magic" and the Secret Road to Pearl Harbor,* 155.

[83] Prange, et al., *At Dawn We Slept: The Untold Story of Pearl Harbor,* 73.

[84] Farago, *The Broken Seal: "Operation Magic" and the Secret Road to Pearl Harbor,* 143.

[85] Ibid.

[86] Congress, *Summary Report,* 148.

[87] Ibid, 149.

[88] The Shincho-ro tea house is now the Natunoya Tea House, the last remaining full-time tea house in Hawaii.

[89]Farago, *The Broken Seal: "Operation Magic" and the Secret Road to Pearl Harbor*, 157.

[90]Prange, et al., *At Dawn We Slept: The Untold Story of Pearl Harbor*, 75.

[91]Ohira, *Natsunoya Tea House Banquet Room*.

[92]Prange, et al., *At Dawn We Slept: The Untold Story of Pearl Harbor*, 148.

[93]Volkman, *Espionage: The Greatest Spy Operation of the 20th Century*, 183.

[94]Ibid, 185.

[95]Prange, et al., *At Dawn We Slept: The Untold Story of Pearl Harbor*, 155.

[96]Farago, *The Broken Seal: "Operation Magic" and the Secret Road to Pearl Harbor*, 239.

[97]Congress, *Summary Report*, Minority View, 22.

[98]Farago, *The Broken Seal: "Operation Magic" and the Secret Road to Pearl Harbor*, 225.

[99]Ibid, 229.

[100]Layton, et al., *"And I Was There," Pearl Harbor and Midway-Breaking the Secrets*, 164.

[101]Ibid.

[102]Farago, *The Broken Seal: "Operation Magic" and the Secret Road to Pearl Harbor*, 233.

[103]Johnson, *An Instance of Treason: Ozaki Hotsumi and the Sorge Spy Ring*, 179. Author's note: Konoe is also spelled Konoye.

[104]Hotta, *Japan 1941: Countdown to Infamy*, 214.

[105]Nelson, *Pearl Harbor: From Infamy to Greatness*, 121.

Chapter 7: Signals in the Night
[106]Farago, *The Broken Seal: "Operation Magic" and the Secret Road to Pearl Harbor*,153.

[107]Kuehn's FBI, File # 65-1574 dated 9-20-1941, 4.

[108]Layton, et al., *"And I Was There," Pearl Harbor and Midway-Breaking the Secrets*,175.

[109]The date of the exchange could have been 18, 25, or 28th October.

[110] Kuehn's FBI File number 65-1574, summary, 27.

[111]Prange, et al., *At Dawn We Slept: The Untold Story of Pearl Harbor*, 311;* Kuehn's FBI file no. 65-414, dated 1-15-42, 3.

[112]Farago, *The Broken Seal: "Operation Magic" and the Secret Road to Pearl Harbor*, 243.

[113]Ibid, 244.

[114]FBI file number 1574, summary, 301.

[115]Barbara [Street] Olsen, 2010 interview.

[116]Ibid.

Chapter 8: The World Turns Gray

[117]*Honolulu Star-Bulletin*, 5 November 1941.

[118]Farago, *The Broken Seal: "Operation Magic" and the Secret Road to Pearl Harbor*, 245.

[119]George Street Archives, Binder 6, page 82, Addendum Item 3, page 4 of Letter to Ladislas Farago dated 14 February 1968.

[120]Ibid.

[121]Ibid, {Entire conversation}

[122]Farago, *Broken Seal: "Operation Magic" and the Secret Road to Pearl Harbor*, 247.

[123] PHH, Vol. 36, 478.

[124]*Honolulu Star-Bulletin*, 6 November 1941, 21.

[125]Ibid.

[126]Ibid, 2.

[127]*The Honolulu Advertiser*, 14 November 1941, 2.

[128]George Street Archives, Binder 6, p. 76, Attachment (a) to Letter to Ladislas Farago, dated 14 February 1968.

[129]Ibid, 64, "Remarks regarding Theobald's book," undated.

[130]*Honolulu Star-Bulletin*, 15 November 1941, 3.

[131]George Street Archives, Binder 6, p. 77. Attachment to Letter addressed to Ladislas Farago, dated 14 February 1968.

[132]*Honolulu Star-Bulletin*, 14 November 1941.

Chapter 9: East with the Wind

[133]*The Honolulu Advertiser*, 13 November 1941.

[134]Marshall, *The Papers of George Catlett Marshall, Vol 2*, 677-678.

[135]Farago, *The Broken Seal: "Operation Magic" and the Secret Road to Pearl Harbor*, 275.

[136]Ibid, 276.

[137]George Street Archives, Binder 5 p. 64, Remarks re Theobald's book dated 9 January 1963.

[138]PHH, Vol. 36, 324.

[139]{Entire conversation} George Street Archives, Binder 5, p. 77, Attachment (a) p.2 to Letter to Ladislas Farago dated 14 February 1968.

[140]Ibid..

[141]PHH, Appendix E, Document 15, Exhibit 63.

[142]Street, Anderson, March, *A Compendium of the Life and Times of George Street Sr.* , 172.

[143]PHH Vol. 29, 2177; Gillon, *Pearl Harbor: FDR Leads the Nation to War*, 27.

[144]Wohlstetter, *Pearl Harbor: Warning and Decision*, Appendix 403-404.

[145]Ibid.

[146]PHH, Vol. 35, 43-44 Affidavits of Robert L. Shivers.

[147]Isonaga, Sue. "*Sue Isonaga's Story*." 7; Colegrove, "The New Order in East Asia," 17.

[148]*The Honolulu Advertiser*, 30 November 1941; *Hilo Tribune-Herald*, 30 November 1941.

[149]Wohlstetter, *Pearl Harbor: Warning and Decision*, Appendix 404.

Chapter 10: Messages in the Wind

[150]PHH, Vol. 39, 462.

[151]Prange, et al., *At Dawn We Slept: The Untold Story of Pearl Harbor*, 445.

[152]Farago, *The Broken Seal: "Operation Magic" and the Secret Road to Pearl Harbor,* 321.

[153]Ibid, 324.

[154]Clausen and Lee, *Pearl Harbor: Final Judgement*, 68.

[155]Layton, et al., *"And I Was There," Pearl Harbor and Midway-Breaking the Secrets*, 240.

[156]Farago, *The Broken Seal*: "Operation Magic" and the Secret Road to Pearl Harbor, 300.

[157]Layton, et al., *"And I Was There," Pearl Harbor and Midway-Breaking the Secrets*, 277-78.

[158]Ibid, 244.

[159]PHH Vol. 36 (Hewitt Inquiry), 498.

[160]Layton, et al., *"And I Was There," Pearl Harbor and Midway-Breaking the Secrets,* 245.

338

[161]PHH, Vol 35, 43-44. Affidavit of Robert L. Shivers.

[162]Clausen and Lee, *Pearl Harbor: Final Judgement*, 207.

[163]Ibid, Kindle location 1576.

[164]Farago, *The Broken Seal: "Operation Magic" and the Secret Road to Pearl Harbor*, 319.

[165]PHH, Vol. 36, 116-141.

[166]Manly, "FDR War Plans!" *Chicago Tribune*, 4 December 1941.

[167]Prange, et al., *At Dawn We Slept: The Untold Story of Pearl Harbor*, 455.

[168]"Too Much Radio Grounds for Divorce," Associated Press, *Los Angeles Times*, 4 December 1941, Shirley, *December 1941: 31 Days That Changed America and Saved the World*, 85.

[169]*Atlanta Constitution*, "Mrs. Roosevelt Speaks on 'Town Meeting' Show, 4 December 4, 1941; Shirley, *December 1941: 31 Days That Changed America and Saved the World*, 86.

[170]Prange, et al., *At Dawn We Slept: The Untold Story of Pearl Harbor*, 457.

[171]Ibid, 455.

[172]Shirley, *December 1941: 31 Days That Changed America and Saved the World*, 92.

[173]Farago, *The Broken Seal: "Operation Magic" and the Secret Road to Pearl Harbor*, 305.

[174]George Street Archives, Binder 5, p.83, Addendum to Letter to Ladislas Farago dated 14 February 1968.

[175]Ibid.

[176]Ibid.

[177]Ibid, 68, Letter to Ladislas Farago, dated 4 August 1967.

[178]Ibid.

[179]Clarke, *Pearl Harbor Ghosts*, 71; *Honolulu Star-Bulletin*, 5 December 1957.

[180]Layton, et al., *"And I Was There," Pearl Harbor and Midway Breaking the Secrets*, 276-277.

[181]See Appendix B for the complete transcript.

Chapter 11: "Why Don't You Run Along..."

[182]Freidel, *Franklin D. Roosevelt* 402.

[183]Morgenthau, "Transcript of Telephone Call between FDR and Treasury Secretary Henry Morgenthau, Jr."

[184]Einstein, Letter to FDR dated 2 August 1939.

[185]Farago, *The Broken Seal: "Operation Magic" and the Secret Road to Pearl Harbor*, 339.

[186]Prange, et al., *At Dawn We Slept: The Untold Story of Pearl Harbor*, 466.

[187]Farago, *The Broken Seal: "Operation Magic" and the Secret Road to Pearl Harbor*, 336-337.

[188]Ibid, 336.

[189] Layton *et al., "And I Was There," Pearl Harbor and Midway Breaking the Secrets*, 281.

[190]Farago, *The Broken Seal: "Operation Magic" and the Secret Road to Pearl Harbor*, 331-332.

[191]Ibid, 332.

[192]Ibid, 340.

[193]PHH, Vol. 14, 1225-1226; Farago, *The Broken Seal: "Operation Magic" and the Secret Road to Pearl Harbor*, 35; Grew, *Ten Years In Japan,* 488.

[194]Farago, *The Broken Seal: "Operation Magic" and the Secret Road to Pearl Harbor*.

[195]Mosley, *Hirohito: Emperor of Japan,* 264; Prange, et al., *At Dawn We Slept: The Untold Story of Pearl Harbor*, 477, cites Exhibit No. 1225, July 30, 1946, Affidavit of Tateki Shirao.

[196]Mosley, *Hirohito: Emperor of Japan*, 266.

[197]Ibid, 266.

[198]Ibid, 267.

[199]Farago, *The Broken Seal: "Operation Magic" and the Secret Road to Pearl Harbor*, 340; PHH Vol. 36, 533; PHH Vol. 36, 315.

[200]Farago, *The Broken Seal: "Operation Magic" and the Secret Road to Pearl Harbor*, 338-340.

Chapter 12: One Last Day in Paradise

[201]Burlingame, *Advance Force Pearl Harbor,* 129.

[202]Ibid, Figure "Advance Force Submarine Deployment December 7, 1941," 155.

[203]Ibid, *Advance Force Pearl Harbor,* 153.

[204]Repplin, "1941 Pearl Harbor Willamette Football Team."

[205]Lord, *Day of Infamy,* 4.

[206]Clarke, *Pearl Harbor Ghosts*, 84.

[207]Farago, *The Broken Seal: "Operation Magic" and the Secret Road to Pearl Harbor*, 311.

[208]Evans, *The Japanese Navy in World War II: In the Words of Former Japanese Naval Officers,* Chapter 2, "The Air Attack On Pearl Harbor," by Mitsuo Fuchida, 51.

[209]Ibid.

[210]Ibid.

[211]Hare, "They Will Always Be Remembered."

[212]PHH, Vol. 39, 1-21.

[213]Street, Anderson, March, *A Compendium of the Life and Times of George Street Sr.*, 173.

Chapter 13: The Rising Sun

[214]Farago, *The Broken Seal: "Operation Magic" and the Secret Road to Pearl Harbor*, 359.

[215]Ibid, 363.

[216]Ibid, 365.

[217]Ibid, 364.

[218]Ibid, 367.

[219]Ibid, 369.

[220]Shinsato, *For That One Day: The Memoirs of Mitsuo Fuchida, Commander of the Attack on Pearl Harbor,* 85.

[221]Farago, *The Broken Seal: "Operation Magic" and the Secret Road to Pearl Harbor*, 370.

[222]Ibid.

[223]Ibid, 371.

[224]PHH Vol. 27, 107-108.

[225]PHH Vol. 34, 33.

[226]PHH Vol. 27, 114 (Paragraph 110-115); Todd, "Early Radio Communications in the Twelfth Naval District, San Francisco.CA," 18.

[227]PHH Vol. 34, 35; George Street Archives Telegram dated 12 December 1941 from Street to TM at RCA New York; PPH Vol. 40, 225; Farago, *The Broken Seal: "Operation Magic" and the Secret Road to Pearl Harbor,* 367, 371.

[228]PHH Vol. 23, 1103-1104.

[229]George Street Archives, Binder 5, p. 11; Memorandum dated 1 April 1957.

[230]George Jr. Interview 11 July 2015.

[231]George Street Archives, Binder 5, p. 11; Memorandum dated 1 April 1957.

[232]Ibid.

[233]Ibid, Binder 5, page 11a; Memorandum dated 1 April 1957.

[234]Fuchida ordered the repeated transmission of the two-syllable signal (in Wabun code, the Japanese analogue of Morse code), which is best represented in English print by lower-case letters, no commas, and a space between each syllable.

[235]Farago, *The Broken Seal: "Operation Magic" and the Secret Road to Pearl Harbor*, 377.

[236]Ibid, 378.

Chapter 14: Lost in the Rising Sun

[237]Street, Anderson, March, *A Compendium of the Life and Times of George Street Sr.*, 177.

[238]Hanyok, *West Wind Clear: Cryptology and the Winds Message Controversy–a Documentary History*, 81-82; Yoshikawa, "Top Secret Assignment," 38.

[239]George Street Archives, Binder 5, p.87; Letter to Ladislas Farago dated 14 February 1968, page 2.

[240]Ibid.

[241]Ibid, Binder 5, page 88 Letter to Ladislas Farago dated 14 February 1968, page 3.

[242]Street, Anderson, March, *A Compendium of the Life and Times of George Street Sr.*, 176.

[243]Ibid.

[244]George Street, Jr. interview 2019.

[245]Street, Anderson, March, *A Compendium of the Life and Times of George Street Sr.*, 176.

[246]Ibid., 177.

[247]Ibid.

[248]Given the time, there were two possible air combats George Jr. could have witnessed. The first, and least likely, was the arrival of the *Enterprise* SBDs over Barbers Point. Combat was high enough for George Jr. to have seen it, but it was brief, not as George Jr. described. The other was a classic one-on-one dogfight involving Lt. Lew Sanders. George Jr. could have seen combat at 3700 to 4500 feet over

K-bay, 8 miles away, if the fight stayed on his side of the mountain ridge. Researched by James R. Olsen.

[249]Street, Anderson, March, *A Compendium of the Life and Times of George Street Sr.*, 182.

Chapter 15: "I'm no Jap: I'm an American"

[250]Lord, *Day of Infamy*, 73.

[251]Willmott et al., *Pearl Harbor*, 115.

[252]Lord, *Day of Infamy*, 73.

[253]Ibid, 73.

[254]Ibid, 74.

[255]Rodriggs, *We Remember Pearl Harbor!*, 333.

[256]Isonaga, The Hawaii Nisei Story: Americans of Japanese Ancestry During WWII.

[257]Ibid.

[258]Ibid.

[259]Ibid.

[260]Ibid.

[261]*Honolulu Star-Bulletin*, 24 July 1962, 1-B.

[262]*Directory of Honolulu and the Territory of Hawaii.* Vol. 1928-9 XXXV.

[263]Clarke, *Pearl Harbor Ghosts*, 188.

[264]"Radiotelegraph and Radiotelephone Codes, Prowords, and Abbreviations" (Third Edition), 130.

[265]George Street Archives, Binder 5, page 18; typed copy of Fuchikami's handwritten statement.

[266]*The Honolulu Advertiser*, 7 December 1951, 6.

[267]George Street Archives, Binder 5, page 18; typed copy of Fuchikami's handwritten statement.

[268]Ibid, Binder 5, 11a; Letter to Ladislas Farago dated 1 April 1957, page 2.

[269]Ibid, Binder 5, page 68; Letter to Ladislas Farago dated 4 August 1967, page 2.

[270]Ibid, Binder 5 page 24, Servicegram dated 9 December 1941.

[271]George Street Archives, Binder 5, page 18; typed copy of Fuchikami's handwritten statement.

[272]Farago, *The Broken Seal: "Operation Magic" and the Secret Road to Pearl Harbor*, 381.

[273]Letter from Mary Stuppy to her mother, Popsie, and Marie, dated Sunday, December 7, 1941 with permission.

[274]Ibid.

[275]Ganske, "To You, Our Fallen," www.thestrategybridge.org/thebridge/2013/12/7/. accessed 6-7-2021.

[276]"NBC Newsroom Bulletin Pearl Harbor Attack." Aired at 2:29 and 50 seconds EST, December 7, 1941 (Exact Broadcast time from Widner, James F., "Bombing of Pearl Harbor.")

[277]Carol Douglass interview 2019.

[278]Gillon, *Pearl Harbor: FDR Leads the Nation to War*, 82-5.

[279]West, *Honolulu Prepares for Japan's Attack: The Oahu Civilian Disaster Preparedness Programs May 15, 1940, to December 8, 1941*, 55.

[280]Limón, *A Pearl Harbor Survivor's Exposé on Pride, Prejudice and Prostitutes*, Kindle location 325.

[281]Ibid.

[282]George Street, Jr. 20 July 2019 interview.

[283]Allen, *Hawaii's War Years*, 26.

[284]Street, Anderson, March, *A Compendium of the Life and Times of George Street Sr.*, 182.

[285]Ibid., 182-184.

[286]*Honolulu Star-Bulletin* 1st extra–December 7, 1941–replica.

[287]George Street Archives, Binder 5, page 88, Letter to Ladislas Farago dated 14 February 1968 page 3.

[288]Odo, *No Sword to Bury: Japanese Americans in Hawai'i during World War II*, Kindle location 1422.

Chapter 16: JIJAY, Duly Delivered

[289]Wortman, *1941: Fighting the Shadow War: A Divided America in a World at War*, Kindle location 5194.

[290]McWilliams, *Sunday in Hell: Pearl Harbor Minute by Minute*, 584.

[291]Olsen, Barbara Jean [Street], Collected works, unpublished.

[292]Allen, "2nd Extra." *Honolulu Star-Bulletin*, 7 December 1941.

[293]Lord, *Day of Infamy*, 164.

[294]Clarke, *Pearl Harbor Ghosts*, Kindle location 2909.

[295]Yoshikawa "Top Secret Assignment," 38.

[296]Gray, *"Our Man of Peace in Time of War: SAC Honolulu Robert Shivers during World War II,"* 8.

[297]Bicknell "Security Measures in Hawaii During World War II."

[298]"Radiotelegraph and Radiotelephone Codes: Prowords, and Abbreviations" (Third Edition), 113.

[299]George Street Archives, Servicegram A298, 7 December 1941 2:43AM.

[300]Ibid, Binder 5 page 69; Letter to Ladislas Farago dated 4 August 1967, page 2.

[301]*Congressional Record* Summary part 4, page 141.

[302]Prange, et al., *At Dawn We Slept: The Untold Story of Pearl Harbor,* 567.

[303]Ibid, 568.

[304]PHH, Part 35, 212.

[305]Schreiber, "Japan Reconsiders and Reinterprets the Pearl Harbor Attack."; Agawa, *The Reluctant Admiral: Yamamoto and the Imperial Navy,* 260.

[306]Kerber, *Women's America: Refocusing the Past,* 435; Thomas, *Hotel Street Harry,* 50.

[307]Lord, *Day of Infamy,* 182; The Censor's name: Soria, *"'The Lost Tapes': My Fathers Secret Pearl Harbor Mission."*

[308]Lord, *Day of Infamy,* 182.

[309]Ibid.

[310]*Honolulu Star-Bulletin* 3rd extra; December. 7, 1941, replica.

Chapter 17: Roundup

[311]Toll, *Pacific Crucible: War at the Sea in the Pacific 1941-1942,* 7-33.

[312]Shirley, *December 1941: 31 Days That Changed America and Saved the World,* 246.

[313]Gillon, *Pearl Harbor: FDR Leads the Nation to War,* 88.

[314]"Current Events, Episode 11." In *The Pan-American Coffee Bureau Series.* NBC 7 December 1941.

[315]Whitehead, *The FBI Story: A Report to the People,* 183.

[316]"Appendix 5 – Presidential Proclamation 2525 Enemy Aliens." Internment Archives; *An Act Concerning Aliens*; 50 U.S. Code §21.

[317]Soga, *Life Behind Barbed Wire: The World War II Internment Memoirs of a Hawaii Issei,* 39; U.S. Census 1940, Honolulu.

[318]Soga, *Life Behind Barbed Wire: The World War II Internment Memoirs of a Hawaii Issei,* 25.

[319]Ibid, 26.

[320]Ibid, 28.

[321]Ogawa, *"Japanese American Internment Unit For Modern History of Hawai'i,"* 32.

Chapter 18: "When it's Time to Panic, Don't"

[322]Street, Anderson, March, *A Compendium of the Life and Times of George Street Sr.*, 185.

[323]Interview George Street, Jr., 20 July 2019.

[324]Street, Anderson, March, *A Compendium of the Life and Times of George Street Sr.*, 185.

[325]Ibid.

[326]Interview, George Street Jr., 20 July 2019.

[327]Street, Anderson, March, *A Compendium of the Life and Times of George Street Sr.,* 186.

[328]Ibid.

[329]Interview, George Street Jr., 20 July 2019.

[330]Rodriggs, *We Remember Pearl Harbor!,* 10; Bicknell "Security Measures in Hawaii During World War II."

[331]Green, *Martial Law in Hawaii December 7, 1941 - April 4, 1943,* Chapter XII.

[332]Rodriggs, *We Remember Pearl Harbor!,* 9-10; Bicknell, "Security Measures in Hawaii During World War II."; Coe, *Wireless Radio: A History*, 127.

[333]Street, Anderson, March, *A Compendium of the Life and Times of George Street Sr.,* 186.

[334]Panko, "VF-6: The Deadly Night of December 7, 1941."

[335] https://www.pearlharboraviationmuseum.org/blog/vf-6-the-deadly-night-of-december-7-1941/ accessed 7-18-21.

[336] *Honolulu Star-Bulletin*, 4 December 1999, 14.

[337] Ibid.

[338]Rottman, *SNAFU: Situation Normal All F***ed Up: Sailor, Airman, and Soldier Slang of World War II*, 62.

[339]The National WWII Museum, *"Remembering Pearl Harbor Fact Sheet"*; Morison, *The Rising Sun in the Pacific, 1931-April 1942*, Vol.3, 126.

Chapter 19: The Morning After
[340] Street, Anderson, March, *A Compendium of the Life and Times of George Street Sr.*, 187.
[341] Ibid.
[342] Ibid.
[343] Ibid.
[344] Ibid.
[345] Street, Anderson, March, *A Compendium of the Life and Times of George Street Sr.*, 190.
[346] Ibid, 190.
[347] George Street Archives, RCA Relay Magazine, public domain.
[348] Allen, *Hawaii's War Years*, 47.
[349] Ibid, 42.
[350] Ibid.
[351] Lyons, *David Sarnoff: A Biography*, 232.
[352] Ibid, 232-233.
[353] Gillon, *Pearl Harbor: FDR Leads the Nation to War*, 94-97.
[354] "*Wants Truth*," *Vidette-Messenger of Porter County* (Valparaiso, Indiana), 9 December 1941.
[355] "*U.S. Acknowledges Heavy Losses In Pacific Raids*," *The Palm Beach Post* (West Palm Beach, Florida), 9 December 1941.
[356] *Call Knox, Stark for Answers; FDR on Radio Tonight, Vidette-Messenger of Porter County* (Valparaiso, Indiana), 9 December 1941.
[357] Shirley, *December 1941: 31 Days That Changed America and Saved the World*, 202.
[358] "Text of president's address:" *Bernardino Daily Sun*, 10 December 1941, 15.
[359] *Oakland Tribune* (Oakland, Ca), 10 December 1941.
[360] *Ibid*, 9 December 1941, 2.
[361] George Street Archives, Letter to Ladislas Farago dated 4 August 1967.
[362] Barbara [Street] Olsen, interview 2011.

Chapter 20: Shell Shocked

[363]Street, Anderson, March, *A Compendium of the Life and Times of George Street Sr.*, 190.

[364]Layton, et al., *"And I Was There," Pearl Harbor and Midway-Breaking the Secrets,* 330-3.

[365]Ibid, 330.

[366]Layton, et al., *"And I Was There," Pearl Harbor and Midway-Breaking the Secrets,* 331.

[367]*The Baltimore Sun,* (Maryland), 3.

[368]Prange, et al., *At Dawn We Slept,* 588.

[369]Commission on Wartime Relocation and Internment of Civilians; Personal Justice Denied, Chapter 11.

[370]Prange, et al., *At Dawn We Slept: The Untold Story of Pearl Harbor,* 590.

[371]Shirley, *December 1941: 31 Days That Changed America and Saved the World,* 211.

[372]Ibid.

[373]*Daily News* (New York, New York) 11 December 1941, 10.

[374]Caphin, *Shaping History, The Role of Newspapers in Hawai'i,* 174.

[375]Layton , et al., *"And I Was There," Pearl Harbor and Midway-Breaking the Secrets,* 277-8; Farago, *The Broken Seal: "Operation Magic" and the Secret Road to Pearl Harbor,* 319-320, 335.

[376]Ibid.

[377]*"Text of President's Request for War on Germany and Italy,"* Associated Press, *St. Louis Post-Dispatch* (Missouri), 11 Dec. 1941.

Chapter 21: Paradise Burned

[378]*Oakland Tribune* (Oakland, CA), 11 December, 26.

[379]Barbara Jean [Street] Olsen, Collected works, unpublished.

[380]Street, Anderson, March, *A Compendium of the Life and Times of George Street Sr.,*185.

[381]*Oakland Tribune,* (Oakland, CA.), 12 December 1941, 26.

[382]George Street Archives, Binder 5, page 80; Letter to Ladislas Farago dated 14 February 1968, Addendum page 2.

[383]Street, Anderson, March, *A Compendium of the Life and Times of George Street Sr.,*185.

[384]Ibid, page 81; Letter to Ladislas Farago dated 14 February 1968, Addendum page 3.

[385]Ibid.

[386]Ibid.

[387]Ibid.

[388]Ibid, page 82; Letter to Ladislas Farago dated 14 February 1968, Addendum page 4.

[389]Tanaka, Attack *on Pearl Harbor*, picture, 52.

[390]Shirley, *December 1941: 31 Days That Changed America and Saved the World*, 179.

[391]Street, Anderson, March, *A Compendium of the Life and Times of George Street Sr.*, 207.

[392]Shivers, *Cooperation of Racial Groups in Hawaii During the War*, 9.

[393]Ibid.

[394]*Honolulu Star-Bulletin* 19 December 1941.

[395]Street, Anderson, March, *A Compendium of the Life and Times of George Street Sr.*, 212.

Chapter 22: The New Reality

[396]*The Honolulu Advertiser* 14 December 1941

[397]Street, Anderson, March, *A Compendium of the Life and Times of George Street Sr.*, 184.

[398]Ibid., 185.

[399]Honolulu Star-Bulletin, 17 December 1941, 6.

[400]Ibid.

[401]Masatake and Caiden, *Zero!*, 51.

[402]RCA *Relay* Magazine, *Letters from Service Men*, March 1942, 14.

[403]*Honolulu Star-Bulletin*, 17 December 1941, George Street archives.

[404]Allen, Gwenfread; *Hawaii's War Year's 1941-1945*, Pacific Monograph, 1999, 168.

[405]*Oakland Tribune* (Oakland, CA), 4 December 1942, 18.

[406]Toll, *Pacific Crucible: War at the Sea in the Pacific 1941-1942*, 149.

[407]Street, Anderson, March, *A Compendium of the Life and Times of George Street Sr.*, 207.

[408]Barbara [Street] Olsen, 4 February 2009 interview.

[409]Street, Anderson, March, *A Compendium of the Life and Times of George Street Sr.*, 207.

[410] 1941-42 *The Roundup* Roosevelt High School yearbook, public domain.

[411]Barbara [Street] Olsen, 2010 interview.

[412]Ibid.

[413]George Street Archives, Letter to Barbara dated 10 February 1945.

[414]O'Hara, *Honolulu Harlot*, vi.

[415]Ibid, Binder 5, page 32; Servicegram dated 23 December 1941.

[416]Ibid.

[417]Willmott, *Pearl Harbor*, 23.

[418]Engineer officer, Commander Bill Olsen, USN (Ret.), 2015 interview.

[419] Theobald, *The Final Secret of Pearl Harbor: The Washington Contribution to the Japanese Attack*, 119.

[420] Weintraub, *Pearl Harbor Christmas: A World at War, December 1941*, Prelude.

Chapter 23: "Nothing Can Change the Facts."

[421] *Valley Morning Star*, (Harlingen, Texas); *The Philadelphia Inquirer*; *Oakland Tribune*, (Oakland, Ca.) 14 December 1941.

[422]Toll, *Pacific Crucible: War at the Sea in the Pacific 1941-1942*, 7-33.

[423]Shirley, *December 1941: 31 Days That Changed America and Saved the World*, 233.

[424]Prange, et al., *At Dawn We Slept: The Untold Story of Pearl Harbor*, 584-586.

[425]Ibid.

[426]*Honolulu Star-Bulletin*, 17 December 1941.

[427]*The Palm Beach Post* (West Palm Beach, FL), 17 Dec. 1941.

[428]Theobald, *The Final Secret of Pearl Harbor: The Washington Contribution to the Japanese Attack*, 154.

[429]Bartlett, *Cover-up: The Politics of Pearl Harbor 1941-1946*, 71.

[430]Congress, *Summary Report*, 226, Footnote 327.

[431]Ibid, 20,

[432]*Oakland Tribune* (Oakland, CA), 13 December, 1941, 1, 3, 11.

[433]Ibid, 14 December 1941, A-9.

[434]Ibid, H-7.

[435]Ibid, 21 December 1941.

[436]*The Honolulu Advertiser*, 21 December 1941.

[437]Ibid.

[438]*Oakland Tribune* (Oakland CA) 20 December 1941, 3.

[439]Ibid.

[440]*The Deseret News*, 20 December 1941.

[441]*Oakland Tribune* (Oakland CA) 20 December 1941, 5.

442*Honolulu Star-Bulletin*, 31 December 1941.
443*The Honolulu Advertiser,* 23 December 1941.
444*Honolulu Star-Bulletin*, 22 December 1941.
445*The Honolulu Advertiser*, 21 December 1941, 8.

Chapter 24: The Cost of War

446George Street Archives, RCA *Relay* Magazine, public domain.
447Street, Anderson, March, *A Compendium of the Life and Times of George Street Sr.,* 202.
448Layton, et al., *"And I Was There," Pearl Harbor and Midway Breaking the Secrets,* 353.
449Ibid, 354.
450McWilliams, *Sunday in Hell: Pearl Harbor Minute by Minute,* photos, 661.
451Cressman, *The Official Chronology of the U. S. Navy in World War II,* 70.
452*Honolulu Star-Bulletin* Evening edition, 29 December 1941.
453Cressman, *The Official Chronology of the U. S. Navy in World War II,* 70.
454*The Honolulu Advertiser*, 31 December 1941, 3.
455Ibid.
456Ibid.
457*The Star-Press* (Muncie, Indiana), 25 December 1941.
458Ibid, 20.
459Ibid.
460Ibid.
461Ibid
462Horodysky, *American Merchant Marine at War, U.S. Merchant Ships Sunk or Damaged in World War II.*
463Whitehead, *The FBI Story: A Report to the People*, 209.
464Ibid, 210.
465George Street Jr., Interview 20 July 2019.
466Ibid.
467*The Honolulu Advertiser*, last edition, 30 December 1941, 2.
468*Oakland Tribune* (Oakland, CA) 31 December 1941.

Chapter 25: A New Year

[469]Rupp, *Mobilizing Women for War: German and American Propaganda, 1939-1945*, 168; Honey, *Creating Rosie the Riveter: Class, Gender, and Propaganda during World War II*, 184.

[470]*The Pittsburgh Courier* (Pittsburgh, PA, 10 Jan 1942, 3.

[471]Honey, *Creating Rosie the Riveter: Class, Gender, and Propaganda during World War II*, 6.

[472]Gose and De Herrer, *Reflecting Freedom: How Fashion Mirrored the Struggle for Women's Rights*, 211.

[473]*Honolulu Star-Bulletin*, 14 April 1942.

[474]Webber, *Retaliation: Japanese Attacks and Allied Countermeasures on the Pacific Coast in World War II*, 24.

[475]Mundy, *Code Girls: The Untold Story of the American Women Code Breakers of World War II*, 27.

[476]Street, Anderson, March, *A Compendium of the Life and Times of George Street Sr.*, 211.

[477]PHH, Vol. 22, 217.

[478]U.S. Congress, 77th Congress, Senate Commission, Document No. 159, 20.

[479]Layton, et al., *"And I Was There," Pearl Harbor and Midway Breaking the Secrets*, 343.

[480] Theobald, *The Final Secret of Pearl Harbor: The Washington Contribution to the Japanese Attack,*154.

[481]Odo, *No Sword to Bury: Japanese Americans in Hawaii during World War II*.

[482]Shirley, *December 1941: 31 Days That Changed America and Saved the World*, 373.

[483]Street, Anderson, March, *A Compendium of the Life and Times of George Street Sr.*, 207.

[484]Ibid.

[485]Chernin, "My Experiences in the Honolulu Chinatown Red-Light District," 213.

[486]George Street Archives, RCA *Relay* Magazine.

[487]Ibid, *Report from Honolulu*, June 1942, 11.

[488]*Honolulu Star-Bulletin*, 8 April 1942, 7.

[489]George Street Archives, RCA *Relay* Magazine, "Radiophoto Service is Now Available between Hawaii and the Mainland," June 1942.

[490]*Honolulu Star-Bulletin*, 22 March 1941, 3.

352

491George Street Archives, *RCA Relay* clipping, March 1942.

Chapter 26: No Goodbyes
492Street, Anderson, March, *A Compendium of the Life and Times of George Street Sr.*, 184.
493Tanaka, *Attack on Pearl Harbor*, 43.
494Street, Anderson, March, *A Compendium of the Life and Times of George Street Sr.*, 211.
495Ibid.
496Ibid.
497*Oakland Tribune*, (Oakland, CA), 17 July 1942, 16.
498Barbara [Street] Olsen, 2010 interview.
499*Honolulu Star-Bulletin*, 3 April 1942.
500George Street Jr., Interview 20 July 2019.
501*San Francisco Examiner*, 19 May 1942.
502Street, Anderson, March, *A Compendium of the Life and Times of George Street Sr.*, 211.
503Allen, *Hawaii's War Years*, 124.
504Street, Anderson, March, *A Compendium of the Life and Times of George Street Sr.*, 212.
505Prange, et al., Miracle at Midway, Kindle location 627.
506Layton, et al., *"And I Was There," Pearl Harbor and Midway - Breaking the Secrets*, 406.
507Ibid., 428.
508Street, Anderson, March, *A Compendium of the Life and Times of George Street Sr.*, 212.
509Ibid. 212-213.
510Barbara [Street] Olsen, 2011 interview.
5111941-42 *The Roundup* Roosevelt High School yearbook, public domain
512Webber, *Retaliation: Japanese Attacks and Allied Countermeasures on the Pacific Coast in World War II*, 55.
513Ibid.
514Ibid.

Chapter 27: Paradise Lost
515Allen, *Hawaii's War Years*, 271.
516Ibid, 269.

[517]Ibid, *278*.

[518]Ibid, 229.

[519]*Honolulu Star-Bulletin*, 22 October 1941, 12.

[520]Ibid, 14 June 1943, 12.

[521]Allen, *Hawaii's War Years,* 194.

[522]*Honolulu Star-Bulletin*, 7 December 1942, 11.

[523]Ibid., 15.

[524]National Park Service, Yosemite's World War II Hospital.

[525]Barbara Jean (Street) Olsen photo album.

Chapter 28: Aftermath: Investigations and Recriminations

[526]George Street Archives, *Honolulu Star-Bulletin* clipping dated 10 January 1945.

[527]Olson, "'2nd Pearl Harbor,' kept top secret until 1962, commemorated"

[528]Prange, et al., *At Dawn We Slept: The Untold Story of Pearl Harbor*, 612.

[529]Ibid, 616.

[530]Ibid.

[531]Layton, et al., *"And I Was There," Pearl Harbor and Midway - Breaking the Secrets,* 512.

[532]Bartlett, *Cover-Up: The Politics of Pearl Harbor 1941-1946,* 76.

[533]Layton, et al., *"And I Was There," Pearl Harbor and Midway - Breaking the Secrets,* 513.

[534]Unger et al., *George Marshall*, 315.

[535]Congress, *Summary Report*, 226.

[536]Ibid, 270-271.

[537]PHH, Vol. 23, 1105

[538]PHH, Vol. 40, 225.

[539]PHH, Vol. 36, 334.

[540]Parker, *A New View of Pearl Harbor: The U.S. Navy and Communications Intelligence*, September 1945, declassified 12-01-2011.

[541]Prange, et al., *At Dawn We Slept: The Untold Story of Pearl Harbor*, 736.

[542]Congress, *Summary Report*, 238.

[543]Ibid, 226.

[544]Ibid, 150.

[545]Prange, et al., *At Dawn We Slept: The Untold Story of Pearl Harbor,* 568.

[546] George Street Archives, Binder 5, page 70, Letter to Ladislas Farago dated 4 August 1967, page 3.

[547] PHH, Hewitt Inquiry, Vol 36, 566.

[548] PHH, Vol. 91, 3389-91.

[549] George Street Archives, Binder 5, page 68; Letter to Ladislas Farago, dated 4 August 1967, page 1.

[550] Lyons, *David Sarnoff: A Biography,* 228.

[551] Victor, *The Pearl Harbor Myth: Rethinking the Unthinkable*, 30.

[552] Street, Anderson, March*, A Compendium of the Life and Times of George Street Sr.,* 242.

Epilogue
[553] George Street Archives, Letter to Barbara [Street] Olsen dated 1951.

Appendix A: Timeline
[554] Clarke, *Pearl Harbor Ghosts, The Legacy of December 7, 1941*, 241.

[555] USS *Curtis* (AV-4) Action report: https://www.history.navy.mil/research/archives/digital-exhibits-highlights/action-reports/wwii-pearl-harbor-attack/ships-a-c/uss-curtiss-av-4-action-report.html. accessed 9 July 2021.

[556] Shinsato and Urabe, *For That One Day: The memories of Mitsuo Fuchida*, Kindle location 1688.

[557] USS *Curtis* (AV-4) Action report: https://www.history.navy.mil/research/archives/digital-exhibits-highlights/action-reports/wwii-pearl-harbor-attack/ships-a-c/uss-curtiss-av-4-action-report.html. accessed 9 July 2021.

Made in USA - North Chelmsford, MA
1309743_9781736706633
03.28.2022 1042